```
> 10 PRINT "David is cool"
> 20 GOTO 10
> RUN
David is cool
David is cool
David is cool
David is cool
David is cool
David is cool
David is cool
David is cool
David is cool
David is cool
David is cool
David is cool
David is cool
David is cool
David is cool
David is cool
David is cool
David is cool
David is cool
David is cool
David is cool
David is cool
David is cool
David is cool
David is cool
David is cool
```

Emergence

A MEMOIR OF BOYHOOD,
COMPUTATION, AND
THE MYSTERIES OF MIND

David Sussillo

GRAND CENTRAL

New York Boston

This book is a memoir with its starting point in my earliest childhood. To the best of my ability, I have tried to re-create events, locales, and conversations from my memories of them, but I acknowledge that time may have blurred my recollections. In order to maintain their privacy and anonymity, in some instances I have changed the names of individuals and places, and I may have changed some identifying characteristics and details such as physical properties, occupations, and places of residence.

Copyright © 2026 by David Sussillo

Illustrations by Robin and David Sussillo

Jacket design by Claire Sullivan. Jacket images by Shutterstock and Getty Images. Jacket copyright © 2026 by Hachette Book Group, Inc.

Hachette Book Group supports the right to free expression and the value of copyright. The purpose of copyright is to encourage writers and artists to produce the creative works that enrich our culture.

The scanning, uploading, and distribution of this book without permission is a theft of the author's intellectual property. If you would like permission to use material from the book (other than for review purposes), please contact permissions@hbgusa.com. Thank you for your support of the author's rights.

Grand Central Publishing
Hachette Book Group
1290 Avenue of the Americas, New York, NY 10104
grandcentralpublishing.com
@grandcentralpub

First Edition: March 2026

Grand Central Publishing is a division of Hachette Book Group, Inc. The Grand Central Publishing name and logo is a registered trademark of Hachette Book Group, Inc.

The publisher is not responsible for websites (or their content) that are not owned by the publisher.

The Hachette Speakers Bureau provides a wide range of authors for speaking events. To find out more, go to hachettespeakersbureau.com or email HachetteSpeakers@hbgusa.com.

Grand Central Publishing books may be purchased in bulk for business, educational, or promotional use. For information, please contact your local bookseller or the Hachette Book Group Special Markets Department at special.markets@hbgusa.com.

Print book interior design by Jeff Stiefel.

Library of Congress Control Number: 2025946850

ISBNs: 9781538768570 (hardcover); 9781538768594 (ebook)

Printed in Canada

MRQ-T

10 9 8 7 6 5 4 3 2 1

This book is dedicated to the family who opened their doors:
my Aunt Maria and Uncle Brad,
Aunt Moira and Uncle Elliot,
and Uncle James and Aunt Beverly;
to my mentors Dr. Laquercia and Larry Abbott,
who guided my healing and discovery;
to Omar, my group-home brother,
who helped me dream of escape;
and above all, to my wife, Robin,
who made that dream a life worth living.

CONTENTS

Prologue—The Princeton Neuroscience Retreat 1

Part 1—Disorder, 1975–1983 5
1—Booting Up 7
2—We Were Perfect 13
3—The War Zone 31
4—A Crumbling House 44

Part 2—Chaos, 1983–1988 51
5—Orphaned by the Living 55
6—Ask and Ye Shall Find 63
7—David Is Cool 71
8—Road to Nowhere 80
9—Omar and the Commitment 91
10—Cholo-Curious 102
11—What If Tomorrow? 117
12—Thirty-Two Years Old 125
13—Did We Even Say Goodbye? 134

Part 3—Order, 1988–1993 141
14—Discover 145
15—Ninety-Nine Problems 152

Contents

16—The Milt 166
17—The Blob and the Brown Zebra 178
18—Inhale, Exhale 191
19—The Utterly Unremarkable Experiences
    of a Mediocre Swimmer 206

Part 4—The Edge of Chaos, 1993–1998 .... **217**
20—Serious Decision Number 3 221
21—A Quarter for Your Past 232
22—Complex Variables 246
23—The Oracle Hive Mind 260
24—Boston Shakers 271

Part 5—Emergence, 1998–Current Day **287**
25—Just Say Everything 291
26—Attractors 305
27—Useful Networks 320
28—What Remains 328
29—Ten Thousand Seats 335
30—Get the Free Life 348

Afterword *363*
Acknowledgments *371*
Notes *373*
About the Author *376*

PROLOGUE

The Princeton Neuroscience Retreat

My heart pounded as I approached the stage. The grand wooden pavilion, filled with two hundred of my academic colleagues, stretched before me. I'd already delivered my keynote address the day before: "Dynamical Motifs as the Link Between Neurons and Cognition," a lecture on how to use tools from artificial intelligence to better understand the human brain.

That talk had been a piece of cake.

It was today's talk, part of the Growing Up in Science series—meant to showcase the human behind the scientist—that had me on edge. Previous speakers had opened up about the challenges of being first-generation Americans or overcoming gender bias in academia. But nobody had a story quite like mine.

I made it to the podium and surveyed the crowd. Waitstaff bustled around the tables, pouring beverages. It had taken forever for my colleagues to make their way through the buffet line, but they were all seated now around large round tables. My sweaty hands clung to my notes as I took a deep breath and tested the microphone. "Howdy, folks," I said as I forced a smile. "This is a first for me, but I'll give it a shot."

Prologue

Here goes nothing.

"When I was a kid, I was told that my hometown of Albuquerque, New Mexico, was the epicenter of the seventies' heroin epidemic. I've no idea if that's true, but it made perfect sense—both my parents were heroin addicts. When I found out as an adult that the television show *Breaking Bad* was filmed in and around Albuquerque, I just nodded and thought, *Yep*."

I looked up. The crowd had gone completely silent.

"For my sister, Esther, and me, having drug-addicted parents meant we grew up largely in orphanages. By the time I was a young adult, I'd been in the system for a decade. I'd lived in two group homes—and with two sets of aunts and uncles. I'd been under the long-term supervision of"—I looked down at my notes—"thirteen sets of houseparents. I called at least sixty other children surrogate siblings: boys and girls, both younger and older, of all races, colors, and creeds."

I looked out at the crowd again. Even the waitstaff were standing still. I took another breath. "I was a bright kid, but I was no iron robot or some hero from another planet. The profound, the beautiful, and the terrible—they all imprinted on me."

For the next thirty minutes, I spoke about group-home life, how I'd managed to attend college, and the struggles of getting my PhD. How I'd ended up in a position to give the Princeton neuroscience keynote. Afterward, there was applause and a few questions. But there was a lot of silence, too.

On my way out, a woman from the waitstaff ran up to me. She was in her early twenties, dressed for work with an apron and hair pulled back into a ponytail. "I was really inspired by your story."

"Thanks! That means a lot," I said. "Honestly, I was wondering how it came off."

Prologue

"I, umm"—she swallowed hard—"grew up in foster care, too, and I always wanted to be a biologist. That was my dream—*is* my dream." The words began to spill out of her. "But I had to drop out of community college to earn money. That's why I have this job." She glanced back at the pavilion and then again at me, waiting for me to say something.

I could relate to veering off course; my journey had been anything but a straight line. I wanted to offer words of support, but I didn't know her at all. Where to even begin?

After a moment of silence, she continued, "I just know I could do something, be *someone*. If I could just get on the right track. How did you do it? I mean, I heard what you said, but how'd you *actually* do it?"

I knew how I'd done it as far as that kind of thing went: I'd done the work, had been in therapy. I'd studied the science. But after a lifetime of receiving bullshit advice from everyone and their mother, I knew generic sentiments were worthless. "Well..." I trailed off. Finally, a few words limped out of my mouth: "Persistence and a lot of luck."

My stupid response haunted me the entire ride back to the airport. To tell my story properly, I would have had to weave together all the threads that had shaped my path: the group homes and friendships that had formed me, the video games that had sparked my love of computers, the mathematics that had taught me to embrace chaos, and the neuroscience that ultimately became my life's work. It was all connected—the personal and the scientific, the emotional and the analytical.

As I thought about it, I realized my journey was like the concept of emergence I'd just lectured about—how complex patterns arise from simple parts, whether in artificial intelligence or in life itself. The same questions that drove my research now pulled at my memories: How does a child from a group home end up studying the brain's complexity? Why do some kids survive trauma while others don't? My science training had taught me that these questions resisted simple explanations—just like the mysteries of mental illness or consciousness that my field struggled to understand. The more I thought about it, the more I realized that my life and my work were inseparable.

PART 1

DISORDER: 1975–1983

> Physics underlies all complexity, including our own existence: how is this possible? How can our own lives emerge from interactions of electrons, protons, and neutrons?
> —*Cosmologist George F. R. Ellis*

Remember the ancients, who believed we were woven from earth, wind, water, and flame? They sensed a hint of the divine in the crashing waves, a soul's echo in leaves swirling in the wind. But modern science unveils an even grander scheme, a miracle within your head, not crafted from the ancients' four elements but from a thousand trillion synapses.

Each neuron, a cell transmitting in this intricate network, sparks with the electrical activity that gives rise to thought. Eighty-six billion neurons, living cables, fire away at one another to ignite constellations of perception and understanding. It's staggering: How can this cacophony of electrical clicks translate into individual human beings like you and me?

Because in this bustling information highway, a marvel unfolds: the essence of you, the *you of right now*—that feeling of nowness with all its immediate sensations, thoughts, and emotions. It arises from chattering between the neurons in your brain taking place this very instant. The precise connections between the neurons in your brain make *you* who you are.

Electrical impulses pass from neuron to neuron through molecular machines, *synapses*. Malleable, increasing and decreasing in their capacity to enable communication, synapses sculpt the dynamic of your being. They change when you pay attention in class, practice the piano, or even when you scroll through a social media feed. In ways we do not yet understand, these synapses—more numerous than the stars contained in a thousand Milky Way galaxies—control the long-term firing patterns of your neurons. They are the physical knobs, the parameters configuring the electrical storm in your brain.

When a neuron receives enough input from other neurons, it activates, contributing its one-millisecond-long electrical pulse to a computational symphony. Some neurons enhance while other neurons suppress. Because a neuron connects to as many as ten thousand more and receives connections from as many as ten thousand others, the *you of right now* is a never-ceasing, always-raging electrical storm of unfathomable complexity.

You are no fixed statue, but a dynamic process: a high-dimensional river of information flowing through the improbable nooks and crannies of an M. C. Escher drawing. You are the traffic congestion in the city, the schooling of fish, the swarming of bees, the murmuration of a million starlings above the skies of Barcelona.

1
Booting Up

I was born in 1975, which means I grew up in the golden age of the personal computer. While millennials claim to be the first generation raised on modern technology, the last five years of Gen X were right there, too. We were kids when the first home computers hit the market, even if such luxuries were beyond some family's means. We lost ourselves in early PC adventure games like *King's Quest* and can still hum along with the 8-bit music from early '80s video games. The two-dimensional sprites of Mario, Donkey Kong, and Link occupy prime real estate in our hearts and on the T-shirts and hoodies we now wear on weekends.

From the neural networks I work with as a scientist to the online dating scene where I met my wife, much of my life has been intertwined with computers and gaming. In high school, I couldn't resist automating every algorithm I learned in my math classes on my trusty TI-81 graphing calculator. Even further back, in elementary school, edutainment games like *The Oregon Trail* introduced me to the wonders of computing.

Yet, the true genesis of my fascination with computers lies in the dazzling, neon-soaked arcades of the early '80s, where classics like *Ms. Pac-Man* and *Defender* captivated my young mind and provided a much-needed escape. The phrase GAME OVER, now forever etched into my psyche, served as a bittersweet reminder that even the most epic gaming sessions—and life's most cherished moments—must eventually come to an end.

My parents were in and out of rehab throughout my early childhood. Whenever they tried to get clean, Esther and I would be placed in a group home or "children's home." My parents would come to get us about a month later, and we'd all live together for a while. Until it would happen again. Wash, rinse, repeat.

When I was five, we moved to an apartment complex called Lori Place in the northeast heights of Albuquerque. It was there that my brain started booting up in earnest, and "I" came online. Whichever neural circuits give rise to a sense of thereness, to the sense of me, had finally wired up.

One of my earliest memories involves helping my parents score drugs. My mother, Esther, and I were walking to our car, the heat radiating off the asphalt and cement, when our mother turned to us with a smile.

"Hey, want to get lollipops?" she asked. "We can get some if you can cough for the doctor—and we need cough medicine."

"But I don't have a cough," Esther said. "And I don't like cough medicine."

My mother's smile faltered for a moment, but she quickly recovered. "Sweetie, *I* need it. If you just *pretend* to have a cough, you can get a lollipop."

And so, as we entered the doctor's office, Esther and I began coughing. The doctor looked at us sympathetically, and our mother played her part perfectly, feigning concern and asking for a prescription.

In the end, we got our Dum-Dums, and our parents got their codeine.

Maybe it was to enjoy codeine or other substances more fully that my parents would frequently use the local movie theaters as a babysitter for us. They'd drop us off at a local dollar theater for the double feature, regardless of what was playing, and we'd be there until they picked us up four hours later. Sometimes we'd linger in the lobby, lying on the red velour couches or limboing under the line ropes. I'd routinely check the pay phone slots for quarters, and—as they were always empty—simply stand in front of the video game in the lobby and pretend to play. We were there a lot. I remember *ET*, *Dragonslayer*, *On Golden Pond*, *Chariots of Fire*, *The Great Muppet Caper*, *Tootsie*, and my favorite, *Annie*. It's fair to say that when the Oscars rolled around, I had opinions.

We couldn't stay at the movies all the time, however. One night, we were at home when I woke up to the sounds of raised voices coming from our apartment's tiny living room.

"Knock it off, Luke!" my mother yelled. "It's not my fault you grabbed the wrong stuff."

I got out of bed to see what was going on. Esther was already up, peeking out behind our bedroom door that was opened just a crack. "Go back to sleep!" Esther whispered. She was a year and a half older than I was and always tried to boss me around. As I wriggled by her, my parents came into view. My mother stood, hands on her wide hips, glaring at my father. Her face was flushed. My father was stumbling around the living room, a half-empty bottle of whiskey in his hand.

"We have to burn," he muttered, his eyes wild. "Time to meet God."

"Luke, you're wasted."

My father pointed a wavering finger at her. "I get it now. You're the problem!" With deliberate menace, he tipped the bottle, letting whiskey spill onto the brown shag carpet. The liquid seeped into the fibers and filled the room with the scent of alcohol.

"You're scaring me, Luke," my mother said, realization dawning on her face that her husband might be out of control. She rushed over and grabbed at the bottle. "Give me the whiskey."

My father shoved her away, sending her crashing onto the floor. "I'm gonna set a fire," he declared, splashing whiskey all over the furniture and walls. Alcohol spilled over my mother's legs as he began a circuit around the small room.

My mother got back to her feet, her clothes disheveled and damp. "Please stop," she said, her voice edged now with fear.

My father completed his circuit. He tottered unsteadily. "Where's the lighter?"

"I'll call the cops. I swear it."

"No, you won't." He snatched the lighter off the coffee table, his fingers fumbling with the small object.

My mother was by his side in an instant. "Luke, give me the lighter now!" She tried to take it, but my father held it up high, his six-foot-two height ensuring there was no way my mother could reach it. As if it were some childhood game, she kept jumping and grabbing for it.

"Get away from me!" My father roared. He threw the empty bottle across the living room, the glass shattering as it hit the far wall, shards scattering across the floor.

My mother backed away from him, eyes wide.

Esther opened our door fully and walked the short distance to the living room. "Mommy? Is Daddy okay?" Her voice was small and uncertain.

"Yes, Esther—go back to your room," said my mother, attempting to project calm, not taking her eyes off her husband.

My sister just stood there.

Booting Up

"Esther, I said go back to your room!"

My father turned and smiled, his eyes unfocused. "Hi, sweetie. You were right to come out. We need to pray for your mother." He took her by the hand and led her back to our bedroom. He saw me by the door and said, "You too. Come on, David."

He sat us down on Esther's bed, the mattress sagging beneath our weight. Then he started us off: "'Our Father which art in heaven.'" He looked at me. "Come on. I know you kids know this one."

From the living room, our mother shouted, "That's it! I'm calling the police!"

"Oh no you're not." My father was up in a flash, stumbling badly, his feet tangling in the sheets. Halfway to my mother and the phone, he tripped and fell, his body hitting the floor with a heavy thud. His hand landed on a shard of glass from the broken whiskey bottle, and blood began pouring out of the gash.

Through the doorway, I saw my mother put the phone down and throw a roll of paper towels at my father. "Goddamn you, Luke!" she exclaimed.

My father grabbed the roll and clutched it between his hands, the white paper slowly turning red. He took a deep breath and lowered his head to the floor. Over the next minute, his eyes slowly closed, and he went silent, his chest rising and falling with shallow breaths.

My mother rescued the lighter from my father, went into the kitchen, and came back smoking a cigarette with shaking hands. After a couple of drags, she sighed and said, "Luke—you okay?"

Nothing.

"Are. You. Okay?"

Still nothing.

My mother knelt next to her husband and tried to wake him. After minutes of shaking him and calling his name, her voice growing ever-more frantic, she got up and paced around, clutching herself. She went back to the phone. "Hi. Yes. A medical emergency." She paused for a few seconds and then continued, her voice barely above a whisper, "Yeah, valium. I'm not sure; definitely more than one." She gave our address and hung up the phone.

It took the EMTs around fifteen minutes to show up at Lori Place. They began resuscitating my father, their voices urgent as they worked on him, the sound of their equipment filling the small apartment. During that time, my mother darted in and out of our room, hastily packing a suitcase. Finally, she said, "Esther, take David's hand. We're leaving." She marched us out of the apartment, down to the parking lot and our brown Ford Pinto.

That fight badly frightened my mother and her parents. Within the week, my grandparents moved my mother, Esther, and me into an apartment complex a short walk from their house. My mother filed for a divorce, which ended my parents' nine-year marriage. She instructed me to run to my grandparents' house should my father ever show up. A few months after the papers went through, things cooled off enough that visiting my father seemed possible. But this quickly became a study in disappointment.

The one time my father agreed to pick me up for the day—just me, not Esther—ostensibly for some father-and-son time—he never showed. It had rained recently, and the scent of rain and dust mixed with juniper was strong in the air. I waited outside, sitting on the sidewalk for an afternoon, throwing pebbles into the street, and looking up at the Sandia Mountains. Eventually, I realized he wasn't coming, so I walked back to our apartment, slamming the door behind me as I went inside.

I never lived with my father again.

2

We Were Perfect

I was about to start second grade in 1982 when my mother announced that we were moving. She was enrolling in the College of Santa Fe to attend nursing school. The fight with my father and their subsequent divorce had made it clear, even to her, that it was time to pull her life together. The entire venture, from college tuition to monthly rent to living expenses, was financed by my grandparents. Aside from the food stamps, which were compliments of Uncle Sam.

We ended up in a tiny, single-story apartment complex just off the main drag through town. We didn't have much in the way of belongings, aside from my mother's piano, so a two-bedroom apartment was fine. We'd moved around so many times, and somehow, my mother always managed to bring that piano.

With high, arid desert meeting jagged twelve-thousand-foot mountain peaks, Santa Fe is a natural beauty. At an elevation of seven thousand feet, it's an ecological mash-up set between the desert of the Galisteo Basin and the wilderness of the Sangre de Cristo ("Blood of Christ") Mountains, the Rockies' southernmost range. Throughout the small city, spindly cholla cacti and soft chamisa with yellow flowers meander alongside the walking trails, and massive cottonwoods grace the banks of the arroyos and streams. Juniper and piñon pine dot the otherwise naked hills on the outskirts of town. Drive higher up the winding mountain roads, and you'll find groves of aspen interspersed with forests of ponderosa pine.

But it's the sky that steals the show: sunsets in wondrous color, and the complexity of the stars in the Milky Way at night conjuring far-off worlds. In the summer, you can spy the afternoon monsoons rolling in from thirty miles away, their fearsome energy reminding you that you are alive and that that means something.

Not long after we'd moved to Santa Fe, I met Shiloh. I was walking the neighborhood by myself, kicking a rock along, when I spotted a short-haired blond kid about my age. He was standing on the curb, unwrapping a pack of Starburst candies.

When he saw me, he called out, waving the colorful package in my direction. "Want one?"

I hesitated for a moment, surprised by the offer, but then shrugged and walked over.

He tossed me an orange Starburst and introduced himself. We soon figured out that we were both in second grade and went to the same school.

Next, Shiloh began ripping through the package of Starbursts and pulled out a yellow candy, holding it up like it was a dead bug. "Wanna see something neat?"

I nodded.

"Yellow ones make me barf."

I raised an eyebrow. "Really?"

"I eat it, and then I puke it right back up," he said, making retching noises.

I couldn't help laughing, impressed and a little grossed out.

Shiloh grinned, a mischievous glint in his blue eyes. "I'll show you." He unwrapped the lemon Starburst, tossed it into his mouth, and chewed deliberately, making a big show of swallowing.

We waited in anticipation, seconds ticking by. Then, just as I was about to call his bluff, Shiloh's eyes widened. "Here it comes!"

He spun around and hurled, the bright yellow candy splattering onto the sidewalk, along with what appeared to be the remains of his lunch.

"Cool!"

Shiloh wiped his mouth with the back of his hand, proud of himself. In that moment, I knew I'd found my first best friend.

Shiloh lived in a trailer near us with his parents, Rose and Steve, and his two siblings, Esmerelda and Dan. Rose didn't work. She was morbidly obese, had a face scarred with pockmarks and acne, and kept her hair back in a greasy bun. Like my mother's, her wardrobe seemed to consist of nothing but purple-and-green-paisley muumuus.

Shiloh's father had a huge red beard and often wore a broad-brimmed felt hat. He was mean and unknowable, thanks to his reluctance to use any form of verbal communication. Steve was largely absent from Shiloh's life, spending all his time working at a carpentry outfit. When he was present, he spoke volumes with his side-eye. I avoided him at all costs.

One remarkable aspect of Shiloh's trailer was that there was no running water. I'd regularly watch as Steve and Dan struggled to carry multiple ten-gallon water tanks into their mobile home, their muscles straining under the weight. The family shat in a two-foot-high green bucket lined with a black plastic garbage bag. They hauled all their waste out—I had no idea to where.

There were many similarities between our two families. Both had just moved to Santa Fe. Two kids of similar ages (Shiloh's sister, Esmerelda, was in third grade like Esther). Both families were dirt poor, and neither had any sense of propriety or boundaries. Not a person was educated beyond high school. In short, my family was poor white trash, just like Shiloh's.

To be fair, we weren't as broke as Shiloh's family, but that's a win on a technicality. Shiloh's father had a job. Beyond welfare, my grandparents were the only thing keeping my family afloat. Without them, my mother, my sister, and I would have been out on the street in the time it took to evict on a month's missed rent.

As Shiloh and I became besties, my mother met and became friends with Rose. She would go over to Rose's trailer, and they'd smoke joints together. When I was a child, my mother's drug use didn't register a conscious thought, but with the hindsight of adulthood, a couple of friends smoking weed doesn't seem like a problem. However, the whole point of our family moving to Santa Fe was so my mother could get clean, educate herself, and become financially independent.

Before long, my mother stopped attending her classes at the College of Santa Fe. She resumed her habit of lying about all day and watching soap operas, high on pharmies, methadone, or heroin.

From the first day we met, Shiloh and I were inseparable. Together and left completely to our own devices, we wandered Santa Fe, discovering where to find free grub, where to get "free" toys, and most importantly, how to play our favorite video games for the low, low cost of nothing. We could find video games in the lobby of nearly any supermarket or movie theater. They were present in pizza parlors, laundromats, and bowling alleys. These were public spaces open even to poor kids who otherwise had no access to computers.

It was a typical day, which meant that Shiloh and I were on our own, trying to scrounge up a quarter to play an arcade game. "Can't you ask your mom?" I suggested. We'd been tearing up his trailer, searching for pennies and nickels under the beds, in jacket pockets, on the floor.

"She already said no," he said, checking one last time behind the sofa cushions. "What about yours?"

"She's asleep," I said. Even if she had been awake, I knew my mother wasn't going to cough up a quarter.

But we had other means. We made our plan as we walked to the Albertsons, stopping in at the laundromat on St. Michaels to ask the ladies there if they would give us a quarter. They'd usually take pity on us if we asked nicely and made sure to smile. But today, there was nobody there, so it was on to plan B: the Albertsons supermarket itself.

Albertsons, like most grocery stores at that time, had a dedicated corner for games where parents could drop their kids while they shopped. Once we were there, we pretended to put money in the *Dig Dug* machine, pressing the buttons, and wriggling the joystick around.

After a minute of this, I started yelling, got down on my knees, and inserted my finger into the coin return. Shiloh chimed in, and soon we'd drawn some attention to ourselves. Then we headed over to the customer service booth, occupied by a heavyset and world-weary woman.

"What now, boys?" she asked.

"*Dig Dug* ate our quarter," Shiloh said.

She shuffled to the back of the booth and returned with a clipboard. "You two, I tell you what. Okay, write your names."

We signed our names, and she opened the register, pulled out a shiny new quarter, and gave it to us.

While Shiloh and I were busy at the customer service counter, the technician responsible for maintaining the video games came into the store. I was familiar with this tech; he was something of a priest in my eyes, and Shiloh and I lurked, watching, whenever he serviced the machines.

We walked up to him, and Shiloh showed him our new shiny quarter. "Check it out. That *Dig Dug* is causing problems again."

"Well, someone's been putting garbage in there, so that might have jammed it," the tech said, eyeing the two of us.

"Garbage just messes things up," I agreed. "But what if you tied a string around a quarter and then pulled it out super quick?" I began to imagine the prospect—hours of unimpeded *Dig Dug*.

"Oh, that definitely won't work." He looked at me. "There are scissors in there—a tiny, tiny little pair of scissors." He mimed a snipping gesture. "They make a cut every time a coin is inserted into the slot."

Shiloh and I stared at him in newfound awe as he finished emptying the coin boxes and strode off, chuckling to himself.

Had Shiloh and I been able to get inside that *Dig Dug* console, we would have discovered a world of wonder. Wires everywhere. Wires that connected the joystick and button inputs to the motherboard, wires that connected the audio and video circuitry to the speakers and TV screen. Our eyes would have then turned to the motherboard—the large, rectangular circuit board—with the read-only memory chip that held the game code and the random-access memory chip that held the details of the game during operation, like the positions of the monsters and the great digger himself, *Dig Dug*.

And in the middle of all of it, we would have discovered the components responsible for powering all that fun and creativity—three Z80 microprocessors: one chip for running the game, one chip for graphics, and the last chip for sound processing.

To look at the Z80, you wouldn't think a simple rectangular chip about the size of a stick of gum could accomplish that much. But it's a legend in the world of computing hardware, perhaps the most successful central processing unit (CPU) of all time. It performs arithmetic and logic operations on its binary 0 and 1 inputs, allowing it to manipulate input/output and orchestrate the interactions of all devices within the video game.

It's no exaggeration that, along with a few other CPUs of the era, the Z80 powered the personal computing revolution, including the state-of-the-art graphical user interfaces and latest software applications, such as spreadsheets, word processors, and, of course, video games. The Z80 was relatively speedy and had low power consumption. But most importantly, it was cheap, selling for about twenty-five bucks, making personal computing accessible to a much wider demographic. It also enabled smaller companies and individuals to participate in the burgeoning computer revolution, which led to further innovations in software and hardware.

The Z80 has always held a special place in my heart because of its role as the great democratizer of computing. Released by Federico Faggin and his team at Zilog in 1976, the chip was ubiquitous—and I mean *everywhere*—from *Ms. Pac-Man* to *Donkey Kong* to *Galaga*. It was also in the personal computers of the time, such as the TRS-80 or the Sinclair ZX Spectrum. Even the Game Boy of the '90s featured a processor based on the Z80 design.

These days, with our laptops, smartphones, and smartwatches always close at hand, it's hard for people to appreciate just how difficult it was back in the '60s and '70s to meaningfully interact with a computer—and difficult to fathom how enormous an impact a microprocessor like the Z80 had on the world. Before the invention of microcomputers, known today as *personal computers*, most programmers worked with laughably misnamed "minicomputers," such as the famous PDP-1, which was about the size of a refrigerator and weighed as much as a Volkswagen Beetle. These monstrosities were only considered miniature relative to the truly colossal mainframes, whose many components could occupy an entire room and sometimes even an entire building floor. Both minicomputers and mainframes were ludicrously expensive and only affordable by businesses or large academic institutions. And using them wasn't simple—interacting with these early computers required mastering punch cards. To use this error-prone and tedious input method, software engineers would feed paper cards into a computer so that the precise ordering of their punched holes could be read as programs and data.

All of which is to say you had to really *want* to use a computer back in the day. So when computers like the Apple or the Commodore 64 came out in the late '70s and early '80s, it was a revelation and a revolution. These machines were smaller, more affordable, and more user-friendly compared to earlier computers, featuring a keyboard for input and a monitor for output. For the first time, what we all now recognize as a modern personal computer was available to the public at a reasonable price.

Gazing at the labyrinthine circuitry of the Z80 chip design specs, one can't help but be reminded of a sprawling, futuristic metropolis—the tightly packed grid of components like a bird's-eye view of bustling city blocks connected by a network of copper-hued highways. The registers—those crucial memory units—stand tall like gleaming skyscrapers. As the eye wanders, the intricacy and interconnectedness of the design become increasingly apparent. The complex web of circuit elements speaks to the nature of our modern world—a place where seemingly disparate elements are inextricably linked, where the work of a visionary engineering team led by Faggin can ripple out to touch the lives of people across the globe, even two seven-year-old deviants in Santa Fe, New Mexico.

Shiloh and I also made the rounds at the arcade right on St. Michaels. There were a couple of tricks to getting free games, tricks Shiloh and I stumbled upon through trial and error. One secret concerned the video game classic *Defender*, where you piloted a sexy Corvette-looking spaceship. The game's noble goal was to preserve humankind by shooting alien ships; it was the way you were meant to play the game. But *Defender* was too difficult for Shiloh and me. More often than not, we'd say screw it and help the aliens out. We'd pilot our ship down to the bottom of the screen and waste all the peaceful humans ourselves, giggling with delight at this corruption of intended gameplay.

So what was the secret that particular *Defender* game held? First, you charged up your body with static electricity by swishing your feet along the shag carpet. Then you touched a metal part of the *Defender* cabinet. Bam! Free credit! We played a lot of *Defender*.

We absolutely loved *Ms. Pac-Man*. We played it as often as possible despite having to cough up a quarter each time. It was exceptionally well balanced and entertaining, popular with video game aficionados, yet simple enough for seven-year-olds like Shiloh and me. We loved *Ms. Pac-Man* because we could get a *free man*, a peculiar turn of phrase given the avatar was not male or even human. Video games in the '80s would give you three lives when you began a game. If you played well enough, the standard formula awarded you a free man after achieving a certain number of points. In the arcade we frequented, that score was set to ten thousand. We could achieve this score on occasion, but it was no sure thing.

Of course, Shiloh and I never had more than a single quarter between the two of us. So, just like brothers, it was essential that we share the experience even steven. This meant, without question, that we had to get the extra life so that three lives became four.

We'd toss our quarter to see who would go first because—trading lives—whoever went first also went third. The first player would begin, intent on the gameplay and the sacred obligation of an even game. Whoever was the second player would scream, "Get the extra man! Get the free life!" Upon hearing the ten high-pitched bell rings that signaled a free life, our gameplay was evenly divided, and all was right in the world.

At some point, Shiloh and I started embarking upon another kind of adventure—dumpster diving. An odd thing about my early childhood is that I don't remember much about food. Nor do I remember going hungry too often. I ate free lunches at school, and Esther and I always made sure to arrive early in the morning to eat the free hot breakfasts. During the summers, local community centers held activities that included lunch, which we attended for the sole purpose of eating.

My mother went to food outlets to purchase subsidized food from the government, things like powdered milk, powdered eggs, processed cheese, and old fruit. Cooking as little as possible, her specialty was Top Ramen, which she'd trick out by tossing a raw egg and maybe some frozen vegetables into the pot. Lots of pinto beans and pasta made their way onto our plates.

Our menu expanded a bit when, one day, Shiloh and I happened across the dumpsters behind Albertsons and figured, what the hell, why not? Shiloh's family ate no better than mine. We were both keen to help out.

The grocery store had an array of long metal dumpsters in the back parking lot. We'd crawl into these through the side door and root around in all manner of rotten filth, looking for edible food. We found all sorts of treasures in those dumpsters: unopened sugary drinks, day-old baked goods still completely wrapped, barely expired food in undamaged bags and boxes, and plenty of canned food with no dents. One afternoon's expedition proved particularly successful.

"Dave, look at this!" Shiloh held up a can of condensed milk, his grin visible even in the dim light filtering through the dumpster's side door.

"No, wait!" I plunged deeper into the pile, cardboard boxes flying. "Here!" I emerged triumphant, thrusting a banged-up but unopened box of Life cereal into the air. "We got breakfast!"

The crunch of gravel made us both freeze. A young man in an Albertsons apron approached with fresh bags of garbage. We pressed ourselves against the dumpster's metal wall. He tossed the bags in without a word, their weight landing with a soft thud. Once his footsteps faded, we went right back to the hunt.

Such encounters with store employees were common, but they never said a word to us. Anyway, Shiloh and I were too young to be ashamed. We believed we were serving a useful purpose: gathering up the goodies into an Albertsons shopping cart, gleeful as we pushed the cart all the way home.

Neither my mother nor Shiloh's ever rejected our windfall. We weren't careless, if such a thing can be said of two seven-year-old boys rooting around in grocery store dumpsters. We didn't take anything moldy or obviously rotten. I don't think we ever took produce and certainly not meat. I'd like to believe that our mothers cast a responsible adult eye over the food, but who the hell knows?

While dumpster diving helped fill our bellies, Shiloh and I soon discovered another way to acquire things we desperately wanted but could never afford. As the year progressed into spring, Shiloh and I became friendly with a trio of brothers living in the mobile home park. I liked the boys a lot, in no small part because they had great toys. I'd never owned more than a single toy, and certainly never any toys of social consequence.

Early in our friendship, Shiloh, the three brothers, and I were playing with *He-Man* and *Star Wars* action figures out in front of their trailer.

"Holy cow! You have Castle Grayskull, too?" Shiloh asked.

The eldest, Adam, called to his brother, "Yep. Hey, Jeff, let's show 'em the Millennium Falcon."

Jeff put down Boba Fett and ran into their trailer. Sure enough, a minute later, he came out with the famous spacecraft and began running around like mad. Clearly, the Falcon had made the jump into hyperspace.

"You guys are rich!" I cried.

Adam nodded. "We sure are."

Jeff stopped in his tracks. Apparently, the Falcon's hyperdrive had failed yet again. "But, Adam…we're not rich."

I was too excited about the battle I was orchestrating between Luke and Darth Vader to think too much about this exchange, and we all continued playing.

A few weeks later, it was the same scene, all five boys outside, this time playing with *Return of the Jedi* action figures.

Shiloh said, "And there's Endor Leia, and there's Jabba's creepy sidekick, and Luke all dressed in black 'cuz he's a Jedi now and—"

"Adam, this movie just came out!" I said. "Your mom really bought all of these for you already?"

"Sure did."

"Nope," said Jeff. "We steal—"

"Jeff!" yelled the middle brother, Joe.

I stopped playing and stood up. "Adam, you *steal* these?" I asked incredulously.

"From where?" Shiloh asked.

Adam gave his youngest brother a dirty look and then turned to us. He said, "Can you keep a secret?"

"Yep. Of course. Uh-huh." Shiloh and I stumbled over ourselves to reassure the brothers of our commitment to secrecy.

"Well"—Adam looked around conspiratorially—"we've been snaking them from the Kmart over on St. Michaels."

Shiloh and I looked at each other and nodded. I turned to Adam. "Teach us."

We all walked over to the Kmart, and when we arrived, Adam briefed us and then gave a final emphatic instruction. "Don't do anything. Just *watch*."

We nodded, and then all five of us walked into the Kmart.

Shiloh and I hung around the front of the store, feigning interest in this or that item. The two younger brothers stood guard at the toy aisle; Joe was at the front, and Jeff was at the back, both pretending to be engrossed in whatever product was right in front of them. Meanwhile, Adam walked down to the middle of the aisle where the good toys were.

The two sentinels gave the nod for the all clear, and then Adam began stuffing action figures into his pants. My heart raced as I watched him, half expecting an alarm to go off or a security guard to materialize out of nowhere. After just ten seconds, Joe made a subtle movement with his hand—the predetermined signal to stop. A clerk was walking to the back of the store in another aisle. Adam put a toy right in front of his face, studied it with exaggerated interest, then shook his head and put the toy back on the rack. A minute later, Joe gave the all clear. Adam went right back to stuffing his pants.

Once at capacity, he walked down the aisle and headed for the door. Joe and Jeff lingered in the store for a few more minutes, and Joe bought a pack of Hubba Bubba bubble gum. Then they exited the Kmart, the automatic doors whooshing closed behind them.

Shoplifting was easy!

Shiloh and I started stealing with the brothers, but eventually, we became confident enough to splinter off our own thieves' guild. The only problem with the plan was that it required three kids. We recruited Shiloh's sister, Esmerelda, who was just as adventurous as we were. The three of us stole a whole mess of toys from that Kmart, including the entire set of My Little Pony dolls for Esmerelda.

Esmerelda inevitably let Esther in on our secret, and for a time, Esther kept quiet. But a few weeks on, when my sister and I had a small fight, she spilled the beans. But my mother didn't punish me. Instead, she told me to knock it off, and surprisingly, I did. I guess I'd started to develop a conscience, or maybe I was growing ever-more nervous about getting busted. In hindsight, there may be another reason my mother let me off the hook. One of my very first memories is of her placing a quart of milk from the supermarket rack directly into her purse.

Shoplifting was just one of many ways Shiloh and I tested the boundaries of what we could get away with that year. For nine months, we'd run all over Santa Fe, had regularly played in the arroyos, a massive no-no in New Mexico because of flash flooding during the summer monsoons. We'd snuck into the pool at the high school many times, fully a mile and a half away. In the winter, I'd dared Shiloh into nearly drowning himself when he walked over—and then fell into—an iced-over swimming pool. And by early summer, the police had been called when a car hit me at a glancing blow while he and I were tangoing in the middle of Cerrillos Road. We teetered on the edge of consequence, yet somehow always landed on our feet. But for all our unbridled freedom, we soon discovered that our actions could have repercussions.

Shiloh's sixteen-year-old brother, Daniel, had a local paper route that he'd service on his bike. Having nothing better to do, Shiloh, Esmerelda, and I trailed him one evening. We followed surreptitiously at first, but he eventually caught on to us, saying he didn't mind if we tagged along. So off we went. We had a grand time roving through parts of the city we'd never explored before.

Daniel's paper route was lengthy, and likely even longer than usual with eight- and nine-year-olds following after him on foot. We didn't arrive back from our adventures until night. Once we got back to Shiloh's trailer, we found all the adults were there in the living space, including my mother. She and Rose did the talking. Steve stood silently in the kitchen, leaning against the wall, watching.

"Where have you been?" Rose asked. "We've been worried!"

"We went with Dan on his paper route," Esmerelda explained.

"You're supposed to be back home by seven," said Rose.

"But we were with Dan. He's old. What's the big whoop?" Esmerelda asked.

Shiloh and I nodded.

"There are dangerous parts of Santa Fe," Rose responded.

My mother joined in. "David, you know you should be home by now."

"I don't get it," I said. "We're out after dark all the time."

Rose shook her head. "You all know better. So you're going to be punished."

Shiloh's father pushed off the wall and stretched.

"David," said my mother. "I've decided to let Steve spank you."

I looked toward the kitchen and gulped. "Why?"

She didn't answer. Instead, she got up, grabbed her purse, and made to leave. "Come straight home when you're finished," she said as she closed the door behind her.

There was a silent menace about my friend's father. For the entirety of my friendship with Shiloh, I'd avoided any interaction with him. He called us into the kitchen. "Esmerelda, you're first. Then you, David. Then Shiloh. You boys sit down there and there," he said, gesturing to two yellow kitchen chairs. He grabbed another of the chairs, pulled it into the middle of the small kitchen, and pointed to it. "Esmerelda, pull your pants down and bend over." She obeyed. She was wearing Wonder Woman Underoos.

He pulled his two-inch-thick leather belt off his own pants. He placed the buckle in his hand and slowly wrapped the belt around a couple of times.

"Daddy, I'm sorry," Esmerelda pleaded as she bent over the chair. "It won't happen again. I promise."

The belt came down across Esmerelda's backside with a *whap!* She screamed, flailing. Steve beat his daughter, full arm stroke after full arm stroke. He was aiming for her backside, but the blows fell indiscriminately.

Esmerelda squirmed all over like a drop of water in a pan of hot oil. She fell off the chair, writhing on the floor, all the while the blows kept falling.

Shiloh and I had front-row seats to this, knowing full well that we were next. We began crying and laughing in turns. On the one hand, it was terrifying, knowing that we would get the same beating as Esmerelda, if not worse. So we cried. On the other hand, it was hilarious to see Esmerelda flopping all over the kitchen floor. So we laughed. Back and forth it went, like a pendulum in a grandfather clock, one boy's hysterical laughter pulling the other in that direction. After reaching a feverish crescendo, the pendulum swung the other way, now with one boy's panicked crying inducing the other boy to cry.

Esmerelda's whooping finally ended. She managed to get up off the floor and pull up her pants. Now it was my turn.

Shiloh's father repeated the instructions he'd given his daughter, and I complied, bending over the chair. Once the blows rained down, I, too, started wailing and crying and begging for him to stop. Soon I was writhing on the floor, just like Esmerelda. I peed myself and finally just covered my head and tuned out. The beating eventually came to an end.

Finally, Shiloh was up. He fared no better than Esmerelda or I had, but I was too spent to pay any attention. Esmerelda and I just stared off into the distance, whimpering.

When I arrived home, my mother was waiting. She said, "I want you to know that I love you, and that's why you got a spanking."

I knew whatever had just happened, it was *not* a spanking. I walked to the bedroom I shared with Esther and opened the door. I looked back at my mother. "You should have done it yourself, then, *Mom*," I said and closed the door behind me.

My mother had to have seen my soiled pants, so I can only conclude she understood what had happened and was okay with it. Either that or she was so high that she didn't notice. Either way, this event marked the beginning of the end of my respect for my mother. I have no memory of cleaning up after myself.

A week or two after the last day of school, my mother informed Esther and me that we were moving back to Albuquerque. Though I didn't understand why at the time, I now realize it was because my mother's attempt to become self-sufficient had failed. It wasn't even a close call. An associate's degree in nursing requires two years of full-time classes. My mother hadn't made it through a single year. As a result, my grandparents saw no reason to fund an unsuccessful experiment further.

Esther and I made a stink about moving back to Albuquerque. We'd each made a best friend and had no desire to leave Santa Fe. We finally stopped objecting when we learned from Esmerelda and Shiloh that they, too, were leaving town. Shiloh's father was moving the family to Madrid ("MAD-rid"), New Mexico, a tiny village in the Ortiz Mountains between Albuquerque and Santa Fe.

It came time to leave, and Shiloh and I had a final game of *Ms. Pac-Man* at the arcade. We had a last rummage through the Albertsons dumpster for good measure, though we didn't take anything home.

Once back at his trailer, we used carbon copy pages, which Shiloh had snaked from school, to write promises to each other and plans for further adventures. Each triplet of pages was composed of white, yellow, and pink paper. If you wrote on the first page and pressed hard enough, some kind of dark coating on the back of each page transferred your words through all three. We wrote on these and buried our promises-in-triplicate behind his trailer, swearing to each other we'd return on our golden birthdays to dig them up. It was lost on our young minds that our birthdays fell on different days of the month, but we both understood it to mean a long time away.

I no longer remember what our plans had been, but I like to imagine they were for adventures so perfect in their childish conception that they're beyond the ability of my adult mind to grasp. A part of me longs to recall them or go back, dig them up, and read them. But I know those days are gone, buried deeper than our carbon-copy promises.

When Shiloh's family pulled out of the trailer park in their pickup, I held back tears, quickly wiping my face as they drove away.

3

The War Zone

Esther and I called our grandparents Mimi and Papa. The Great Depression and World War II had shaped their entire worldview. Papa emerged from the war determined to live righteously under God, provide steadily for his family, and spend frugally. When they moved to Albuquerque in the early '60s, they joined the ultraconservative Abraham Avenue Church of Christ and stayed there for decades.

Whenever the topic of my father came up, Papa would take a deep breath and close his eyes in search of patience, reciting his mantra, "The Bible says, 'If a man does not work, he does not eat.'" As an adult, I came to understand this line as metaphorical, about the work a person puts into their relationship with God, but Papa wielded it as a weapon against my father, using it in a literal sense.

My grandfather was smart but uneducated. He held the same job for most of his adult life—chief engineer at the Happy Cow Milk Company. I've no idea what responsibilities a chief engineer of a milk plant entails, but he was good at it, and they paid him a living wage.

I loved Papa because he was kind and spent time with me. He taught me long multiplication but not long division (he didn't understand the latter). We played rummy 500, checkers, and occasionally chess. This last was more "chess-adjacent" than actual chess, as neither one of us had a firm grasp of the rules. We'd often play past the point where the king was captured, just mowing down each other's pieces in a free-for-all.

Mimi was beautiful and rail thin with a tremendous 1950s beehive hairdo that stood out five inches in all directions from her delicate cranium. Between her figure and her old-white-lady blowout, she always reminded me of a Q-tip. Mimi applied base from her compact at least four or five times a day and was generally uninterested in Esther and me. She never ate dinner, which, growing up poor, I found highly suspicious. Papa did all the cooking in their household.

As for my mother, what I remember most about her is that she made doilies. They were intricate little things that seemed to appear out of thin air. She used fine, cream-colored yarn and a set of tiny metal crochet hooks. She'd follow a pattern for a few weeks, and once they were completed, she'd put them out in our apartment, little islands of prettiness in otherwise unadorned spaces.

I'd say my mother was kind and soft-spoken. She called herself a hippie and seemed a free spirit who loved rock and roll and the mountains, who despised littering in the wilderness but couldn't care less about it in the city streets. She hated authority: "Pigs," she'd mutter under her breath whenever we passed a police officer. Beyond the brief attempt at a nursing degree, I have no knowledge of her hopes or dreams. I never knew her to vote; I never saw her read.

She was also tall—five ten, to be exact—and heavyset. She had thick, straight, brown hair that ended past the small of her back. She always wore makeup when she left the house, and I thought she was pretty.

My mother's descent into heroin addiction is a mystery to me. By all accounts, she was a good student early on. As an adolescent, she enjoyed tennis, even winning a local tournament. She was a gifted piano player, and my grandparents held hopes she'd have a career in music. But something happened midway through high school; whether it was the onset of a mental illness or a crisis at home, I don't know. Regardless, she dropped out and ran away. The truth is I never really knew my mother.

When we moved back to Albuquerque, our grandfather arranged an apartment for us located in a neighborhood called La Mesa. Despite the city's recent efforts to rebrand the area as the "International District," locals still refer to it by its notorious nickname, the War Zone. My new life was smack in the middle.

We lived on Virginia Street, a block off Central and Wyoming, where sirens sounded a nighttime chorus against which gunshots could occasionally be heard. Each side of our street was lined with single-story dilapidated houses. All had wrought iron bars running vertically in front of the windows to keep would-be burglars out and desperate dreamers in. The landscaping consisted of dirt, old living room furniture, and broken-down cars. There were no parks or playgrounds—I can't remember a single tree on the block—just parking lots with dumpsters and weeds growing through the cracks in the patched asphalt. At one end of the block, behind a chain-link fence with razor wire along the top, was a hubcap scrapyard where two rabid Doberman pinschers kept guard.

We moved into our apartment complex, its stucco facade split by enormous cracks, and placed my mother's piano against the living room wall. The silent, out-of-tune instrument stood as a mockery of promises—of music, of a nursing degree, of normalcy—that would never materialize. That first night, when the lights went out, the cockroaches emerged, claiming their dominion.

Beyond adjusting to the new physical environment, I had to come to terms with being alone again. Early on, Esther made a friend next door, and they entertained themselves by watching music videos and lip-syncing to Bonnie Tyler's "Total Eclipse of the Heart." There was no room for me in their friendship. I was constantly and gnawingly lonely, like I was missing a part of myself. I missed Shiloh.

My mother's response to my complaints of boredom was the inevitable: "Go outside and meet someone."

So I went outside. Within a week, I received my first ass-kicking from a boy with whom I thought I was becoming friends.

I could have made another "friend" one time as I walked through the parking lot of a large country music club on Central Avenue. A trucker rolled down his window, called me over to his cab, and said, "Hey, kid, come here a second."

I walked over.

He looked down at me, smiled, and said, "Do you want to see the inside of my truck?"

I shook my head. Somewhere, sometime, someone had instructed me that the combination of children, strangers, and vehicles led to few positive outcomes.

"Are you sure? It's nice in here, plus I have dirty magazines we can look at!"

"No, thanks," I responded and continued my shortcut through the parking lot and on to my destination.

To occupy my time and combat loneliness, I took to leaving the War Zone to play video games, which meant walking to the Coronado mall, a solid three-mile walk through the barrio and over the I-40 interstate into a different part of Albuquerque. My mother's concerns in Santa Fe about my wandering the streets were apparently no longer operational, though I was eight years old and still believed in Santa Claus.

I'd usually have three or four quarters when I set out because my mother would sometimes give me a dollar if I nagged hard enough. Later in the month, she'd more likely give me a dollar food stamp, which I'd found a way to swap for quarters.

The currency exchange went like this: I'd go to the Circle K convenience store, use the food stamp to buy a single piece of Bazooka bubble gum for three cents, and get that bad boy into my mouth as soon as possible. I'd receive ninety-seven cents back. That's three quarters, two dimes, and two pennies. Then, having earlier found three pennies in the couch or on the street, I'd trade the two dimes and five pennies for another quarter. In this way, I'd launder my single food stamp into four quarters. Not every store clerk would allow this, but I knew which clerks at which Circle Ks would, and I timed my machinations accordingly. (Today, the storefront of one of those former Circle Ks is infamous in Albuquerque, a harrowing scene of fentanyl use, violence, and even murder, with drug users shambling through the parking lot and dozens of folks living there on the street.)

The only reason I went to the mall was to go to the arcade. Toy stores held little interest for me since I couldn't afford anything. Clothing stores didn't even rise to the level of conscious awareness. I did wander into Tower Records from time to time or sit down on a bench to people-watch. Still, the mall was just a lavish mansion to hold the arcade.

And what a magnificent arcade it was! Just approaching, it gave me goose bumps as I heard the beeps and boops and saw the flashing lights. It was ecstasy through sensory overload.

The physical space was enormous; there were hundreds of games. All the great games eventually made their way through that arcade, including *Super Mario Bros.* and my all-time personal favorite, *720°*, a skateboarding game of immense creativity and playability easily ten years ahead of its time. The mall arcade also had some newfangled games, such as *Space Harrier* and *After Burner*, which featured moving cabinets that you'd sit in for a more immersive experience. Too expensive for me, but I loved to watch.

A casual observer walking through the promenade might glance in and see a bunch of kids standing around, apparently doing nothing. But on screen after screen, life-and-death dramas played out, each person actively participating through well-timed joystick maneuvers and button presses. Here a teenager piloted his crew with precision through the peaks of the Himalayas, and there a girl just released POWs from a Soviet prison camp. One boy from the War Zone escaped his desperately lonely homelife.

I still recall the reek of that arcade, the aromas of Orange Julius, corn dogs, and french fries wafting in from the promenade. They combined with the sharp, metallic tang of quarters held securely in hand and the odor of teenage boys.

That's how I passed that summer in the War Zone, making daily trips to the mall to play video games. Mostly, I watched highly skilled teenagers kick ass on all the best arcade games of the '80s and played an occasional game myself. In those moments, I didn't notice my isolation or begrudge my circumstances.

"Mom, someone's here!" Esther yelled back into the apartment as she opened the door. Though we'd been in the new apartment for almost four months, we rarely had visitors. There stood two women in their mid-thirties. One had short, curly hair and wore a blue blouse while the other had her long, dark hair pulled back into a neat ponytail.

"Hi there. Is your mom home?" asked the woman with the curly hair.

Esther looked at them suspiciously. "What do you want?"

"We're teachers."

Esther called out again for my mother, and there was a long silence. My mother finally made her way from her bedroom over to the door.

The woman with the ponytail spoke up. "Hello. We're teachers over at La Mesa Elementary School. Now that fall's here, we're making the rounds through the neighborhood, just so everyone knows that school has started and that children need to be enrolled and attending regularly."

"Oh," said my mother.

"I see you have a daughter. Have you enrolled her yet?"

"Not yet."

"Ma'am, it's important that you enroll your children in school."

"You think I don't know that?"

"Of course, ma'am. We look forward to seeing your daughter in classes next week." With that, the teachers left.

I don't know if teachers were just "making the rounds" or if they'd caught wind that there were two kids absent from school. Regardless, after the teachers' visit, our mother organized herself enough to purchase the required school accessories and enroll us. Thus, my sister and I began our daily routine of walking to La Mesa Elementary, a fifteen-minute walk through the War Zone, always sure to cross the street to avoid the menace of the Dobermans.

I was placed in Mr. Gomez's third-grade class, and I liked him straightaway. He was young, engaging, and obsessed with Van Halen. He regularly strutted around in front of the classroom, showing off his air guitar technique. Plus, he extended music lessons for an extra thirty minutes on Fridays, which engendered endless goodwill with us kids.

A curious thing happened in Mr. Gomez's class that fall. One day, all the kids were working on their multiplication tables. I'd finished mine in about thirty seconds and had moved on to pestering the girl in front of me by poking her in the back.

Mr. Gomez spotted me and said, "David, can you come up here for a minute?"

I approached his desk.

"Listen, you're *really* quick on the uptake, and you can be a real... challenge...when you're bored. So I have an idea. How would you like to be my assistant?"

"What do you mean?"

"Well, when you're done with an exercise, you can come up to my desk and let me know. Then, maybe you could help some of the kids with their work."

"Like explain why three times five is fifteen?"

"Exactly! What do you think?"

I smiled. "Okay!"

So in an act of effortless genius, Mr. Gomez deputized me to be the class tutor. I'm sure he thought it was a win-win: His student was no longer bored and was no longer acting out, and he could kick his feet up on his desk and practice his air guitar. PA-NA-MA!

Later that fall, La Mesa held a science fair. The open secret of a science fair is that the best projects are almost always heavily aided—or even completed—by the parents. Moreover, every parent knows that the key to a good project is a solid plan. I was highly disorganized, and my mother was barely participating in my life. It was obvious that both Esther and I were going to fail at the science fair.

But an amazing thing happened! The same two teachers who had come around to our apartment helped Esther and me organize our science fair projects. We all agreed to go to the resource room each day after school and work on them. I don't remember my sister being there often, but I loved female attention, and the attention of these two teachers, in particular.

I chose a project on "oxidation in nickel versus iron metals." What this meant is that I put a few different types of nails into glass jars full of vinegar, sealed the tops, and observed day over day which nails disintegrated and which didn't. Esther chose that most time-tested of science fair chestnuts, "Do plants grow better in artificial or natural light?"

The teachers procured the necessary materials, and I began my experiments. After a couple of weeks of observation and with plenty of luxuriant supervision, I collated my results and wrote them up on a poster board in my best script. When the project was finished, I carried the presentation to the gym with the care a parent gives their newborn.

As it turned out, Esther and I both won the science fair for our grades that year. Had those teachers worked the refs in our favor? Who knows? It was a huge positive boost for me, as it was, I assume, for my sister. I don't remember my mother's reaction; I like to think we remembered to tell her.

The third-grade science fair was my first exposure to science. It was a revelation to me that one could learn about the inner workings of the world through systematic exploration, that simply writing down a hypothesis—an educated guess—and then setting up the conditions to test it could be so powerful. But even as I marveled at this new understanding, I couldn't have known that science itself struggles with questions central to my own life: How do minds emerge from matter? What is mental illness? Why do some kids thrive while others falter? These are the kinds of questions that challenge science's very foundations, so it's worth briefly examining these foundations.

Our modern lives are predicated on the success of science and the scientific method. At the smallest scale, twentieth-century physicists smashed all manner of particles together to explain how matter behaves. That work led to understanding of how electrons move in different materials. Building on this knowledge, scientists invented devices that control electron flow—leading to the microprocessors that power our modern computers. Twentieth-century biologists isolated the chemical compound of DNA, and now we understand genetics so well that a biotech industry is growing up around personalized medicine. From power lines to penicillin to the internet, science and technology have changed the daily fabric of our lives.

Yet, for all these triumphs, science faces a surprising and essential failure. This failure becomes particularly evident in fields close to my own work: biology, neuroscience, and artificial intelligence—all attempts to understand how complex systems emerge from simpler parts.

The scientific method employs observation of the natural world. For example, a third grader might think that nickel nails should last longer than iron nails in water or vinegar because he saw many rusty iron nails in his trips roaming through Santa Fe with his buddy. Our little scientist devises an experiment that tests the conjecture by removing all extraneous variables. So he fills a bunch of mason jars, each with a different liquid, then adds nickel nails to some jars and iron nails to others and watches what happens. In this way, the scientific method has been used time and again to successfully explain how natural phenomena behave in highly controlled and simplified settings.

But critically, science *requires* highly controlled and simplified settings. And this is precisely its weakness. For our young scientist to extrapolate his findings to the everyday world, he must make a subtle and far-reaching assumption: that what works in the controlled setting of the mason jar applies to nails in wooden boards that have been rained on for years, scraped by rocks during flash floods, and buried and dug up by coyotes.

The real world is never simple. It's filled with a diversity of objects and processes: coffee cups, cacti, waterfalls, prairie dogs, quartz crystals, and stars. While a cactus and a prairie dog live very different lives, we believe the foundations of life—composition from cells, DNA, and so forth—are shared. Even the force of gravity, which keeps a prairie dog's feet on the ground, operates on a grander scale to hold together the nuclear furnace of our sun. In short, despite wildly different sizes, time scales, and contexts, scientists believe that an object's features and behaviors depend on the material and processes from which they are built, all governed by universal physical laws, such as gravity.

But let's look at an extreme example, where the scientist's perspective becomes obviously tenuous. *You*. You are a human who has a mind with the capacity to read and reflect. While you arose from a combination of just two cells, an egg and sperm—now long gone—you have an identity that lasts over a span of decades. What if we wanted to use the scientific method to explain your sense of yourself? Could we really reduce your conscious mind to a set of underlying processes that, when composed, create the feeling of you, the *you of right now*? It sounds preposterous, but neuroscientists and philosophers ponder the question in earnest.

In all but the simplest cases, science struggles to explain or predict the behavior of a whole from its parts. Sure, we can find correlations—statistical relationships between variables—and make predictions based on patterns. A genetic test might suggest predispositions to certain illnesses without ever explaining how specific genes create the condition. But constructing understanding from the ground up—the idea that knowing fundamental laws means you can explain everything—proves impossible with today's methods.

In 1972, the Nobel laureate P. W. Anderson addressed this limitation when he argued that while scientists accept reductionism—the idea that everything can be reduced to fundamental physical laws—constructionism should be viewed with more skepticism. Constructionism is the idea that the world can be built up and understood from these fundamental laws alone. Anderson argues you can't build biology from chemistry alone, just as you couldn't have predicted DNA's double helix from basic chemical principles. The history and context of evolution matters. Each level of complexity requires its own framework of understanding.

Anderson argued his point using a joke that summarized an exchange between two famous authors:

> Fitzgerald: "The rich are different than us."
> Hemingway: "Yes, they have more money than us."

The quip highlights a fundamental truth about complexity in the physical world: What appears to be merely quantitative (having more money) can become qualitative (being a different kind of person). This same principle applies to one of science's greatest challenges: explaining how parts become wholes. The title of Anderson's essay says it all: "More Is Different."

In summary, as we move up through the hierarchy of physical matter, the increasing complexity and quantity of interactions at each successive level make constructionism ineffective and thereby make reductionism less valuable. Just as having more money fundamentally changes one's experience, the sheer number of components and their interactions at higher levels of organization make it challenging for science to explain phenomena using the same principles that work at lower levels.

These limitations don't diminish science's astounding achievements. From the smartphone in your pocket to the medicines extending our lives, scientific understanding has fundamentally transformed human existence. But when we confront questions about how complex wholes arise from simpler parts—whether in living systems, conscious minds, artificial intelligence, or society—we must approach with humility.

I didn't know it then, but as I stood in the gym with my jars of disintegrating nails, I was already brushing up against these fundamental limits of science. Not with my simple science fair project; that offered clean, predictable results. Rather, the really interesting questions in my eight-year-old life revolved around why my mother wasn't working and why we lived in a neighborhood called the War Zone. These belonged to a realm of complexity that science has yet to disentangle.

4

A Crumbling House

Through the second half of the year in Santa Fe and the entirety of our time in the War Zone, my mother's mental health was in decline. She was on drugs, whether prescribed, illicit, or both, I'm unsure. She began to gain weight and rarely got off the couch except to go to bed or to warm something up to eat. She had nothing to occupy her time beyond the chore of parenting, in which she was no more than minimally engaged.

The truth was my mother's life was falling apart. Like a house that goes neglected for a long while, any individual observation seems no different from the day before. But compare across years, and you observe that the roof is caving, the paint is all peeled away, and the windows broken, leaving you to wonder what shadows lurk inside. It was hard to believe that just two years earlier, my mother had been fired up to get a nursing degree.

Although my grandparents handled the larger expenses and made sure we weren't thrown out on the street, my mother nonetheless contended with crushing poverty. She wouldn't or couldn't work, and my father wouldn't or couldn't pay child support. He hadn't been seen by anyone since the night he'd tried to burn down our apartment. On the single occasion that he wrote to Esther and me, he asked *us* to send *him* some money. The letter read something like this:

A Crumbling House

Hey kids,

I'm away in Denver taking care of some things. But I love you a whole bunch! By the way, if you find any money, maybe a dollar in the couch, will you write a letter and send it to me?

Love,
Dad

I don't remember being put out by this correspondence, but Esther and I did respond to it. My sister penned the letter, and I contributed ideas. It read along the lines of:

Hi Dad,

We miss you! We don't have any money to send you. David says you can get a food stamp if you ask Mom real nice. By the way, we have a question, too. Do you really love us? Please check the box below and send the letter back.

[ ] Yes   [ ] No

Love,
Esther and David

I don't think our father replied.

The TV was always on in our house. In the morning, it was Phil Donahue, then *The Young and the Restless*, then *Days of Our Lives*. A break for lunch, then *Guiding Light* and *General Hospital*, followed by Judge Wapner and *The People's Court*. Then a few comedy reruns before the local news at five. We had *Knots Landing, Dynasty, Dallas, The Love Boat,* and *Fantasy Island* on weeknights.

My mother's one lifeline was my grandmother. There was a phone next to her La-Z-Boy chair so she could answer my grandmother's phone calls without getting up. These calls came three or four times a day, minimum. I overheard only small talk: soap opera storylines, events in my grandmother's circle. But in hindsight, I'm sure my grandmother was keeping tabs on her very ill daughter and, indirectly, on Esther and me.

All of which meant that, by third grade, my mother wasn't an emotional presence in my life. Yes, there was a bit of food in the fridge, and the heat and electricity worked. It was as if Esther and I were latchkey kids, except that my mother never *left* home. I mostly ignored her. Esther got stuck with the housework. Our mother expected her to clean up everything, only ever asking me to "pick up the carpet." We didn't own a vacuum, so that meant I was to get down on all fours and pick up any crud by hand.

Our small family's precarious situation finally fell apart sometime in late fall. I knew something was up because my mother had her friend Anna come stay with us. She was a thin, brown-haired woman from Farmington, in the northwest corner of New Mexico. She and my mother went way back to their hippie Christian commune days. Anna arrived with her kids, a boy and a girl of roughly the same age as my sister and I.

We all crammed into our tiny apartment, and at first, this was a welcome change. There were other kids to hang out with, and there was more food on the table. Anna knew an old hombre named Eagle, who she and my mother talked openly about flirting with, in the hopes that he'd buy us groceries.

One morning, a couple of days into Anna's visit, I woke up to find my mother gone. Anna sat Esther and me down and explained that my mother needed a break, but not to worry, because she'd be back soon. In the meantime, Anna would be taking care of us.

Anna was an excellent short-term surrogate, and at first, I didn't really notice my mother's absence. Anna made us popcorn balls and attempted to keep us busy with educational activities. But after a few days, I began to miss my mother. There was that time she let me crawl into bed with her after the *Poltergeist* trailers started showing on television. And we did occasionally play *Pac-Man* together on the Atari 2600 that my grandparents had purchased; I'd have to play with the joystick upside down to make it competitive because she was awful at it. But still.

To my eight-year-old self, my mother was simultaneously everything and nothing. Invisible, but ever present. She was a part of me that I never knew was separate from me. Until the moment she went away.

I started getting into trouble, the form of my misbehavior shaped by my mother's neglect. Outside the classroom's imposed organization, I was used to doing as I pleased, when I pleased. A few days into Anna's supervision, she sent me to my room for the afternoon for some misdeed I'd undoubtedly committed. While my mother forced us to take long naps in our room throughout our childhood, perhaps so she could get high or just to get us out of her hair, she'd never sent us to our room as a form of punishment.

I didn't much care to stay in my room, so I decided to "run away." I had no intention of going far, but I thought my sneaking out might give Anna a good fright. So I slipped out of my bedroom window.

A teenager from the neighborhood often played *Pac-Land* at one of the Circle Ks where I regularly laundered my food stamps. *Pac-Land* was an intriguing side scroller featuring multistage levels and is credited by some for influencing the greatest video game ever made,

Super Mario Bros. I went to Circle K, hoping to catch a bit of this kid's awesomeness. I hung out for the better part of an hour, appreciating his skill and learning new secrets and warp tunnels in the later levels.

When I finally returned to our apartment, my grandfather was waiting for me. Anna had panicked and called my grandparents when she noticed I wasn't in my room and saw the window was open. I'd never considered my grandfather to be an imposing man. But at that moment, with his six-three build, severely receding hairline, and stern look on his face, I became frightened. He didn't lay a hand on me, though. He just took me aside and lectured me on why what I'd done was wrong. That was the end of it.

Or so I thought.

What I'd really done was set off a life-changing sequence of events.

It turns out that my mother wasn't "taking a break" but in a psychiatric hospital, seeking relief from severe depression. She'd asked Anna to watch us, and their friendship was clearly strong enough that Anna had agreed. She must have even pulled her own children out of school for a short time.

My grandparents must have known that my mother was going into the hospital, because it's preposterous to think she could have managed it on her own. From there, I infer that my grandparents were aware that Anna was watching us, hoping that my mother would quickly get back on her feet. Finally, I take it that they were nervous about the whole damned thing.

So, when Anna was forced to call my grandparents and explain to them that I'd run away, the gig was up. My grandparents realized the crumbling house of their daughter's life had collapsed. They immediately began considering alternative living arrangements for Esther and me.

My grandparents were longtime attendees at the Abraham Avenue Church of Christ. Through the church, they'd heard of an orphanage called the Albuquerque Christian Children's Home (ACCH). My grandfather made some calls, and I'm guessing a timely donation, and the ACCH agreed to take Esther and me that very night.

We threw our clothes into black trash bags and got into the back seat of our grandparents' Cadillac. My grandparents drove us across the Rio Grande, to the west side of Albuquerque and the children's home. I never saw Anna or her children again.

Our grandparents never explained why they weren't taking us in—they were well off enough to own a Cadillac and a middle-class home in a middle-class neighborhood, after all—but I was too young to ask questions. I don't remember any conversation about what the ACCH was or what going there might mean for me. Our mother went to the hospital; therefore, Esther and I went to the Albuquerque Christian Children's Home.

It was dark outside by the time our grandparents drove Esther and me out of the War Zone. The uncertainty of not knowing our destination made it seem like we were driving forever; the final few minutes on a dirt road through the desert felt as if we'd left Albuquerque far behind. In a sense, we had. Everything we'd known, everything we'd thought about ourselves and our family, was changing as fast as the Cadillac could carry us.

At the ACCH, a small group of adults awaited our arrival. We were ushered into Cottage 3, where Esther and I met our new houseparents, Mr. and Mrs. Christiansen. After a brief exchange of pleasantries, my grandparents vanished into the night.

Mr. Christiansen took charge of me while Mrs. Christiansen tended to Esther. He instructed me to address them by their surnames, "Mr.

and Mrs. Christiansen," emphasizing their roles as "housefather" and "housemother." Due to our short-notice arrival, a room hadn't been prepared for me. I was to share a space with two brothers, Willie and Merle, for the night. When I mentioned that Esther and I had always shared a room, Mr. Christiansen firmly asserted that boys roomed with boys and girls with girls.

We dragged a mattress into Willie and Merle's room, where the brothers were already settled. Merle, a redheaded kid my age, and Willie, a few years older and blond, occupied a bunk bed at the far end of the room. The space, like all the rooms in the cottage, measured about fifteen by ten feet, designed to accommodate up to four children, with bunk beds on each side. We positioned my mattress on the lower bunk near the door. As Mr. Christiansen provided a basic orientation, I did my best making my bed; I couldn't remember ever doing it. Once finished, he retreated to the houseparents' apartments.

The moment Mr. Christiansen's footsteps faded, Willie approached, his face contorted. "You little twerp!" He punched me as hard as he could in the stomach.

I crumpled to the floor; he'd knocked the wind out of me.

Later that night, I cried myself to sleep. In my dreams, I found myself atop a mountain, peeing on everyone below in an act of glorious revenge. When I awoke in the morning, I found I'd wet the bed.

PART 2

CHAOS: 1983–1988

Time is the very fabric of our reality. There's no stopping it, no escaping it, and no changing it. From the firing of neurons to a swirling rainstorm, physical systems move to time's rhythm, so we give them a name when we're focused on how they change: *dynamical systems*. It was through the study of the weather that mathematician and meteorologist Edward Lorenz made an accidental discovery about the nature of our world. He stumbled upon a mathematical phenomenon lurking in dynamical systems called *chaos*.

In 1961, Lorenz and his team at the Massachusetts Institute of Technology were tinkering with a computer simulation of a weather system on a Royal Bee LGP-30, a clunky beast about the size of a washing machine, weighing a hefty eight hundred pounds. To save time, they fed the computer's final output from one simulation back in as the next simulation's starting point. Not with perfect precision, mind you. They rounded the numbers off to one-thousandth of a decimal. So instead of entering 4.2315, for example, they entered 4.231. This seemingly trivial shortcut unleashed a whirlwind, and they ended up with wildly different results from what they had expected.

After analyzing the code, the weather simulation results, and the underlying mathematical model, Lorenz understood there had been no mistake. The simulation results *did* depend on the truncated portion, the miniscule 0.0005 they had failed to type in. He realized the weather, and by extension, our world, danced to a tune so intricate that even the tiniest tremor could throw it into an unpredictable tailspin.

Across the Atlantic, in the early 1970s, David Ruelle and Floris Takens expanded Lorenz's discovery, showing that chaos wasn't confined to computer weather models but was woven into real-world phenomena—like the turbulent flow of fluids. Thus, a new lens on reality came into focus, revealing the web of interdependence that binds the weather, ecosystems, and even societies.

Not all dynamical systems are chaotic. The grandfather clock's pendulum, a steadfast metronome, keeps time with predictable precision. But hang another pendulum onto the end of the first pendulum, creating a swinging duo locked in a wild waltz, and the rhythm fractures. Imagine you push this double pendulum, and it embarks on a spree, looping and barrel-rolling until it finally settles at the bottom. Then, you push it again, just the same as before, but its path forks, diverging completely from the first in a chaotic choreography.

In these chaotic systems, you cannot know in any practical sense how the past shapes the future. If only you could start the double pendulum in *precisely* the same state, it would repeat its first path; it contains no inherent randomness that might vary the trajectories. But you cannot. For the double pendulum to repeat two trials exactly would require an *infinite* degree of precision, which simply doesn't exist. If you altered the second run's initial position from the first by even one miniscule part in a thousand—just as Lorenz did—then sooner or later, the paths of the two runs will diverge.

The brain's activity, too, is an intricate waltz. We are no simple creatures of stimulus and response: Neurons activate other neurons that activate yet other neurons, which feed back to reactivate the first. In this way, feedback loops amplify thoughts into being. This electrical polyphony allows us to hold on to a phone number or street address after hearing it. And within this polyphony, chaos also rears its head.

Imagine running the experiment, making the tiniest changes to my brain state when I was young, tweaking the millisecond timing of the electrical pulse of a single neuron. Better still, imagine that Federico Faggin and his engineering team missed their deadline of releasing the Z80 microprocessor, resulting in a delay in the arrival of *Ms. Pac-Man* to our arcade in Santa Fe by a single day. Shiloh and I end up blowing our quarter on an impossibly difficult game like *Gravitar*.

Either of these changes might birth two Davids. The first, initially a ghost of the other, mimics the second in precise lockstep: experiencing the same emotions, playing the same video games, stealing the same toys. Over the years, the two Davids become ever so slightly out of sync. Then one day, one of the twelve-year-old Davids doesn't laugh at a joke while the other does. The two Davids no longer dance in lockstep although they still attend the same classes, perhaps one David sitting in the front while the other hunches down in the back row. Five years later, one David allows his girlfriend to pull him away from a terrible idea while the other smokes meth for the first time. From this point forward, their lives are on different trajectories along a spectrum of possibilities. Ultimately, one David soars to academic heights on the East Coast, graduating magna cum laude from the Massachusetts Institute of Technology. The other remains in New Mexico and stumbles into darker paths, ultimately panhandling on the streets of Santa Fe and sleeping in the dry arroyo beds on the outskirts of town.

Hidden in the staggeringly complex dynamics of our chaotic world, both outcomes were possibilities for me.

5

Orphaned by the Living

The Albuquerque Christian Children's Home was located on the west side of town, on the edge of the Rio Grande bosque. While *bosque* means "forest" in Spanish, in New Mexico, it's a regional term for that rare treasure in the desert—the green strips of woodlands that grow along both sides of the river. The ACCH was pushed up against the bosque, which went back a quarter of a mile to the Rio Grande, while the front side of the compound faced the open desert and the ass end of a strip mall. We kids were greeted every morning by dumpsters filled with refuse from the local Albertsons.

The campus was a ten-acre square plot, fenced in on three sides to delineate the property's boundaries. The back side abutted a canal, which you could cross thanks to a narrow, wooden bridge. I crossed it regularly to go wandering in the bosque, which the houseparents permitted if you asked. Aside from the local public schools we attended, it was the only physical escape allowed.

There were three houses for kids, unimaginatively called Cottage 1, Cottage 2, and Cottage 3. The word *cottage* is highly misleading here as it implies a charming, breezy home with light construction, possibly on the edge of an idyllic body of water. Each ACCH "cottage" was a redbrick ranch-style house with a footprint of over six thousand square feet. The floor plan was a single-story rectangle with shared living spaces in the middle and bedrooms along the perimeter. Each cottage comfortably housed twenty people and came complete with an industrial kitchen and a living room so large you had to raise your voice to be heard across it.

The cottages were lined up in a row, 1, 2, 3, at the front of the property, just behind the Albertsons. Huge cottonwood trees intermingled with the houses to provide shade. Behind the cottages, there was a concrete basketball court, aging but serviceable. Farther back was a small playground with seesaws and enormous tractor tires to play on for the younger kids. You could find black widow spiders the size of silver dollars earning a tidy living in the interior of those tires. Alongside the houses, court, and playground were about five acres of undeveloped desert. You could tromp around there if you had a mind, but you were guaranteed to fill your shoes with sand. At the back end of the property, tucked in the corner near the bridge to the bosque, was a little administrative building where the group-home executives labored to keep the ACCH above water.

Houseparents ran the individual households in the orphanage, one set per cottage. They lived there with the kids, typically in a separate wing called the *houseparents' apartments*. A couple oversaw as many as sixteen kids, so across three cottages, there'd be between thirty and fifty kids at the ACCH at any given time.

If the houseparents were so inclined, the children would sometimes call them by their first names, as we did with Jake and Tania Lovato. In other cases, such as Mr. and Mrs. Christiansen, the houseparents required you to use their surnames. One set of houseparents at the ACCH, the Guzzlers, who lasted just a few months, said it would be okay if we called them *Mom* and *Dad*. These newbies had unwittingly overstepped a sacred boundary. These adults might have been our chaperones—might have even wielded power over us—but they weren't our parents, and we sure as hell weren't their children. Smelling blood, we kids began calling them Mommy and Daddy, explicitly baiting them (and perhaps subconsciously flirting with the luxurious possibility of actually having parents). The confrontation finally came to a head in the group-home van.

"Mommy, do you love me?" asked Diamond. Diamond was a thirteen-year-old girl.

Mrs. Guzzler hesitated and then replied, "Yes, Diamond."

"Mommy, would you still love me if I peed my pants?"

"Now, Diamond."

"I think I have to go right now, Mommy."

Mrs. Guzzler said nothing but looked over at Mr. Guzzler, who was driving.

At once comprehending Diamond's brilliant ploy, I joined in: "Daddy, I want a lollipop!"

Nothing.

"Daddy! *I want a lollipop!*" I yelled with my voice all pouty.

Then Omar joined in. *"Lol-li-pop!"* Next thing you know, all the group-home kids were pounding the van seats and chanting in unison, *"Lol-li-pop! Lol-li-pop!"*

Though every kid got a few days' restrictions for that stunt, it worked. That night, "Mom and Dad" went back to being "Mrs. and Mr. Guzzler." Both sides were relieved.

It was a miracle if a set of houseparents lasted a year. During my time, I lived with the Christiansens, the Lovatos, the Carpenters, the Blankenships, the Guzzlers, the Gonzalezes, the Johnsons, the Texieras, and the Machos. There was also the relief housemother, Grandma, a tough-as-nails middle-aged lady who always had an apron tied around her hips.

Houseparenting inevitably focused on the practical aspects of parenting at the expense of the emotional. It was a simple matter of math. A 16:1 kid-to-adult ratio left very little one-on-one time (typically only one houseparent at a time was on duty). We kids didn't much give a shit about them, and given how many kids they had to contend with, the feeling seemed to be mutual. Other than anger related to discipline, in my experience, the emotions between children and houseparents were for the most part no different from those between kids at a school dance and the PTA chaperones. There's no sugarcoating it—we lived alone emotionally and fended for ourselves. I recall early on in my stay at the home, I was convinced there was a man under my bed with a knife. I called and called for the housefather, but he never came. He thought I was throwing a fit to get attention.

Looking back now, I suspect many of the houseparents genuinely valued mentoring kids and helping them grow in challenging circumstances. But they had to contend with children who had significant emotional and behavioral issues. The worst-behaved kids consumed wildly disproportionate amounts of houseparents' time and emotional bandwidth. In a world where attention was the most valuable currency, it paid to be bad.

For the most part, group-home life for children revolves around chores. (Movies have nailed this aspect of the orphanage experience.) Life there is simultaneously the same as in an ordinary family household and yet totally different. On the one hand, there are still dishes to wash and garbage to take out. On the other, there are twenty people at every single meal, so each of these jobs is a real effort. Children do just about all the chores in a group home, with one of the houseparents supervising the process and checking the work afterward. Since the group home is a legal entity that must satisfy health inspections, the standard of cleanliness is exceptionally high.

Good ol' Grandma, the relief housemother, actually wore a white glove. No bullshit. She'd run her hand lightly over a counter and inspect the glove. If she saw anything amiss, you'd have to redo everything.

Chores in the group home were viewed as character building, and boy howdy, did we build character! We built character in the morning before breakfast; we built character after breakfast. We strengthened our moral fiber when we got home from school, before dinner, and after dinner. There were special character-building workshops on the weekends that involved less common kinds of work on the ACCH grounds. The one I hated the most was the Sisyphean task of hoeing weeds in the desert under the beating summer sun. I mean, who thought that one up?

Esther and I would beg our mother to take us out, and early on, she would often yield to our pleading, removing us from the group home three times that first year and a half. But each time, she brought us back, no better able to look after us than she'd been when we first arrived.

We quickly learned that the first rule of living in an orphanage is you don't talk about living in an orphanage. We literally never used the term. In fact, there was an entire calculus of syllables when it came to referring to the Albuquerque Christian Children's Home. We kids alluded to it in many ways, depending on context. Sometimes we just used the full name: "Al-bu-quer-que Chris-tian Child-ren's Home." That's nine damned syllables! Totally unwieldy. Plus, it sure sounds like an orphanage. Most often, we called it "the A-C-C-H." Five syllables. Okay, we're getting somewhere. We also called the ACCH "the group home," three syllables, but potentially understood by outsiders. Finally, we just shortened it to "the home." Two syllables, near maximal efficiency, and total obfuscation.

Note there was always the word *the* at the beginning, even though it cost a syllable. For example, we never got on the public school bus to "go home" but to "go to *the* home." As surely as we knew how to breathe, every one of us instinctively understood that *the home* was in no way *home*.

What the hell *is* an orphan in modern times, anyway? The current approach in the United States to the issue of imperiled children no longer involves orphanages. Rather, the goal is to place children in long-term foster care in the hope of finding a safe, nurturing environment that approximates the family unit. But group homes still exist as a last resort for children who would otherwise end up on the street. I don't think the ACCH was ever intended to be a long-term living facility, although that did happen—as it happened for Esther and me. Most often, there was a constant flux, with children coming and going.

These days, most kids in children's homes are "orphaned by the living"—social orphans. You can find these phrases on the ACCH website and in promotional material that group homes across the United States put together when soliciting donations. The expressions are intended to capture the complexities of modern society. Over 150 years ago, when orphanages became fixtures, deaths of people with dependent children were commonplace. But the US doesn't suffer from disease in the same way we used to. Nor, thankfully, have we endured a deadly war on our own soil in modern times.

But there's no shortage of problems. There are no meaningful cures for the worst mental illnesses. Over 12 percent of the US population lives in poverty, and 1 in 175 Americans is incarcerated. Prescription opioids, fentanyl, and meth make quick addicts of their users, destroying families in the process.

So now most modern group homes are filled with the children of the poor, drug addicts, or the mentally ill, and typically some combination of the three. Esther and I were a classic example. Our mother was in a psychiatric ward, battling severe depression and addiction, while our father was nowhere to be found, possibly running from the law for drug-related misdeeds. Though both our parents were alive, Esther and I were, by any functional definition of the word, orphans.

In some ways, our fate might have been worse. When parents are deceased, there's a sense of finality that allows others to feel like they can intercede on behalf of the children. Instead, Esther and I found ourselves in a yearslong limbo, where no one was willing to step in because our parents were still living, albeit unable or unwilling to care for us.

Children were occasionally adopted or entered long-term foster care. A couple of times, a child at the ACCH ended up on the local news channel's Wednesday's Child program, which aired during the evening news and promoted children in search of adoptive parents. Two brothers at the ACCH were featured on the program and adopted a year later. Sometimes, adults affiliated with the group home took an interest in a particular child, providing a break by taking the kid out on weekends. These were ACCH volunteers, members from the Church of Christ community, and sometimes even houseparents. If things went well and if the kid's parents consented, these folks, on rare occasions, adopted the child.

We *wanted* to be taken by new parents. We *wanted* to be in foster care. But for those of us who'd lived a long time at the ACCH, it was always complicated. There was a mother, a father, who just might… maybe…someday…be able to take us back.

Plenty of kids ran away. Sometimes, you never saw them again. Most often, they were found by the police and brought back. One time, Jake Lovato had to track down a sixteen-year-old girl and a ten-year-old boy who'd run away together. The kids had made it as far as the Greyhound bus stop in Rio Rancho, about five miles north on Coors Boulevard. When Jake found them, they were holding up a sign that read, "We'll go anywhere."

I never seriously considered running away, my little stunt in the War Zone with my mother's friend Anna, our brief caretaker, notwithstanding. While light-years away from perfect, I understood that the ACCH provided protection from the elements, was a reliable source of food, and kept me in school. But for the last thirty-five years, I still dream about running away from the ACCH. These days, my dreams are filled with negotiations with my former houseparents about why I don't need to be there any longer. Perhaps in the future, I'll just up and leave.

6

Ask and Ye Shall Find

Within a week of living at the ACCH, I discovered that the "Christian" in Albuquerque Christian Children's Home was no bullshit. The place was insanely religious. When I'd lived with my mother, we'd occasionally attended church with our grandparents, but that was it. At the ACCH, every single morning, before we even did our chores, all the kids in a cottage congregated for a ten-minute devotional. We prayed before every meal, and the prayer always ended in Jesus's name.

We also had our thrice-weekly doses of vitamin church. Most important was Sunday morning, which included Sunday school for kids, followed by the regular service and perhaps a potluck dinner afterward. Church was only canceled once a year: the evening service on Super Bowl Sunday.

The ACCH attended the University Church of Christ congregation right near the University of New Mexico. Our church consisted of perhaps four hundred souls who regularly attended, mostly old folks plus some middle-aged couples and a few younger families recruited to help revitalize the aging congregation.

One of the congregants was an old man—I never knew his name—but we called him the Candyman. Every week after church let out, the young kids would run up to him and ask him for candy. He would dig into his suit jacket pocket, procuring an individually wrapped piece for each kid. Sometimes it was a mint or a cherry-flavored Jolly Rancher. I was partial to butterscotch. The Candyman knew he'd get hit up by at least three dozen kids each and every week. His pockets were very full, as was his heart.

Like Santa Claus or the tooth fairy, the Candyman was one of those childhood institutions that you sadly aged out of. At some point, each child would come to the realization that they were too old to ask for a piece of candy. But the young kids loved that bald old man, with his brown suit and bowlegged walk. I'd like to think Saint Peter gave him a piece of nicely wrapped, old-fashioned divinity when he made it through the Pearly Gates.

The pastor was a balding man with gray hair in his late fifties named Jim Aaronson. He dressed well, typically in a slick gray jacket with a white turtleneck underneath. He had a degree from Pepperdine University in Malibu, which is affiliated with the Churches of Christ. I thought Rev. Aaronson was a smart, hip dude given his sharp dress, academic bona fides, and occasional mentions of exotic Southern California.

To an external observer, I would have looked like a fidgety kid who was spacing out during church. But I was picking up what Rev. Aaronson was putting down, and I got my fair share of the Good News. By the time I had made it to fourth grade, I'd started believing in Jesus.

I also noticed conflicts and contradictions between what I learned in the Bible and commonly known scientific facts. In particular, Genesis states that the creation of the universe and the world was pretty much all buttoned up after six days. Six days doesn't exactly square with the modern scientific consensus that our planet is 4.5 billion years old or that dinosaurs dominated life on Earth for 165 million years.

Ask and Ye Shall Find

My houseparents didn't believe in evolution, and when I asked about the dinosaurs and their relation to the Old Testament, their answers made no sense. So I went up the chain of command to get to the bottom of the dinosaur conundrum.

Following service one Sunday, I made sure to quickstep it to hit up the Candyman before any of the other kids. Then I ran up to the front of the church, where the pastor was greeting other members of the congregation. After I waited around impatiently for a few minutes, the crowd finally cleared, and I had my opportunity to put my important queries forward to our pastor.

"I have questions about the dinosaurs."

"You're from the group home, aren't you?" he asked.

"Yes. See, the Bible says the world was created in six days, and then God rested for a day, and that's it. But in the science books I read..."

"I bet I can guess...that dinosaurs existed a lot longer than five thousand years ago, and for a lot longer than seven days?"

"Yeah. But my houseparents..." I trailed off again.

"I wouldn't worry too much about the dinosaurs. They were definitely here, and they existed for millions of years."

I was excited to hear this. "But what about Genesis?" I asked.

"People interpret things differently. For my part, I think the dinosaurs were here for millions of years."

I didn't fully understand, but I thanked the pastor and split to catch up with the others before the group-home van pulled away.

I realize now that I unconsciously interpreted my pastor's answer as giving me permission to think for myself. Though he didn't come out and say it, the message I heard was that I shouldn't accept at face value everything that my houseparents asserted as true.

Sometime in the fourth grade, I decided I wanted a Bible to dig a little more deeply into the stories for myself. One afternoon, I mentioned this to Bobby, who lived in my cottage. Bobby was a gorgeous Hispanic boy with bright blue eyes who'd quickly figured out his good looks and friendly disposition could get him whatever he needed in our small world.

"Why would you want a Bible, anyway?" Bobby asked around a big wad of bubble gum. "Wanna be a preacher?"

"I don't know; I just want one. The stories are good."

"Well, there's a lady at church who gives kids free Bibles if you learn the names of the books by heart."

"Really? Like, *all* of them?"

"Yep."

In the Protestant Bible, there are thirty-nine books in the Old Testament and twenty-seven in the New Testament. I started studying.

A few days later, we were climbing one of the enormous cottonwood trees on the ACCH property. After we'd found some branches to hang from, Bobby said, "All right, Preacher Tippy-Toes, let's hear it."

"*Tippy-Toes?*"

"That's how you walk, and you want to be a preacher, so that's your name now."

"Okay. Whatever." I filled my lungs to capacity. In a droning voice, I ticked off all the books of the Bible: "Genesis, Exodus, Leviticus, Numbers, Deuteronomy, Joshua, Judges, Ruth, First and Second Samuel, First and Second Kings, First and Second Chronicles, Ezra, Nehemiah, Esther."

I took another huge deep breath and finished the Old Testament. I took one last gulp of air and then switched to singing the New Testament song, which we'd learned in Sunday school.

Bobby grinned. "I think you're ready."

The next Sunday, I approached the pew where the old lady was sitting and did my thing.

A few weeks later, the nice old lady caught up with me after Sunday service. "Here you go, David. A brand-new Bible."

"Thank you so much!" I said, accepting the gift and giving her my best smile.

She'd had the Bible covered in a sweet black leather case with a white dove that had my full name sewn into it. I unzipped the case and rapidly paged through the front of the book. It was the King James version.

That Bible was the first possession I ever valued. I treasured it. I read a large portion of it and highlighted quite a bit of the scripture. I like to imagine that the first verse I ever highlighted was "Ask, and it shall be given you; seek, and ye shall find."

Esther and I were in and out of the group home quite a bit that first year. My mother would be stable enough to leave the hospital, and after a couple of weeks back on her feet, she'd take Esther and me out of the ACCH. We'd unenroll at Marie Hughes Elementary—the school we went to when we were at the home—pack up all our belongings, move back to the War Zone, and reenroll at La Mesa. A month or two would roll by, and my mother would again become depressed enough to go back to the psych ward. Unenroll, pack, move, reenroll. Eventually, all three of us realized this wasn't working, so our mother decided we should remain at the ACCH even when she wasn't in the hospital.

During one of the periods when Esther and I were living with our mother, we drove out to visit Shiloh's family. I hadn't seen him for nearly a year, so I was near bursting with excitement. I still considered him my best friend.

Shiloh's family lived in Madrid, New Mexico, a tiny village of about two hundred souls in the Ortiz Mountains halfway between

Albuquerque and Santa Fe. The town ran about a third of a mile through a few dry, narrow hills before opening up on either side. Madrid was originally a coal mining outfit in the late 1800s, but the operation closed in the 1950s, and most or all the miners left. By the early '80s, the town was downright seedy, with a highly fluid boundary between grizzled drug users and avant-garde artists.

When we arrived in town, I noticed that most houses appeared to be run-down or abandoned. There was no adobe; instead, the house exteriors were made of wood clapboard siding. The paint was gone on most dwellings, revealing graying, weather-stained wood underneath. Here and there, a porch lurched at an awkward angle. A couple of stray dogs ran through the streets.

Our mother pulled into the dirt driveway of one dilapidated house and parked. Shiloh ran out to greet us. The moment we arrived, the adults and my sister scattered: My mother went inside to visit with Rose, where they proceeded to get high, while Esther went off to play with Esmerelda. It was just Shiloh and me.

"Wanna smoke?" Shiloh asked.

"Smoke?"

"You know, a cigarette."

"Is it fun?" I asked.

"Yeah, makes you all woozy."

"Okay!"

Once we were safely hidden behind someone else's house, he took out a tin, and I watched him roll a cigarette with Zig-Zag rolling paper and Top tobacco. Shiloh finished rolling the cigarette, lit it, and took a big drag. He passed the cigarette to me, its end all wet from his lips. I'd never smoked, but if Shiloh vouched for it, I was sure it'd be awesome. The cigarette smoke tasted gross, but as promised, I became pleasantly buzzed.

"Esther and me mostly don't live with our mom anymore," I said as I exhaled. I told Shiloh some more about living at the ACCH: the chores, the shared rooms, occasionally getting beat up.

"Why don't you run away?" Shiloh asked. "I got a buddy who's going to run away tomorrow." Shiloh thought for a second. "I know! We can help him. Maybe he'll show you how to do it."

"Really?"

"Yeah, he does it whenever he's mad at his mom. He always comes back, though."

I thought back to the two kids who'd run away from the ACCH recently. "That's not really running away."

That night, we stayed over, and I got to sleep in Shiloh's house. It stank of unwashed bodies, and the air held a moldy, unidentifiable funk. But I didn't mind; it was great to see my best friend again.

The next day, we explored a derelict mine shaft, and then Shiloh took me up one side of the canyon that hemmed Madrid in to look for geodes. Back at the house, he broke out his slingshot, and we took turns breaking windows of an old, abandoned car next door, an orange station wagon from the '70s. The fun ended after we started pelting the tin roof of the house adjacent to Shiloh's. A grown man with a bald head, glasses, and a goatee came running out, chased Shiloh around the orange car, grabbed the slingshot, smashed it underneath his feet, and then went back inside.

We indeed helped Shiloh's buddy run away and then negotiated with his mother for good terms to secure the boy's return. We tried to buy menthol cigarettes from the general store, but the clerk knew that Shiloh's parents smoked Winstons, so we bought and smoked those instead.

All in a day's work.

At the end of the second day, we said goodbye to one another, and Esther and I hopped up into our car. I'd had a great time with Shiloh, but something was different. I put my forehead against the car window and watched the desert go by as I thought it over. In second grade, I hadn't understood the poverty in which we'd all lived. Nor had I experienced those conditions as shameful. Yet thinking of Shiloh living in a shack in the middle of nowhere, his family barely scratching out a living, I was sad for him, and ashamed. Whether from increased maturity or the civilizing effects of religious group-home life, I understood that our lives were diverging rapidly.

7

David Is Cool

Back at the ACCH, the Christiansens tapped out, and Jake and Tania Lovato replaced them. Jake had been born into an old New Mexican Hispanic family and rocked a rancher/cowboy aesthetic to great effect. Tania had a vibrant smile and bright eyes that were framed by hair styled in a feathered '80s look. They were young, idealistic, and energetic. I liked them as soon as I met them.

Their arrival, coming a year or so after my own at the ACCH, coincided with dramatic changes in the way I thought and behaved—especially around girls. Almost immediately upon arriving at the ACCH, I had begun having crushes on girls at the public elementary school. The first was Arlene, whose great attraction to me revolved around the profound shared experience of being born on the same day. In fourth grade, I developed a crush on Debbie because she had a nifty Trapper Keeper.

I didn't think of these girls as pretty, per se, as I was too young. Nor was I concerned with how we'd interact were I to profess my undying love. I think my attraction was rooted in a longing for the female affection I'd lost. They weren't just crushes but symbols of the nurturing and care I desperately but unconsciously craved. Seriously, stop for a second and imagine the impact it might have on a young child if they didn't receive hugs or kisses from a mother (or father) for years on end. For the remainder of my childhood, I would select a girl in school and pine away.

I decided that I needed to become *perfect*, which, to my fourth-grade mind, was to be like Jesus Christ—who I was being taught to view as *the* shining example of how to live. At age nine, in a desperate act of completionism, I set out to read my new Bible all the way through. I made it out of the first bunch of books of the Old Testament easily enough. If you weren't moved by the stories of the Israelites escaping the tyranny of the Egyptian pharaoh, you just weren't paying attention. But somewhere between the scripture laying down the laws governing proper goat sacrifice and the "X begat Y begat Z" for pages at a go, I lost the thread.

Still, my reading of the Bible made me receptive to Jake and Tania's suggestion that rock and roll was the music of the devil. Such was our prudish group-home culture that they once marched the entire cottage of children out of the roller-skating rink not ten minutes after we'd arrived because the DJ played Marvin Gaye's mildly suggestive "Let's Get It On." So I decided to eschew the evil influences of popular music and instead tune in to the local classical station on the tiny FM radio I kept in my bunk bed. It wasn't because I dug the music but because I wanted to be *perfect*. For a couple of months, if you'd walked into my room, you'd have seen a nine-year-old boy doing whatever it is that nine-year-old boys in a group home do—but with classical music playing in the background.

I learned somewhere that immersing oneself in freezing-cold water was meant to be healthy. For the better part of that year, I took ice-cold showers. Every morning, I'd step into the bathtub and stand right under the showerhead, steeling myself. Then I'd quickly turn on the cold water full blast before I lost my nerve. My heart rate would jump as I went into a few seconds of mild hyperventilation. I'd take the quickest shower possible, muttering and cursing and shivering. All the while, I'd tell myself I was doing something healthy.

One day, Tania told me I was to be tested for the gifted and talented (G&T) program at school, a decision based either on my teacher's feedback or her own observations. Since the G&T program was state-run, we went to some rando government building in downtown Albuquerque to take the test.

The test had four categories with questions related to verbal and spatial reasoning. Which of these doodles doesn't belong? Pick the cartoon that completes the sequence, that kind of thing. I hadn't ever seen a test like this before, and I thought it was a hoot.

Afterward, Tania said, "Great job! You passed!"

"Wow! Really?" I asked, beaming.

"Yep, all four sections. They said you got the highest score of anyone in the last five thousand times they've given this test. Get ready for some new classes," she said, high-fiving me.

I high-fived her right back as we hopped into our white E-350 Econoline group-home van to return to the home. It was just us, so I even got to ride shotgun.

The G&T program met a few times a week in its own classroom. We learned a far more advanced, conceptual curriculum, which saved me a lot of boredom and gave my regular teacher a break from my constant interruptions. What I learned in the G&T classes could best be described as *metacognition*—learning how to learn or thinking about thinking. The focus wasn't about knowing the answer; it was about *finding* the answer, about debugging the thinking process. There I learned how to brainstorm, when to let the creativity flow, and when to be more critical. I learned how to write an outline and summarize a topic. All these tools helped me organize the thoughts swirling in my head. Thoughts that had nothing to do with schoolwork.

Along the way, I learned the laws of probability as explained through a kind of *Encyclopedia Brown* mystery story. It followed a kid who began to think about his chances of getting his favorite type of candy from his Halloween stash. This kid made reasonable inferences about pulling a chocolate or caramel out of his bag, and he was right more often than not. I found it fascinating because knowing math seemed akin to having Jedi powers. There's no way I could have verbalized it at the time, but I intuitively grasped that understanding how the world worked gave you power. As I had no control over my daily life at the ACCH, I was attracted to whatever forms of power were available to me. Plus, I knew math was just freaking cool.

But survival in the group home entailed a different kind of intelligence, something of a more social and emotional nature: street smarts, situational cleverness, reading people's faces and body language, the ability to communicate or crack jokes, knowing when to fight or hide, the ability to delay gratification. Maybe solving an algebra problem isn't that useful in and of itself, but tutor another boy in the topic to avoid detentions for poor grades, now you've made an ally, possibly even a friend. Maybe the detention teacher will even take you out for pizza afterward as a thank-you.

Eventually, our gifted and talented instruction involved a computer lab once a week. We'd team up, two students assigned to a single Apple IIe. Aside from video games, I hadn't meaningfully interacted with computers before, but the computer lab was an appropriately light introduction for ten-year-olds. We mostly played so-called edutainment games, such as *The Oregon Trail*. This was a comically difficult simulation set in the mid-1800s, in which you tried to make it across the country in a covered wagon to set up your family on the West Coast.

Sadly, I always died of dysentery. One of the coinventors of the game, Don Rawitsch, was responsible for the historical content. He test-played it with teachers, and fully 50 percent died on their first playthrough. This matched the actual survival rate of pioneers on the real Oregon Trail, so Rawitsch figured that was about the right difficulty setting.

We also learned about programming languages by playing around in a graphical computing environment called LOGO. There was a triangular cursor—meant to invoke an image of a turtle—on a 2D virtual paper rendered on the screen. Using keyboard commands, you manually entered instructions to drive the "turtle" around and draw. You'd input commands like "Go forward so many inches," "Set the pen down to write," "Move forward some more," and "Bring the pen up to stop writing." Then you'd hit Run and watch the cursor follow the sequence of commands you'd entered, painting whatever picture you'd managed to conceive.

I always programmed the cursor to paint bizarre patterns by using huge numbers when coding the pen strokes, going full-on chaos agent: turn right 50,302 degrees, go forward 1,739,395 inches, and so forth. Luckily, if the cursor went off the screen, it wrapped around to the other side. Then I'd sit back and admire the psychedelic, kaleidoscopic patterns unfold. The cool kids would program the cursor to spell out logos for heavy metal bands like Twisted Sister (a stylized *TS*), or have it write *Shit* before the teacher could catch them.

While LOGO was a simple programming language, its creators had lofty ambitions. Creators Wally Feurzeig, Seymour Papert, and Cynthia Solomon believed that computers would one day revolutionize the way we teach and so set out in 1967 to create a programming language accessible to children. They believed that kids learn not by receiving knowledge from on high but by constructing it through their trial-and-error interactions with the world.

Papert went on to write an influential book on education called *Mindstorms* (1980), whose opening paragraph reads, "In most contemporary educational situations where children come into contact with computers the computer is...programming the child. In the LOGO environment the relationship is reversed....The child programs the computer. And in teaching the computer how to think, children embark on an education about how they themselves think....Thinking about thinking turns the child into an epistemologist, an experience not even shared by most adults."

In short, Papert believed that a child constructs theories about the world and then falsifies, or "debugs," those theories along their own personal journey to create a constructed knowledge base relevant to them. He further believed that simplified computing environments such as LOGO were ideal media to allow children to build that knowledge and subsequently falsify it. I can only imagine that Papert and the other creators of LOGO would be over the moon with how much today's kids love to build, explore, and create with their friends in sandbox games like *Minecraft* or *Roblox*.

I must have been getting a huge kick out of all that epistemologizing, because my teacher pinned a note to my shirt one day to take home to my houseparents. It read, "David refuses to share the computer with his partner. Please talk to him about the value of sharing."

How could I possibly share my computer? I'd loved them since I was five years old, when I saw a long-haired teenager messing around on a TRS-80 computer at a Radio Shack. Affectionately known as a "Trash-80," the model was an inexpensive home computer popular in the late '70s and early '80s. It had a whopping 4 KB of computer memory. For reference, a modern iPhone takes a *single picture* that requires about 4 MB of storage, one thousand times larger than the *entire computer memory* of the Trash-80. Here again, Federico Faggin, the inventor of the Z80 computer microprocessor, touched my life from afar, for the Trash-80 was powered by none other than the beloved Z80.

I approached the teenager to see what he was up to. He was hacking a bit of BASIC—an easy-to-learn programming language popular in the early '80s—not that I understood any of that at the age of five. I watched him, and eventually, he looked down at me.

"What's your name?" he asked.

"David," I said.

He typed in

```
> 10 PRINT "David is cool"
> 20 GOTO 10
```

Then he paused to make sure I understood what was going on.

"The first line tells the computer to print your name." He pointed to line 10. "The second line makes the program go back to the first line. So this son of a gun is going to print out your name. A *lot*."

I nodded that I understood, and I think I did.

Then the boy typed

```
> RUN
David is cool
David is cool
David is cool
David is cool
David is cool
```

```
David is cool
David is cool
David is cool
David is cool
David is cool
...
```

This was the first time in my life I ever saw true magic.

The computer monitor displayed that phrase tens of times, hundreds of times, a million! It wasn't simply a line of text; it was a story about me, one amplified through an infinite loop. After a few seconds, the teenager keyed in the break sequence, and the program returned to the BASIC prompt.

```
>
```

The computer was waiting for more input, ready to execute further commands.

I got it! Computers made you like an army general or master chef. You gave the PC carefully written recipes, and it executed those recipes faithfully and without complaint, forever and ever.

In time, my interest in computers helped me connect with Dana, an alumnus of the group home who was finishing up a computer science degree and touted as a shining example for us group-home kids. Despite having been out of the ACCH for a couple of years, Dana still attended the University Church of Christ. I first met him as he was sitting, legs crossed, in the middle of the church parking lot, poring over hundreds of pages of C code printed out on striped green-and-white paper from a dot-matrix printer. He was searching for bugs in his program. I instantly thought the guy was a genius.

For a short while, Dana took me under his wing, teaching me a bit of programming and introducing me to the famous *King's Quest* games from Sierra On-Line. He and his wife even took me home with them one weekend, where I spent the entire time in front of their computer playing the famous text-based adventure game *Zork* in zoned-out bliss.

Dana also gave me a book on Pascal, which I took back to the ACCH. Pascal was another '80s-era programming language developed both for large-scale applications and for teaching good programming practices. As I sat there back in my room in Cottage 3, staring at the book Dana had bestowed upon me, I couldn't help but feel a mix of intrigue and frustration. Here was a tome that promised to unlock the secrets of the universe. I'd made it through the first three chapters, enough to understand basic syntax and simple commands. But then I'd hit a wall. I'd only spent that one weekend with Dana, and he wasn't around to answer any of my questions. At the age of nine, without any instruction, I got stuck. Story of my life at the ACCH.

8

Road to Nowhere

The tragedy of my father's life began with his own father's untimely death. My grandfather, a captain in the air force, was killed during a routine training exercise over Phoenix in 1953 when his plane collided with another. Although he managed to bail out with the rest of the flight crew, he was struck by wreckage as he parachuted down to earth.

Within seventy-two hours of the accident, my grandmother, now a single parent of five children under the age of eight, moved the family back to her childhood home of Bay Ridge, Brooklyn. The kids left behind the Sonoran Desert of Tucson, where they had spent their early childhood on the edge of an air force base chasing lizards and playing hide-and-seek between the saguaro and ocotillo. In Brooklyn, they found themselves thrust into a world of unending brownstones, cement sidewalks, and asphalt streets. The comfort and familiarity my grandmother experienced in returning to her childhood neighborhood came at the expense of the children, for whom the foreign surroundings were a constant reminder of their father's death.

The youngest children, Daisy, Maria, and my father, Luke—who were only a few months, a year and a half, and three years, respectively—never knew their father except as a vague memory, the hint of a man who turns the street corner before you can catch sight of his face. As for the two eldest children, Moira and James, ages six and seven, their mother pressed them into service to babysit and manage the household. The stark reality of their new roles was made clear when, six months after his father died, my grandmother took my Uncle James by both shoulders and said, "Your father is gone now. I need *you* to be the man of the family and help me raise your sisters and your brother."

Raising five kids is exhausting work, but it doesn't pay the bills. My grandmother received a pension and nothing else, leaving the children to grow up in poverty. When prompted, my aunts and uncles recount stories of food scarcity and hardship, their tales imbued with the gnawing, corrosive worry of barely making ends meet month after month, year over year, across two decades.

And so the children also effectively lost their mother, who emotionally withdrew, devastated both by her beloved husband's unexpected death and the overwhelming responsibility of raising five children alone. She became brittle and unpredictable, flying into rages and regularly striking out at her children. Perhaps because he was more of a handful than the others, my father caught the brunt of my grandmother's wrath. Their fights often ended with my father locked in the bathroom and my grandmother pounding on the door, screaming bloody murder.

That's the life my father experienced as he became a teenager. Arguably the smartest of the five siblings, his behavioral problems led him to learn every lesson the hard way, if he learned at all. He was a total goof in school and couldn't be bothered to study. By age thirteen, he was hiding pill bottles from his mother in his fish tank and experimenting with the heroin his friends had given him. At fifteen, he'd likely developed a habit, and by seventeen, he'd been arrested for possessing an ounce of marijuana. After being remanded to a weekday reform school, he decided he'd seen enough of Brooklyn and split town, never to return.

My father was completely absent from my life between kindergarten and fifth grade. It's impossible to know what dark, drug-addled corners of his mind he retreated to in those years, but one Saturday, he reemerged, rolling into the ACCH in a red VW Bug.

Esther and I were expecting him, so we were sitting out on the basketball court. Once he'd parked, he hopped out of his car, jogged over, and called out, "Hey, kiddos!"

"Hi, Dad," we said, hugging the man we hadn't seen for five years.

"It's been so long. You've both really grown." My father looked around. "This place is great!" He looked across the court at a bunch of kids playing basketball. "Who's that?" my father asked.

"Other kids who live here," I said.

He walked over to say hello to them.

Esther cocked her eyebrow at me, and I mouthed, *What the eff?* Our father was a goddamned weirdo; I remembered this nearly pathological need to chat people up from when we'd lived with him. As my father talked with the other kids, asking where they were from, what grades they were in, what sports they liked, I scoped him out. He looked about the same as I'd remembered him. Still thin, still had a mustache. But he'd cut his long brown hair. It used to hang below his shoulders; now, he kept it in a bowl cut. Eventually, the other group-home kids returned to their basketball game, and our father walked back over to us.

"Is that your car?" Esther asked.

My father looked over at the parked VW. "Oh, that's my girlfriend's car."

Esther's eyes popped out of her head. "You have a *girlfriend*?"

"Sure do! Holly. Maybe I'll introduce you to her sometime."

That day, our father took us out to Petroglyph National Monument, just a few miles away in the desert on the outskirts of town. While hiking, Esther and I learned that he'd moved back to Albuquerque. He'd landed a cheap apartment a stone's throw from the University Church of Christ we attended every Sunday.

For a while after that day, he'd occasionally borrow a car and pick Esther and me up from the group home. Each and every time he arrived, he'd make an ostentatious show of friendliness toward any kid he came across. This pissed me off something awful. Didn't my father know he was supposed to put aside his "suffer the children to come unto me" routine and pay attention to his son for once in his life? Ultimately, I made my peace with his weirdness; I'd observed many adults visit the ACCH campus, and their reactions to the plight of us kids were all over the map.

Now and then, I'd walk over to his apartment and spend a Sunday with him, returning to church for evening worship and connecting with the group home there. Most of my memories of my father during this time were of just the two of us. I don't know why my sister only came now and again. Maybe she'd quickly tired of his broke, overly religious ass. Perhaps she had better options, as it was at about this time that she started regularly going out on Sundays with a family from church.

My father lived in an efficiency apartment and never locked his door, proudly proclaiming that Jesus protected him and all his belongings. Yet the briefest glance inside his apartment revealed that my father did not require the Good Lord's services. His apartment had no furniture whatsoever, aside from a single kitchen chair, a mattress on the floor of the bedroom, and, of all things, a thin, wooden lectern.

On it, he kept a six-inch-thick dictionary and a Bible. The Bible always lay on top of the dictionary.

During a Sunday-afternoon outing with my father, he'd prepare our lunch: a can of Campbell's tomato soup and "cheesy bread," a slice of Wonder Bread with a piece of Kraft American cheese warmed up in the broiler of his oven. Often, we'd go to the movies afterward. My father didn't own a car, so we walked everywhere, hitchhiked a bunch, and took buses.

As my years at the home wore on, he lost that apartment, disappeared for long periods, reemerged, and disappeared again.

My father would occasionally take me out for the entire weekend. We'd go to his place, get settled, and he'd pass out on his mattress, invariably saying he was fatigued. After this happened the first time, I started taking my Nintendo to have something to do. My father's siblings from the East Coast had sprung for it as a Christmas gift. I'd sit on the floor playing *Super Mario Bros.* for the whole weekend on a tiny TV my dad had found somewhere. I became so skillful I could beat all eight worlds without warping, with only a single Mario. And I discovered every extra life in the game.

No number of extra lives, though, could counter the fact that at some point during the fifth grade, I realized I was going to die and that my life couldn't possibly amount to anything. Not that I *could* potentially amount to something but would not, thanks to my circumstances or mistakes I might make. I hadn't considered that yet. Rather, I began to contemplate the nihilistic belief that our lives are fundamentally meaningless. That nothing we do by our actions or words can change this cold, hard fact. Strangely, my faith in Jesus provided no comfort against these thoughts; other than a growing fear of nuclear holocaust that was vaguely associated with religion, they existed in entirely separate compartments of my mind.

These rosy ideas were brought to consciousness thanks to the pop song "Road to Nowhere" by Talking Heads, which was receiving heavy airplay on the radio at the time. Every time I heard it or watched the video—which featured David Byrne walking along a highway through a desert not dissimilar from the one I lived in—I'd remember there was no point to anything, and my stomach would roil.

There were other contributors to my budding nihilism. The topic of death was foregrounded several times in public school that year. This must have been a conscious curriculum choice, though perhaps one better suited to children ensconced in the warm nest of parental love. My fifth-grade teacher, Mr. Romero, read to us *Where the Red Fern Grows*, the story about a boy with two hunting dogs, and the boy's coming of age based on the events surrounding an accidental death. We also read *Bridge to Terabithia*, which screwed me up real good. I was caught entirely by surprise when Leslie fell into the ditch and drowned.

That same year, the *Challenger* space shuttle blew up. Because Christa McAuliffe, a high school teacher, was onboard, the *Challenger* launch was televised live in most classrooms in the United States, including mine. Mr. Romero wheeled out the TV on its cart to the front of the room. And so I and a generation of children watched seven astronauts get blown to bits when the *Challenger* shuttle exploded seventy-three seconds after launch. Mr. Romero rolled the TV to the back of the classroom, and it was on to grammar lessons.

After a few months of brooding alone in my room over these thoughts, I started drifting away from reality and having minor panic attacks on the school bus. Each attack left me hollow, convinced that at any moment I might simply cease to exist—not just someday but right there on that bus with its vinyl seats and shouting children.

Outwardly, life went on as usual. I'd spend recess by myself on a swing and have my everyday group-home adventures. But inside, I was a mess.

I didn't talk to anyone about this—I didn't even have words for what I was experiencing. Obviously, my parents weren't around. Esther was out of the question. By the sixth grade, she'd gotten her period and had grown six inches. She had some boy from church on a string and was comparing herself to normal girls from school. I was her shrimpy, nerdy younger brother. The truth is that once we arrived at the ACCH, Esther and I didn't room together, and often, we didn't even live in the same cottage. Because of this and the fact that we had so little in common, my sister and I grew further apart: closer than two random kids at the home, but nothing like typical siblings.

A therapist might have helped with my dread, but we were too poor for those, nor would they have been culturally acceptable at the ACCH in the 1980s.

What about my houseparents? No, not really. The houseparents provided essential supervision only, mostly meting out punishment to ensure group-home life never went straight-up *Lord of the Flies*. If Jake and Tania Lovato had still been at the ACCH, they might have helped, but they had gone on to have their own children. Apart from the Lovatos, I have no memory of ever engaging in a one-on-one conversation with a houseparent that wasn't related to discipline or Jesus Christ.

I finally snapped out of my funk during my fifth-grade summer thanks to the intervention of my family from the East Coast. We'd reconnected the year before. During my fourth-grade summer, my then-housemother, Tania, had walked into my room. I was hunched over on the floor, working on a puzzle filled with wizards, goblins, and magic.

Tania said, "David, it's time to meet your aunt and uncle from New York."

"Who are they again?" I asked, looking up at my housemother.

Tania explained that Moira was my dad's sister and Elliot was her husband.

"Oh yeah." I went back to studying my puzzle piece.

"Come on, don't be shy. They're excited to meet their nephew!"

I put my puzzle piece down, got up, and followed Tania out into the common area. My aunt and uncle were sitting on the couch. Esther was already there, hugging Moira.

I stayed back; I didn't know these two from Tuesday. They sure didn't look like family. Moira was beautiful, though, and dressed well; she had what I would later learn was Manhattan city polish. And she did have a large forehead, just like Esther and I did. I looked over at Elliot. He wore thick glasses and a full, brown beard—like an intellectual fisherman.

Moira asked if she and Elliot could take us out for the afternoon.

"Did you ask our mom?" I asked.

Esther flashed me her *Shut up, David* look.

"She thinks it's a great idea!" Moira said. "She'd love for you to get to know us."

My sister explained that we'd always wanted to go to this water park with lots of slides and tunnels. I don't think our aunt and uncle were overly excited about this prospect, but they took us, and we had a blast. I clogged up the tunnels and caused traffic jams. It was good, clean family fun.

Later that day, Moira and Elliot brought Esther and me back to the ACCH, and we all hugged goodbye. I went back to my chores. Time dragged on *forever* at the ACCH during the summer, so I was thankful they'd taken us out.

The next day, Tania pulled Esther and me aside after lunch. "How would you two like to see the Four Corners region with your aunt and uncle?"

"Yes!" we both exclaimed.

So my sister and I boarded a Greyhound bus headed for Farmington, New Mexico, a town right on the edge of the Navajo Nation. Over the next few days, Moira, Elliot, Esther, and I went exploring. From ancient ruins up on Mesa Verde in Colorado over to Monument Valley in Arizona, down to the Painted Desert, and back to Shiprock, New Mexico, the area is a desert gem of the United States.

The four of us camped near Canyon de Chelly and ended up chatting with some Navajo boys riding bareback. As we hiked down the side of the canyon, I'd run far ahead of my aunt and uncle. I had to know if I could handle sprinting down the switchbacks without falling over the canyon's edge. Plus, there were signs everywhere claiming that the local squirrels and chipmunks carried the plague. I wanted to find a plague-ridden rodent myself and see what all the fuss was about.

Moira would yell ahead to Elliot nervously, "Be sure and keep up with him!"

"I'm trying, dear," Uncle Elliot would reply as he'd again break into a jog to catch up to me.

Our trip took us down to Window Rock, a town in Arizona that features an arch in the sandstone. There, Elliot and I took a hike, just the two of us. We hiked up a trail along a stream for about a mile, with the cottonwoods providing shade, and came out onto an enormous clearing. We found ourselves looking over a vast, deep bowl carved in the sandstone.

"Can we go up to the edge?" I asked.

"Okay, but let's be careful." Elliot got down on his stomach, and I followed his example. We both crawled up to the edge, our elbows scraping against rock.

"*ECHO!*" I yelled, my voice echoing in the bowl below.

Elliot's hand found my shoulder, steadying me. "Look at that." He pointed with his free hand. "I think it's bats!"

"So cool," I said, full of wonder.

Elliot turned his head to look at me, his eyes gentle behind his thick glasses. "This will be our special place, David. For just you and me." His grip on my shoulder tightened. "Any time you're feeling lonely, just remember the two of us here, looking out at the world together."

Finally, we drove south to Gallup, New Mexico, for our last night together. Esther and I hopped into the hotel's pool as soon as we were able. Esther often worried about her blond hair turning green in the summer if she was in the pool too often. But as she cannonballed into the water, it seemed the furthest thing from her mind.

We splashed around and caused a ruckus. After we'd calmed down, Moira tentatively waded in.

"Who wants a ride?" she said, moving through the water to my sister. She went over to Esther and gathered her up the way a person might carry a small child. It wasn't so much a ride as a tender embrace. Esther held on to her, arms wrapped around our aunt's neck, eyes locked with hers. They moved this way through the water, that eye contact holding the entire time. It was the happiest I'd seen my sister in years.

The following day, after a tearful goodbye, we were back on a Greyhound bus bound for Albuquerque and the ACCH, having made a real connection with our aunt and uncle.

For a long time after their visit, I thought that Moira and Elliot had dropped by the ACCH because they were vacationing in the area. Turns out that they had come out explicitly to check on us. My aunt and uncle were both psychotherapists, and they didn't buy my grandparents' story of a cozy Christian happy home.

Moira reported back to all my father's four siblings, who lived on the East Coast. Upon hearing Moira and Elliot's report of our lives at the ACCH, they decided to act, agreeing that Esther and I should visit them in New York for a month the following summer.

That year—when I was in fifth grade—Talking Heads came on the radio singing about roads to nowhere, and my teacher read to us stories about kids dying in ditches. And for six months, I wigged the fuck out. Then Moira extended the invitation, and our mother consented.

That summer, Esther and I left our group-home reality behind as we boarded our first-ever plane bound for New York to meet our aunts and uncles.

We plunged into a world utterly different from our own, filled with restaurants and the endless wonders of New York City. With Daisy, we navigated the bustling streets of Manhattan, sampling delicacies I'd never even heard of. We walked along the water in Bay Ridge with Maria and James, marveling at the Verrazzano-Narrows Bridge, and felt the salty spray of the harbor as we passed the Statue of Liberty on a ferry ride. In the Berkshires, north of the city, Moira and Elliot's home became our stage as Esther and I played dress-up, danced, and sang our hearts out.

Amid the towering trees of upstate New York and the labyrinthine playgrounds of Central Park, I forgot about my anxiety, plain and simple. The old saying "No matter where you go, there you are" didn't hold true. I had escaped my existential dread, not through some profound realization born of hard work but through the sheer joy of being swept up in my very first vacation with a family I never knew I had. For those brief weeks, I felt what normal might be like—to exist in a world where adults saw you, where your presence mattered, where someone might actually grieve your absence.

9

Omar and the Commitment

Omar arrived at the ACCH when I was in fourth grade. A twelve-year-old Mexican American boy, he came from a neighborhood in downtown Albuquerque that rivaled the War Zone for danger. The cops had busted him for gang-related activity, and the judge handling his case had given him a choice: go to juvenile hall or go to the ACCH. Omar chose the home, bringing with him the survival skills of the streets—a stocky build maintained through constant weight lifting, perpetually clenched fists, and the instinct to secure his position through physical dominance. For him, safety meant constantly working the angles, including the fourteen different ways he could beat your ass if worse came to worst.

The first thing Omar did when he got to the ACCH was kick my ass. Afterward, to reduce the trouble he'd be in with the houseparents, he went into the bathroom, checked out his reflection in the medicine cabinet mirror, and then smashed his face into it. This was to make it appear as if we'd had something of an even fight, which was laughable given our differences in size and the fact that I was nine.

Notwithstanding this first, inevitable ass whooping, Omar and I became good friends. Early on, Omar shared a few pearls of wisdom with me. "Always have a roll of pennies or at least a lighter in your fist when you punch someone. It's not brass knuckles, but it'll hurt way more than nothing." He told me if our housefather, Jake, came at me, I should kick him in the right knee. "He was in a bad car accident, and that knee has metal bolts in it."

"Ummmm, okay, Omar," I'd responded. It had never once crossed my mind to strike my housefather.

Over the years of our shared stay at the group home, we ended up rooming together more often than not, I think because our houseparents discovered we were compatible. It's one thing to be in the same cottage with other kids; you get to know them well enough. It's another thing entirely to room with someone. You learn about his hopes and fears. Who he has a crush on. Whether he's a bully, asshole, or pushover. You find out who's more intelligent, who can do more push-ups. Who bothers to shower, who smells. Who cries in his sleep.

Our friendship followed the contours of a relationship between an older and younger brother. I looked up to Omar; he tolerated me. We talked about everything. I was precocious, so our conversations were more balanced than those typically held between nine- and twelve-year-old kids.

But Omar would still tire of my company. He'd look back over his shoulder, not at me but right behind his butt. He'd say, "I have a tail. Why do I have a tail? You want some *chingasos*?"

That was my cue to scram.

Another significant feature of our friendship was a kind of friendly-until-it's-definitely-not-friendly bullying. Omar would put me in the Camel Clutch until I cried mercy, then wallop me or threaten a beating if I didn't do thirty push-ups on the spot. He spoke fluent Spanish, and anytime this kind of shit was about to go down, he'd yell, *Chingasos!* or *Jodasotes!* both of which translate to vulgar versions of "Beat down!" in this context. I could never get these words out straight, so I'd say things like, "No Wallasotays, Omar, please!"

Perhaps a year after Omar arrived, I was shooting hoops by myself on the basketball court. Omar walked out of Cottage 3 and headed my way, eyes blazing.

"*Pinche cabrón!* Were you talking about me to Bart?" he asked.

I had no idea what Omar was talking about. Put on the spot, I just stood there, looking at him.

Omar got in my face. "Don't talk about my business!" he yelled. Then he punched me in the face as hard as he could. A one-two combo, first in the mouth and then again in my eye. The second punch hit me on my way to the ground.

Seeing stars, blood began dripping from my split lip, and I started crying.

Omar turned and walked back toward Cottage 3. No one else was around; Omar being Omar, this was likely by design.

I thought about what the hell had just happened. What might I have said? Nothing had come to mind when Omar questioned me, but the taste of blood has a way of opening new neural pathways. As I lay there, I remembered I had indeed gossiped.

A week earlier, while walking between Cottage 2 and Cottage 3, I'd seen Bart. He was a couple of years older than I was, and though we weren't great friends, I knew him well enough because we'd lived together with the Lovatos. So we'd ended up chatting for a few minutes. During our brief conversation, I'd mentioned that Omar and Samantha were "boyfriend and girlfriend."

There were politics here. Samantha was the attractive teenage daughter of the Johnsons, the houseparents du jour in Cottage 3, where Omar and I lived. For the most part, the houseparents' kids and the group-home kids didn't mix. While I always thought it was unlucky to be a houseparents' kid relative to normal kids, I was keenly aware that they held a vastly superior rank in the overall pecking order at the ACCH.

For example, suppose a violent kid like Omar had thrown a couple of unexpected punches at the houseparents' son. I'm certain Omar would have been tossed in juvenile detention faster than you can say *rebar motel*. Likewise, any romantic dalliance with the houseparents' daughter would have been grounds for immediate removal from the ACCH. Keep in mind, we had *literally nowhere* else to go, so getting booted was tantamount to being put out on the street.

I could see why Omar was pissed. He was probably worried about word getting back to the Johnsons. The Johnsons were strict disciplinarians; Mr. Johnson was a downright hard-assed son of a bitch.

But after a few moments, lying there on the basketball court and bleeding, I shut down my momentary identification with Omar and instead contemplated options for revenge. Physical retribution was out of the question. He was bigger and stronger than I was and a seasoned fighter. I couldn't punch my way out of a wet paper bag. Maybe I could find a bat and coldcock him across the head when he wasn't looking? While a delicious fantasy, I was too levelheaded for that. On the other hand, if I ratted on him for punching me, he'd likely get significant detentions.

But again, the problem was politics. Not only had I gossiped about Omar, I'd also opened my big mouth about Samantha. From the Johnsons' perspective, they were players in this drama. Gossiping about their daughter would factor in as large as, if not larger than, Omar kicking the crap out of me.

My options narrowing to nothing, I pulled my face off the ground, wiped the blood off my chin, and went back to my room. I'd take my licks, be quiet, and move on.

Having concluded that avoiding the houseparents was best, I had yet another problem. My black eye was getting darker by the minute, and the split in my swollen lip was there for all to admire. It was expected in the group home that everyone would come together for dinner. We'd say grace, eat, make simple conversation, and then clean up. How could I manage all of that without being noticed?

That night, I sat at the farthest end of the table from the houseparents. Our single table could seat more than twenty people, so I thought it plausible that I could hide my bruised face from Mr. and Mrs. Johnson. I ate my food quietly with my head down—already a tell, thanks to my habit of never shutting up.

After dinner, I was vacuuming around the dinner table when my housemother pulled me aside. Mrs. Johnson was a thin Southern woman in her late forties, with long, flowing hair. We walked to my unoccupied room; she followed behind me and closed the door.

"Who gave you the shiner?" she asked with concern.

"Omar," I replied.

"Well, why'd he go and do a thing like that?"

"I told Bart that Omar and Samantha are having a relationship."

Mrs. Johnson's face transformed from kindly to outraged. She smacked me hard across my bruised face.

"I cannot believe you would say something like that!" she exclaimed. "I mean, it'd be one thing if you'd said they were boyfriend and girlfriend, but to say they have a relationship!" She put her finger right in my face. "Don't you ever say anything like that again!" My housemother left, slamming the door behind her, leaving me once again to figure out what the hell had just happened.

I concluded that Mrs. Johnson thought I was implying that Omar and her daughter were having sex. To be clear, my ten-year-old mind hadn't even begun to grapple with physical intimacy. I may have been mentally precocious, but physically, I was delayed. I'd been intrigued when I saw a porno mag getting passed around by some of the boys in the home, and the old heads at church were always going on about the evils of fornication. But otherwise, I was ignorant.

I don't know why I switched the wording in speaking to Mrs. Johnson. In my mind, the phrase *having a relationship* was a reasonable, even superior substitute for *were boyfriend and girlfriend*. What I hadn't reckoned with was that a generic statement could be taken in a thousand different directions.

If there were any repercussions for Omar and Samantha, I never learned of them. Neither he nor I ever brought the subject up again. That incident with Omar taught me about consequences and keeping secrets—lessons I'd need as I began to understand the harder truths about what my life at the ACCH really meant.

My most important conversations with Omar were yet to come.

I went through many changes in my first few years at the ACCH. Still, none were more consequential or long-lasting than my growing awareness of my parents' problems and, therefore, my own. By the age of ten, I finally understood that my parents were drug addicts and that my mother had severe mental health issues. My father was useless. Before then, I hadn't been consciously aware of their addictions. Few things seem odd if they're all you've ever known.

By this point, I'd developed my own opinions about my mother as a person, concluding that she was a taker, only interested in the easy path in life. When I visited her, she'd discuss her two ambitions: applying for public housing and suing the pants off the person who'd crashed into her car. Neither ever materialized. I couldn't help but think about the New Testament maxim my grandfather wielded against my father—"If a man does not work, he does not eat"—and how it could just as easily apply to my mother.

After contemplating my mother's problems, it didn't take much of a leap to consider my own. I was living in a goddamned orphanage! Kids on the school bus looked at me funny, and I was a loner during recess. When the ACCH wanted to take a trip, we'd collect cans on the side of the highway to get the money from recycling, or we'd humiliate ourselves by selling lollipops in bank vestibules. "It's for a good cause" sure feels like begging when *you're* the good cause.

All of this is by way of noting that by the age of ten, I'd come to realize the obvious truth of my situation: I was well and truly fucked. I might not make it out.

I broached these topics with the local leader in my community, Omar. It's true that he beat my ass with some regularity, and a couple of times, he hurt me badly. But he was my roommate. And I was growing to love him as an older brother, though I'd never have used those words at the time. But despite our increasing closeness, any discussion of our circumstances was problematic for several reasons.

I never once had a meaningful conversation at the group home with another kid, boy or girl, where the intimate details of our parents' failures were discussed. As a rule, we avoided conversations involving parents. If parents were brought up, they were inevitably lionized, mothers especially.

I remember a conversation I'd had with another longtime resident of the ACCH, Jackson. We were both in the kitchen doing our perpetual chores. The sink overflowed with greasy plates, and my sleeves were rolled up, hands deep in the basin, scrubbing.

"My mom's coming to visit next week," Jackson told me as he loaded glasses into the sterilizer.

"That's cool."

"For my birthday. She's bringing me new jeans."

"Great."

He nodded. "She's in construction now. Says she's making loads."

"Awesome."

"So she's buying me new jeans."

"Yeah, you told me."

"She's bringing me twenty pairs of Levi's 501s, David."

I stopped washing and looked over at him. "What?"

"Yup, twenty pairs. Blue, black, stonewashed, acid—"

"Yeah, right."

Jackson, too, stopped loading and looked at me. "She is too!"

"But you're always wearing those Wranglers."

"You calling me a liar?"

I didn't say anything.

"My mother's bringing me twenty pairs of Levi's 501s, David, and if you say anything against her, I'll kick your ass!"

Jackson had once nearly knocked me out when he'd popped me right in the eye in front of a girl we both liked. So I capitulated. "Okay, Jackson. Your mom's bringing you twenty pairs of Levi's 501s."

Despite Jackson's claims about his mother's newfound income, that mofo wore the same old busted pair of Wranglers—year in and year out—just like the rest of us.

Just as the topic of parents was avoided, none of the children ever discussed *why* they were at the group home. If pressed, the most common answers were "Better than home," "Better than the barrio," or "Better than juvie." Undoubtedly true, but more honest responses might have included "My dad hit me" or "My mom shoots up." Our shared and unspoken truth was that our parents had failed us, and they bore the responsibility for our circumstances.

There was a period in which the group home didn't have as many kids as usual, so Omar and I had a room to ourselves. Having not much else to do, we played Risk. He'd beat me three times out of four, employing a strategy whereby he took Australia and then Asia. Being deeply patriotic, naturally I occupied North America first and then attempted to overtake South America before attacking Asia. But anyone who's ever played Risk knows that's a shit strategy.

One Saturday afternoon, we had the game spread out all over the floor of our room. Things were looking up in this particular game; I'd just claimed Kamchatka by an all-out attack over the Bering Strait.

"Omar, we're screwed, aren't we?" I said as I finished my turn.

"We? No. *You're* screwed. I'm about to take Asia."

"I mean us. Here. At the home."

"*Oh.*" He rolled the dice. "Yeah, I've been wondering how to get out for a while now."

I looked up from the game. "What do you think we should do?"

"Don't know. We'll talk after lights-out and work the angles. Now shut up and play."

Omar had a mixtape of early hip-hop with rap artists like Whodini, Kurtis Blow, Melle Mel, UTFO, Roxanne Shanté, and the Real Roxanne. He'd throw that on after the housefather came around to check that everyone was in bed. That night, Roxanne Shanté was absolutely wrecking some fool.

"I think you can get out using your brain," Omar said.

"You think so?"

"Everyone knows you're the smartest kid here."

"So, how's it work?"

"You might be able to get a scholarship to college. Remember that karate instructor that came for a couple of months?" Omar asked.

"Yeah."

"He got money to go to college with the GI Bill. He said he was enlisted in the military or the reserves or something."

"You think I should go into the military?"

"No, dumbass," he said. "I'm saying there are ways to pay for college."

"Oh." I thought for a minute. "Like Dana went to the University of New Mexico?"

"Exactly."

I listened to the song for a bit. Roxanne was now laying the smackdown on some other dude.

"What about you?" I asked.

Omar was silent for a minute. "Beats me," he finally admitted.

"Maybe you can find money for college, too."

"I doubt it. I don't have your book smarts."

"Sorry," I said, "but you *are* smart."

"Not like you. If smart was basketball, you'd make the NBA. I'm cool if I have a good game when we play against Cottage 2."

A few nights later, Kurtis Blow's "The Breaks" was playing.

"I have an idea, Omar. What about that internship you heard about at Coca-Cola?"

"What about it?" Omar asked.

"Well, couldn't you get a job there? You know, work there for a long time?"

"Like stick in one place and work my way up the ladder?"

"Yeah. Kids at the home follow you no matter what. They play the games you want to play, do the stuff you want to do. I play Risk with you, even though you always kick my ass."

Omar thought for a minute. "So, leadership."

I'd never used that word before, but it's what I was driving at. "Leadership," I repeated.

And so we hatched our plans. Omar would get an entry-level job at the Coca-Cola Company and work his way up the ladder. I'd get a scholarship to college.

These conversations established a commitment, the most significant commitment of my life. Not between Omar and me—although he was always kicking around in the back of my head—but to myself. If I made good grades, I'd get a college scholarship.

I kneaded and worked this fantasy in my mind until it became something larger than escape, larger than college. In my ten-year-old imagination, I would become extraordinary—an Einstein, a Jesus-like figure—someone so remarkable they couldn't help but be seen. It was the kind of grandiose dream that could only arise from desperate need—a form of positive narcissism that provided the emotional sustenance required to survive. The fantasy itself became a kind of shelter.

At ten, a college education was vague and far away and would remain so for many years. So this commitment didn't entail a single change in my day-to-day life. The truth was that I didn't have to work to get good grades. But in my head, this commitment was everything—an aspiration, a projection of myself into the future that kept me focused on a positive outcome and helped me ignore the madness that would surround me over the next decade. After those conversations with Omar, I never doubted that I'd survive.

10

Cholo-Curious

At the end of my fifth-grade summer, I mysteriously became aware of my appearance. I'm not sure how it happened, but one day, standing in front of the mirror with a hairbrush—and why was I even looking in the mirror?—I realized my clothing was shabby, my hair was unkempt, and that I used my toothbrush about as often as I saw my father. My thoughts turned to the VoTech building and some clothing I knew was there.

The ACCH had recently finished construction on what they termed the *vocational technology* (VoTech) *building*. It was a redbrick, ranch-style house, just like the three cottages, but instead of housing kids, it was meant for activities like sewing classes or furniture construction. On the recent tour, I remembered seeing a huge pile of donated secondhand clothing, probably from one of the local churches. So I found my housemother and asked her if it was okay if I rummaged through the clothing pile. No problem, so off I went.

I entered the building and caught a whiff of sawdust and varnish as I found my way to the room where I remembered the clothing to be. I opened the door, and there, sitting on a tidy brown desk, was a personal computer. Oh my fucking god. A personal computer. At the ACCH. For a moment, I forgot to breathe.

All thoughts of my appearance fled from my mind. I had no idea there was a computer in the VoTech building! Why hadn't anybody told me? Was it donated? Was it purchased?

I listened intently for a moment, straining to hear if anyone else was in the building. Satisfied by the silence, I approached the computer and studied it. A boxy monitor with a twelve-inch screen sat atop a wide, beige, rectangular chassis, its front adorned with horizontal air vents and an IBM logo. On the right side, two large, rectangular slots housed the 5.25-inch floppy disk drives; a prominent red rocker switch controlled the power.

The consequences of getting caught messing around with the computer were unclear, but I knew they wouldn't be good. The year before, I'd hot-wired the ACCH's tractor (no memory how) and had driven it around the property, smiling and waving at all the other kids, which had resulted in multiple days of restrictions.

Throwing caution to the wind, I flipped the red switch, my heart pounding with anticipation. The computer hummed and beeped, the monitor flickering to life with the text:

```
IBM Personal Computer BIOS
ROM BASIC Version C-1.10 Copyright IBM
  Corp 1981
64K Ram Ok
```

Then, a minute later, it read:

```
Non-System disk or disk error
Replace and strike any key when ready
```

Okay, clearly the computer expected a disk. I looked around, and on the nearby shelf among the baskets of sewing materials was a box of floppy disks. I flipped through the 5.25-inch floppies, and that's when I saw them: *Space Quest (Disk 1 of 3)*, *Space Quest (Disk 2 of 3)*, and *Space Quest (Disk 3 of 3)*. This had to be a game. I inserted the first disk into the left drive, closed it, and hit Return. The disk drive whirred, and after a minute, the monitor read:

```
Non-System disk or disk error
Replace and strike any key when ready
```

I hit the Return key again. Same error. I tried putting the disk into the other drive. Same error. I took out the disk and inserted the second and third disks and hit Return. Same error.

"Farts," I cursed.

I continued paging through the floppies and saw a disk that read *MS-DOS with BASIC*. I put the disk into the drive. Again, the machine whirred and chugged as it attempted to read the disk, but this time, a prompt finally showed up on the monitor:

```
A:\>
```

Progress! On a hunch, I typed *BASIC* and pressed the Return key.

```
Ok
```

Yes! Having no better idea, I keyed in my favorite BASIC program.

```
> 10 PRINT "David is cool"
> 20 GOTO 10
> RUN
```

I folded my arms and smiled in self-satisfaction as my name spilled across the screen. Life was good.

Just then, footsteps echoed through the building. I raced over to the pile of clothing, frantically pretending to rummage through it as the footsteps grew nearer.

The door opened, but it was just Bobby. "Hey, Mrs. Johnson sent me over to get you. Dinner's almost ready."

After powering down the computer, I returned to Cottage 3 and found my housemother in the kitchen fixing dinner.

"Mrs. Johnson, there's a computer in the VoTech building. Do you know how it got there?"

"Oh, Dana dropped by earlier this week. He thought some of the kids—he mentioned you, actually—might enjoy his old computer. I was going to tell you, but it slipped my mind. Dana said there's a couple of games there, too."

"We're allowed to use it?"

"That's right."

"*Really?*"

My housemother continued stirring sauce into a huge bowl of rice. "That's what I said."

"So, like, right now?"

"No, supper's almost ready. But you can go tomorrow after school."

So began my great escape from the ACCH. For the next couple of years, whenever other kids were watching cartoons after school or killing time by tormenting one another, I'd head to the VoTech building and mess around on that PC. I learned the DOS operating system and played through a bunch of games, including *Space Quest*. (It turns out *Space Quest* didn't load that first time because you had to stick the floppy in the drive *before* booting up the computer.)

I also remembered that book on the Pascal programming language that Dana had given me a year or two earlier. It had been too advanced for me then, but now that there was a computer at the home, I thought I'd take another whack at learning the language.

Nope, still too hard. While designed as a teaching tool, Pascal is a significantly more advanced language than BASIC. It uses modular chunks of code called *functions*, which help organize programs by breaking them into smaller, reusable parts that each do one specific job, kind of like one recipe for marinara sauce and another for fried eggplant, which you then combine to make eggplant parm. I understood Pascal's idea of functions easily enough, but the notion of data types threw me. What really was the difference between a Boolean (0 or 1) and an integer (…, -1, 0, 1, 2,…), and why did it matter? Wasn't a number just a number? How the hell did the computer have a notion of numbers in the first place? What actually *was* a goddamned computer? Did normal kids have someone to answer these kinds of questions?

Ultimately, I put the book down in frustration again, but I held on to it. I'd page through it from time to time as my years in the group home wore on. It became a symbol of all the shortcomings of my childhood there, all the opportunities unavailable to me, and I eventually grew to hate it.

I couldn't have known it then, but there is a rich theoretical framework for what a computer is, of what it means to compute. *Computation* is the process of using a set of rules to take information as input—like raw eggplant—perform operations on it—sweating it, covering it in batter, then frying it—and producing a useful output or result—like eggplant parm. It's recipes, but for information. You compute all the time, even in your head, by navigating the roads to get to work or playing a favorite card game with friends.

Cholo-Curious

Let's say you wanted to build the world's simplest computer. Here are your minimal requirements: a memory system to store information, a bit of arithmetic to perform calculations, and *if* and *goto* statements to make decisions. Let's break this down with a simple example.

Imagine you are stranded on a desert island, so you have lots of time to kill and aren't concerned with speed. The first thing you'd need is memory, so you find a stick about arm's length. Using your stick, you can scrawl words into the sand. If you need to remember another word, you just step to the right and scratch out a new one. The beach has become your burgeoning computer's memory tape, storing information that can be written and read. Thanks to your stick, you can *write* whatever words you like into memory, and thanks to your eyes, you can *read* whatever word is in front of you.

Let's say you wanted to write an SOS message. You get out of your hammock under the palm trees higher up on the shore and see the number 23 that you'd previously written in a patch of sand. You walk down to the beach and write "Help!"

Next, you need an *if* statement to execute commands conditionally, allowing your program to make decisions. *If* the sand in front of you already reads "Help!" move to the right and write "I've." You execute these kinds of conditional statements until you write out "Help! I've been stranded on this island for." You also need to do basic arithmetic, but you learned that as a kid. So you recall the number 23 you saw earlier. You *add* 1 to 23 in your head and *write* "24" in the sand next to "for." This simple calculation demonstrates the arithmetic component of your beach computer. Finally, you move one more step to the right and write "days."

Having appreciated your handiwork—"Help, I've been stranded on this island for 24 days"—you're done. You *halt* in the jargon of computer science and walk back into the shade of the palm trees. There, you update the number in the high-shore sand patch to "24." Tomorrow, after the tide washes away your message, you'll *goto* the beginning of the program, meaning you'll grab your stick, walk to the beach, and execute your simple program again.

That's it. That's computing. Yet, anything that can possibly be computed—anything whatsoever—can be calculated by your beach computer. This computer has a name, a *Turing machine*, after the great computer scientist Alan Turing.

The Turing machine you made on the beach isn't much in the way of speed, but it's a terrific theoretical tool. Using it and formalisms like it, computer scientists have proven that some kinds of computation are more computationally expensive than others. So-called *computational complexity* defines the limits of what problems can be solved efficiently. Just as some math problems are harder than others, some computational tasks require significantly more time or resources as the problem grows in size, regardless of how powerful the computer is. This concept is crucial for understanding the capabilities and limitations of both artificial and biological computing systems, including artificial intelligence (AI) and the human brain.

For example, we intuitively understand that addition isn't as hard as multiplication. It turns out that addition is what we call *order N*, while multiplication we learned in grade school is "order N^2" (N-squared). The word *order* just means "on the order of" and indicates that we're only interested in the general trend, while N in these cases reflects the length of the numbers you want to add or multiply.

To understand the difference between order N or order N^2, imagine you had N friends come to your house for a casual Super Bowl party. Everyone lets themselves into your apartment and shouts, "What up, dudes!" They grab a beer from the fridge and plop down on the sofa. That's order N because N people broadcast a single, simple greeting to everyone in the room all at once. Imagine, instead, you are hosting a formal Thanksgiving dinner. Whenever someone comes in from the cold, they warmly greet every single person who's already arrived, one-on-one. This is order N^2 because each of N people has to say hello to about N people separately. Clearly, this scenario is fundamentally more effortful than the one where your friends at the Super Bowl party shouted a quick hello.

This ranking of computational complexity creates a hierarchy of difficulty, at the top of which are the most challenging, the so-called *NP-complete problems*. The most famous NP-complete problem is that of the traveling salesman, whereby a logistics expert wants to minimize fuel costs, so she needs to compute the shortest route for a truck driver that visits N cities once and only once. There are no known shortcuts to a guaranteed perfect solution that work in all cases. The most obvious way to solve it is to list every single option (New York to Saratoga to Buffalo is 450 miles, Buffalo to New York to Saratoga is 580 miles, and so forth) and then choose the route with the shortest distance. This may be feasible with, say, seven cities, as there are 360 possible routes to check. With fifteen cities, however, there are over 43 billion possibilities! Problems like the traveling salesman problem abound, and while solvable in principle, the computational cost of such problems can be incredibly high, making an exact solution effectively unknowable.

The traveling salesman problem represents a boundary on what is solvable in practical or absolute terms with a computer—or, for that matter, an AI. These limits apply even to human brains and even to you.

Even with perfect information, some things are just unknowable.

The discovery of the personal computer in the VoTech building aside, I continued to find myself in front of the mirror, questioning my clothing and my appearance and wondering if there wasn't some recipe or tonic that might make me more appealing to girls. Esther had defined herself in terms of her appearance and was full of ideas for how I should dress. But I was disinclined to follow her advice because our relationship had changed so much over the years we were at the ACCH.

By the time I was in sixth grade, my sister and I barely interacted. I no longer confided in her, if I ever truly had, and she didn't confide in me. When I did check in with her, she'd yammer on about the popular girls in middle school. She called them *privileged* and was always sure to emphasize the differences in circumstances between herself and these girls. With the hindsight of adulthood, much of this could be written off as typical teenage stuff. But while most kids at the home were aware of being on one of the lowest rungs in society, Esther was obsessed with it.

With each passing year, Esther and I looked less and less alike. She'd taken after my father, while I looked like my mother. Like many girls in the '80s, she'd permed her blond hair, which I thought looked awful. But underneath that bad hairdo and bit of teenage acne was a beautiful girl. About this time, a modeling school awarded her a scholarship upon finding out she was in the ACCH. Esther relished those lessons, and in those moments, I believe she was happy.

For my part, I had some honest confusion regarding clothing because deciding how to dress required understanding my identity in the broader social context. The predominant culture at the ACCH was given from the top down: white with a Southern, Bible-thumping twang, and ultraconservative. The children's racial mix was evenly matched between white, Hispanic (descendants of the Spaniards who explored and then conquered the region over four hundred years ago), Mexican, and Native American. As a result, many influences shaped what I thought was cool or stylish.

I roomed almost exclusively with kids of color at the group home: Omar (Mexican), Rob (Navajo), Bobby (Hispanic), or Charn (Thai). When I lived in the War Zone, my only two friends were Native Americans, Apache and Pueblo boys, respectively.

To complicate matters further, our public middle school, John Adams, was filled with older kids who'd already made up their minds about which identity and social groups were right for them. In the 1980s, on Albuquerque's west side, four groups stood out: the skaters, the new wavers, the rockers, and the cholos.

Not participating in this dress-up game was out of the question. If I didn't choose a clique, it meant I was a loser. I'd been a loser throughout elementary school, and I was sick of hanging out on the swing sets by myself.

Like any reasonable kid, I decided to dress like other kids I was growing up around. So I dressed like a cholo. The *cholos* and *cholas*, as they called themselves, were Mexican American and Hispanic kids whose clothing was predominantly influenced by their cultural heritage. The boys wore khaki chinos and white tank tops. In cooler weather, they'd wear loose-fitting flannel shirts with only the top button buttoned. They wore their hair straight back; some of the boys wore hairnets. The girls wore black china-doll shoes with a red rose at the front near the toes. Both boys and girls regularly wore Mexican ponchos, which typically had geometric patterns on them.

Sometime very early in my sixth grade, I asked Omar about training my hair to go straight back. Both he and Antonio, another Mexican kid, trained their hair. I'm unsure what Omar thought of my line of questioning, but he graciously explained how it worked. You did it by using a hairnet and constant grooming. The idea was that sooner or later, your hair would learn to lie backward and flat.

I don't remember ever putting a hairnet on, but I worked hard to train my hair in our bathroom. I combed it backward incessantly while wetting it down, just as Omar had instructed. It's fair to say my fine, blond gringo hair couldn't give two lazy shits about lying flat. It was a lost cause.

I also had to dress the part. I'd coincidentally received a couple of cutoff tank tops from my Aunt Maria on the East Coast, and I found some khaki pants. Between using hairspray to make my hair lie flat (training never worked) and my newfound clothing, my style started heading in the direction of a cholo. But it was never fully realized; you might say I was cholo-curious. I was a sight to behold.

I was ultimately saved from this embarrassing cultural misfire thanks to poverty. Since I had no money, I was unable to fully realize the look. My clothing just wasn't right, and my hair never cooperated. I looked it up years later, by the way. It turns out that training your hair isn't really a thing. It's going to do what it wants unless you use hair products.

My cholo aspirations came to an end midway through my sixth-grade year when I developed a crush on a skater girl named Stephanie in my gifted and talented class. I took one look at how she was dressed and compared it to what I was wearing. Welp, it was time to find a cheapo skateboard somewhere!

I spiked my hair with toothpaste and grew long bleached bangs at the front and a mullet in the back (that was all one haircut). I begged my grandparents to buy me some inexpensive fluorescent Chuck Taylors and pegged my jeans. And that's where my sorry ass stayed for the remainder of middle school.

One night, Omar was watching *MacGyver*. Noticing me walk through the living room, he got up and pulled me aside.

"David, don't say anything," he whispered, "but Juanita and Jessica are coming over."

"At night?" As an eleven-year-old in a ridiculously religious group home, I was shocked.

Omar nodded. "Dude, Jessica is coming over for *you*."

"What do you mean?"

"She wants to make out."

"With me?"

"Yeah." Omar smiled knowingly. "You'll like it."

"Won't we get caught?"

Omar put his hand on my shoulder. "Easy, hombre. Just be cool."

As Omar walked away, I stood there, my palms sweating as I assessed the situation. I'd never kissed a girl in my life. A crush was abstract; making out was...well, physical. Perhaps any boy of eleven might have been nervous. But I'd been punched more times than I'd been hugged or kissed in the last in four years. I had no idea what kissing a girl would be like.

Plus, there was a real risk of getting caught. The cottages were coed, but boys weren't allowed in girls' rooms or vice versa, and it was a major offense if you got caught. All of this being arranged for me, thanks to Jessica's palace intrigues, only served to increase my hesitation.

A curly-haired ginger, Jess had an inviting smile and always found a way to laugh. She lived in Cottage 2 and was friendly with Esther; they'd been on-and-off-again roommates over the years. She was two years older than I was and, like my sister, totally boy crazy. She'd chase me around under the cottonwoods in the late afternoon when nobody was around, trying to pin me to one of the wide tree trunks to steal kisses.

Juanita was Omar's girl; she also lived in Cottage 2. She was Mexican and spoke only broken English, but Omar spoke fluent Spanish. Juanita was attractive, with dark brown skin and luxurious long black hair. She kept very long, pointed fingernails, explicitly filed into claws, but nicely manicured and painted. I asked her about it one time; she made a swiping motion like a cat and responded that they were for protection against anyone who might fuck with her. Plus, she noted with a sweet smile, they were great for picking up hot items in the kitchen.

That night, we all went to bed as usual. In the group home, we had mandatory lights-out at 10:00 p.m. At about 10:02, the housefather, Mr. Johnson, would walk from room to room, ensuring everything was in order.

After he came and went, I waited a minute and then got up. With the lights still off, I quietly went inside the closet I shared with Omar, closed the door, sat down on the floor, and switched on our secret television. We'd found it on a trip out to the Albuquerque dump, an ancient, tiny black-and-white television that received a single channel. After lights-out, if we weren't tired, we'd get up and go into the closet to watch whatever was on—in this case, reruns of *M*A*S*H*. That night, I was mainly focused on Major Margaret "Hot Lips" Houlihan.

As the credits rolled, I heard the girls attempting to enter our room via the window. This was no small feat; the windows swung out only so far, probably to prevent precisely what was happening just then. The girls made an ungodly racket getting in, and I thought for sure we'd all get busted.

After a few minutes, the noise ceased, and the closet door opened. I could see by the white light of the small TV screen that it was Jess. She came into the closet, closed the door, and sat down alongside me. It was a big closet meant for the belongings of two boys, so there was just enough room for the two of us on the floor.

Without saying a word, she bent over and turned off the TV set. The image on the cathode ray tube shrank down to a horizontal line,

Cholo-Curious

which then narrowed to a single point in the middle of the screen. The tube continued to emit an afterglow, which slowly faded.

Jess put her hand on mine.

"Jess, I—"

She put her finger to my lips. She kept her hand there for a few seconds, and then slowly dropped it to my shoulder and then down to my hand.

There we were, a boy and a girl sitting next to each other in the pitch-blackness, on a closet floor in an orphanage in Albuquerque, New Mexico. On a planet hurtling through an ever-expanding, chaotic universe. A boy and a girl holding hands. Her palm was soft and warm against mine, and I could feel the gentle rise and fall of her breath beside me. The smell of her shampoo filled the confined space.

We remained this way, silent for a few minutes of electric anticipation. I was acutely aware of every point where our bodies touched, and I wondered if she could sense my nervousness. Suddenly, we heard a door close loudly, and we both froze, straining to hear if anyone was approaching. The seconds ticked by.

Finally, when no one came, Jessica turned my face toward hers and kissed me. I kissed her back. We made out that night in the closet for an hour. I doubt five words were said between us.

Later, after the girls had gone, Omar put one hand on my shoulder and smiled. *"Órale!* Pretty cool, huh?" he asked.

"Yeah," I said.

"Dude." Omar's demeanor became serious, and he made a fist, which he put right in my face. "Don't breathe a word of this. Otherwise, *chingasos!*"

I thought back to the time Omar had dropped me with a one-two combo for gossiping about him, and my cosmic high collapsed back to the here and now.

I nodded. "Okay, Omar."

We never spoke of it again, not even among ourselves. No houseparents found out, and no trouble ever came of it.

Not a week later, Jess left the ACCH abruptly and without reason, and I never saw her again. That first kiss would linger in my memory for decades as a bittersweet reminder of human connection and the way in which life in the system was utterly unpredictable.

11

What If Tomorrow?

My spiritual crisis finally came when I was twelve years old, at the Ponderosa Bible Camp. The camp was nestled in a valley of the Sangre de Cristo Mountains, a three-hour drive north of Albuquerque. It was a world away from the dust and heat, a place where the pine trees towered overhead and the air was crisp and thin. We slept in rows of rustic cabins, played in splashing streams, and hiked long, winding trails through green meadows.

Every kid at the ACCH loved Bible camp because it gave us a break from the daily grind of group-home life. But beneath the surface, there was a deeper purpose to the camp. It was a place of spiritual awakening and even reckoning, where young minds were molded—sometimes forcibly—to the teachings of the Bible.

At the ACCH, we'd been taught that baptism was the moment of salvation—when your sins were washed away and you were born again in Christ. Without it, there was no hope of heaven. Bible camp was where most kids at the ACCH were baptized, and I'd seen plenty of the older kids going under the water, each in their own time. The previous summer, a teenager named John had been baptized in a freezing mountain stream. When the preacher had pulled him out, John had proclaimed loudly, "Call me Robert!" He'd gone under a sinner and had come out desiring—literally—to be a new young man. The older kids had taunted "Robert" mercilessly until he went back to answering to John.

For the past four years, I'd thrown myself into Christianity. Where some kids merely endured church services and Bible study, I'd found genuine comfort in the rituals, the songs, and the sense of belonging to something greater than myself. I was utterly enthralled, having been an apt pupil and striving for Jesus-like perfection. I was sold to the extent that I'd ad-lib scripture in my daily life. To the women serving food in the lunch line at school, I'd say shit like "Man does not live on bread alone but on every extra drumstick given to me by the friendly lunch ladies." Lord only knows what those lovely women in their hairnets thought of me, but they gave me the extra chicken. Or to my houseparents, when asking for a later bedtime, I'd try out: "The Lord is my shepherd; I shall not want. He makes me lie down in green pastures, but definitely not before 11:00 p.m." That one never worked.

Yet for all my devotion, I hadn't yet taken the final step of baptism. Something had always held me back—maybe just the sense that I wasn't quite ready. And I'd never really understood what had made other kids pull the trigger. But one summer night at Ponderosa, I found out.

We collected around the bonfire under the stars and ponderosa pines. The familiar worship songs felt different in the mountain air, their meaning heightened by the natural beauty and the presence of normal kids from Albuquerque—a larger, less familiar group of worshippers. As the sky darkened and the night grew colder, the youth minister began his sermon. "What happens when Jesus Christ comes back and you're not saved?" He paused, studying his group of a hundred or so kids around the bonfire. "I have bad news for you. You'll burn in hell forever!"

The flames cast eerie shadows around the minister as he walked around the bonfire to address other members of his flock. "I know what you're thinking," he continued. "'I'm a good person; he's not talking about me.' So you think you're a good person? That doesn't matter one bit to our Lord Jesus Christ. He will cast you down into the eternal fires unless you are saved in his name."

He studied us for a minute. "What if Jesus Christ comes back *tomorrow?*"

The question hit me like a physical blow. Until that point, Jesus returning had never felt real—in my mind, his return meant the end of the world, something that would happen when I was older. *Much* older. But suddenly, the possibility of Jesus returning tomorrow felt terrifyingly concrete.

I don't know how the other kids took all this. Maybe Omar was rolling his eyes or off somewhere kissing Juanita. Esther regularly laughed out loud at what she considered complete nonsense. Two Native American kids, Arlene and Arthur, weren't even Christian. Being from one of the Pueblo tribes, they had an entirely different set of religious rituals and beliefs. And perhaps the non-group-home kids at camp were inoculated because they had parents who loved them and spent time with them.

What if Jesus comes back tomorrow?

As the minister's words sank in, all my childhood religious education came flooding back—especially the book of Revelation we'd studied in Sunday school. The apostle John has a vision in which the end of the world is revealed to him. All manner of mayhem and destruction befalls humanity as the seven seals are broken, releasing God's judgment upon the earth. The Four Horsemen of the Apocalypse ride forth, bringing war, famine, plague, and death.

Our Sunday school teacher had also introduced us to the idea of the Rapture, when all the long-dead faithful Christians will literally rise out of the ground. Then, along with living Christians, they will literally float up into the air to meet Jesus. Together, they will enter the kingdom of heaven.

I'd never been sure what I thought about the Rapture. On the one hand, dead people rising out of the ground sounded creepy. On the other, meeting Jesus did seem like something to be excited about. After all, aside from Omar, Jesus was my main man at the ACCH.

Unfortunately, the Rapture also comes with the Tribulation. The Tribulation is reserved for nonbelievers and follows immediately on the heels of the Rapture. It's a period of extreme suffering and includes plagues, famines, and war. I seem to recall that it involves Satan ruling over the earth. It's bad. Very, very bad.

At the group home, they showed us movies about the Rapture and Tribulation tailored to teenagers. The storyline inevitably followed an older teen who realizes that something is off. People are disappearing. After the mystery unfolds for a bit, we come to learn that our protagonist's saved parents are gone. His baptized Christian friends are also nowhere to be found; they all went to heaven with Jesus in the Rapture. Only the rotten kids remain. The movie wraps up with Russian tanks rolling over American soil. Our protagonist is imprisoned in an internment camp and forced to get the number 666, the mark of the beast, tattooed onto his arm in binary digits, 1010011010.

The images from those movies, which had seemed distant and almost entertaining before, now felt terrifyingly real. Each night after the sermon, I lay in my cabin bunk, my mind spinning with visions of empty beds where the saved children should have been, of tanks crashing through the forest around us.

What if Jesus comes back tomorrow?

After asking around, I learned that they weren't holding any more baptisms at Bible camp. For the next two weeks, I couldn't focus on anything due to this overwhelming fear that I wasn't saved. Despite my increasingly poor behavior, I'd always thought of myself as a fundamentally good person. Yet I was being told if I wasn't baptized *today*, I'd be damned forever.

The moment we returned to the ACCH, before even unpacking my bag, I immediately reserved a time to speak with my housefather.

As soon as we sat down, I said, "I want to be baptized."

The following Sunday evening, I found myself in a white baptismal robe, waiting for the last prayer in church to finish. I descended the steps into the pool with the entire congregation watching. The water was warm, and in my heart, I felt a sense of relief. I was saved.

But as the one and only Rev. Jim Aaronson submerged me under the water and I professed my willingness to take Jesus Christ into my heart, I couldn't help but remember that this was the very same pastor who, nearly four years earlier, had liberated me to think for myself by explaining that the dinosaurs had actually roamed the earth for millions of years—that I shouldn't take the Bible literally. Yet here I was, choosing to be baptized for fear of being left behind to face the Tribulation at the hands of Russian infantry.

A few weeks after my baptism, my housemother, Paulette Macho, informed me that I was wanted in the administrative office. I was only ever called there for two reasons: Either I was in serious trouble, or I was meant to help assemble the tens of thousands of donation mailers we sent out each year.

As I racked my brain thinking of all the things I'd recently done wrong, Paulette explained, "Gerald Strong wants to talk to you about Wednesday-night church service."

I breathed a sigh of relief. That anarchy symbol I'd burned into the back of my bathroom door using a can of lit aerosol hair spray hadn't been discovered yet.

I walked over to the administrative building, where all the business of the ACCH was conducted: recruiting houseparents, managing relationships with the families of the children, and, most importantly, drumming up donations. This last was the domain of financial director Gerald Strong. Since the home was a religious nonprofit, we were 100 percent reliant on private donations.

When I arrived in Gerald's office, he was sitting in a swiveling leather office chair behind a huge oak desk. He had a smile full of beautiful white teeth, brown hair neatly parted to the side, and a Southern accent. He was a born rainmaker, and—I'm guessing here—the only person at the ACCH who made anything remotely close to a real living.

Gerald invited me to sit. "Congratulations on your baptism, son. That's a big step forward, and we're all real proud of you."

"Thank you, Mr. Strong," I said.

He brought out a book. "I thought you might like to read *The Screwtape Letters* by C. S. Lewis. Have you ever come across it?"

I shook my head, trying not to fidget and wondering where this was going.

"Give it a read. Perhaps you'll get something out of it." He pushed the book across the desk and then hit me with the real reason I was there. "David, I was wondering if you'd be interested in giving the sermon at church this Wednesday."

"*Me?* I've never done anything like that."

Gerald's smile widened. "Not to worry, son. I've got an outline right here." He looked down at a couple of handwritten pages stapled together on his desk. "I hear you're a bright kid. You read through this and see if it makes sense. Come on back if you have any questions."

I took the papers, thanked Gerald, and scrammed before trouble could find me.

What If Tomorrow?

As I walked back to Cottage 2—I had recently moved there from Cottage 3—I decided I was up for this unexpected request. My need for attention of whatever kind had only grown. I'd taken drama classes in school, had always sung in church, and had no trouble whatsoever projecting my voice. Add to this my knowledge of the Bible, and I figured I could pull it off.

Over the next few days, I studied the notes and looked up the relevant scripture. Gerald and I met one more time to make sure I'd wrapped my head around the material.

At the following Wednesday-night church service, Gerald introduced me to the congregation.

"Good evening, neighbors. I'd like to introduce y'all to David Sussillo; maybe some of you've met him. He's twelve years old, and both he and his sister, Esther, have been with us at the Albuquerque Christian Children's Home for a good long time now. He'll be delivering the sermon tonight." He motioned me up to the stage.

It was out of the question that anyone would clap, but folks gave nods and smiles, and there was a murmur as I headed up to the pulpit.

After my introduction, I got up there and did my thing. And all I can say is: In your time of need, may the Good Lord grant you the same confidence I had that night as I sermonized on a topic about which I had only the flimsiest understanding. Still, I'd studied the notes, and I'd connected the dots. I delivered that sermon like I meant it. I even paced about and shook my pointed finger above my head once or twice.

Back at the ACCH, I got to thinking about the experience. *Why did they ask me to do this? In particular, why had Mr. Strong been the one to ask?* No kid of any age from the group home had ever led a song or given the prayer at church, much less delivered the sermon. The only conclusion I could draw was that it was good optics. After all,

I'd preached to the people who were primarily responsible for keeping the group home afloat. I could just imagine Gerald glad-handing members of the church afterward: *"This* is what you produce when you donate to the ACCH."

Maybe I'd been used; maybe I hadn't. I couldn't make up my mind. But since it was for a good cause, I decided I didn't care. I was happy to help out. Regardless, that experience opened up new possibilities for me. I started considering what life would be like as a pastor. If Rev. Aaronson had attended Pepperdine University, why couldn't I?

12

Thirty-Two Years Old

As my years at the ACCH wore on, my mother spent ever-less time at her apartment and increasingly more time in the psychiatric ward of an Albuquerque hospital. Occasionally, my grandparents would bring Esther and me there to visit her. I hated going because it was so fucking depressing, and trust me, after four years of being "orphaned by the living" in a group home, my assessment here was well calibrated.

Our grandparents would pick us up at the ACCH and drive us across the Rio Grande to the hospital. These car rides were cheerless, and nobody worked at conversation.

"Your mother is really looking forward to this visit," our grandmother would tell us.

Not me.

We would enter the facility via an elevator that let out into a small lobby with chairs along the walls and a couple of unconvincing artificial plants. The white metal doors leading into the ward were locked; we'd have to wait until the nurse buzzed us in.

Upon entering, the hall opened into a large common area covered in wall-to-wall brown carpet. There were chairs and card tables for eating or activities, and along one wall stood a counter with a microwave, coffeepot, and kettle. Nearby was the nurses' station.

Inevitably, my mother would be waiting for us, her smile strained and her eyes tired. We'd all greet one another with hugs that still had connection, but with each passing year, it was less clear to me what that connection was. With Esther and me living in a group home, my mother in the psych ward, and my father in and out of either prison or halfway homes, my entire nuclear family had been institutionalized.

We'd spend our visit with her in her room. It had carpets and a couch that doubled as a pullout bed, not too dissimilar from my room at the ACCH. We'd make small talk. I'd do my best to tune out. School. Movies. Stilted conversation. Life in the ward. Roommates. My mother complaining. Me killing time. Annoying Esther. Thinking of video games.

After forty-five minutes, we'd return our chairs to the common area, say our goodbyes, and get another round of hugs. Esther would cry; I wouldn't. I'd subconsciously learned to push my emotions down, I guess to numb myself to the pain of seeing my mother in this state. Or maybe that's just what years of group-home life did to some kids.

Then the nurse would buzz us out, and we'd load up into our grandparents' car for another silent ride back over the Rio Grande.

It was never clear to me if we visited the hospital to get some mothering or so that our mother could get some childrening. Perhaps my grandparents brought Esther and me because they understood the simple truth that mothers and their kids should be together, even in circumstances like ours.

By the time I was in seventh grade, Esther and I had been in the group home longer than any other kids. Bobby was a close second. Omar, who'd arrived at the ACCH a year after we did, wasn't far behind. We were the lifers, the forgotten kids, the ones who'd been at the home for so many years that we couldn't remember anything else. We'd been warped, bent, only able to interpret the world through the filter of our group-home experience.

Omar and I were spending more time than ever together, roommates again, in Cottage 2. One early fall day, we were playing hacky sack out on the concrete patio. It was Friday, and as we kicked the footbag around, we got it into our heads that we wanted to camp out on the porch for the night, something almost certain to be denied. But having nothing to lose, we sought out our housemother, Paulette Macho.

"Okay, why not?" she said. "Just don't do anything stupid," she warned as she walked back to the houseparents' apartments.

Surely no houseparent in the history of the ACCH had ever granted anyone else such a privilege. Still, the universe is filled with miracles, and the tiny ones are no less significant simply because they're kid-size.

So that night, Omar and I laid out our blankets and pillows on the concrete front porch and spent the night outside. We stayed up looking at the stars, telling stories, and talking about girls. The monsoon season had ended, so instead of lightning, thunder, and whipping rain, the leaves of the cottonwoods rustled softly in the breeze. The next morning, we woke up, put our blankets and pillows away, and resumed our everyday routines.

Around noon, Paulette pulled Esther and me aside to tell us that our grandparents were coming over. I wasn't too surprised by this; my mother had been out of the psych ward for the last couple of months and, earlier in the week, she'd promised to take us out of the home for the weekend but had canceled. I'd assumed it was because she didn't want to spend money on us, so I'd harbored a grudge all week. But when I found out my grandparents were coming to see us, I'd figured

I'd been wrong—that they wanted to tell us in person that our mother was back in the psych ward.

When my grandparents arrived, the Machos told everyone to go to their rooms except Esther and me. Then they excused themselves.

Oh shit, something's definitely up.

My grandfather, grandmother, Esther, and I sat down on the couches in the living room.

My grandfather opened with, "There are times in a person's life when they have to face some hard facts." He swallowed hard. "Your mother passed away yesterday."

My sister began screaming. Her grieving was immediate and physical, as if she were receiving a beating.

For me, there were no feelings and no tears. I felt like I was falling backward through an endless cloud of cotton. Sounds diminished the way an explosion is portrayed in war movies. *Something's missing.* I looked down at the open wound in my chest to survey the damage. *Oh, Mom isn't there anymore.* I looked up. Then my senses returned, and I was back in the living room.

My grandfather looked away, forcing himself to continue speaking. "With your mother dead and your father out of your lives, you'll have to be strong. You're orphans now." My grandmother, who'd clearly been crying all morning, I now noticed, began crying again. She pulled out a tissue to dab at her eyes and gave one to Esther.

I'll never forget my grandfather's final words or his deep, somber tone. "No parent should live to see the death of their daughter." It was the most emotionally naked statement I'd ever heard him utter. He put his head into his hands and began to cry.

After a few minutes of silent grief, our grandmother told us we'd be staying with them for the weekend, so we should go gather our things. I walked back to my room in a daze, my feet moving on autopilot.

Thirty-Two Years Old

As I entered my room, I saw Omar was standing in front of his desk, looking down, rolling the hacky sack back and forth.

I stood there looking at him blankly.

He continued to roll the hacky sack across the desk until he looked up and toward me. "I'm sorry about your mom, Dave."

It turns out that my grandparents had informed the Machos of my mother's death the night before, and Paulette had privately told Omar. That's why I'd been allowed to sleep outside.

That weekend, my sister and I spent most of the time in the back bedroom of my grandparents' house. It had been our mother's room when she was a kid.

My sister was totally into New Wave music, so she played a mixtape with the Cure's "Just Like Heaven" on it. She played it over and over and over, practicing her one '80s dance move—that one with the finger snap and swinging arms on beats two and four.

Esther looked over at me lying on the bed. "What do you think is going to happen to us now that Mom's dead? Do you think Mimi and Papa will take us in?"

"Who even has control of us now?" I asked. "Dad?"

"I'm pretty sure it's Mimi and Papa."

"Then no way. They're not taking us in," I responded.

"Yeah, probably not. Do you think we'll be adopted?"

"Why would Mimi and Papa go for it? We've been at the home for years. They've had the chance for a while."

Esther stopped dancing and spaced out at the wall for a minute. Finally, she turned to me and said, "But Mom's dead now."

I saw Esther's point and considered it. Our grandparents had been the decision-makers, influencing our mother to keep us at the group home on the chance that she might return to health, perhaps even with the idea that keeping us around would improve the chances of her returning to health. Still, their appetite for a second go at raising teenagers—as retirees, no less—had to be somewhere between "no fucking way" and "would rather chew glass." I figured they were dubious about adoption, and frankly, so was I. Neither Esther nor I were in that phase held most dear by those looking to adopt: cherubic and malleable.

On top of the standard adolescent challenge—having a half-baked frontal cortex with executive function lagging far behind other capacities—Esther and I had years of trauma, neglect, prolonged stress, all kinds of privation, and possibly a problematic genetic inheritance, all of which would give even the most intrepid potential adoptive parents serious pause. In my heart, I knew that somebody would have to be batshit crazy to take us in.

During our time at their house, Esther and I only occasionally headed into the den to listen to the conversations concerning the practical details of our mother's death. To get from the bedrooms to the den, you had to pass through the lifeless living room with the out-of-tune piano and the dining room that was only ever used on Thanksgiving. It had always felt like ghosts might haunt those rooms, but it felt especially so then.

Upon entering the den, I observed that my grandparents had set on the fireplace mantel a silver-framed eight-by-ten picture of my mother from when she was sixteen. The picture was black and white; my mother was thin and beautiful and had a huge beehive hairdo. I thought it looked nothing like her. My mother had been a freewheeling hippie, not some beauty queen replica of her own mother.

We learned that, indeed, my mother had planned to return to the psychiatric hospital, which was why she had canceled her weekend visit. By Friday afternoon, my grandparents had expected a call regarding her departure. But the call never came.

Thirty-Two Years Old

After a few hours, my grandfather grew worried enough to head over to her apartment. He let himself in, and there, lying face down on the living room carpet, long brown hair in disarray, was his daughter, obviously dead. He dialed 911 and then called my grandmother, who made her way over.

On Sunday, they received a call from the doctor who'd completed the autopsy. My mother's heart had failed, likely based on interactions between the prescribed drugs in her system. She was on methadone, as well as medicines to combat severe depression. She'd become morbidly obese. It was only a matter of time before one of her many problems killed her. The age on the autopsy report read thirty-two years old.

Just days later, we arrived early at the funeral and sat up front. By the time the service started, the chapel was filled. I couldn't believe it. Despite my mother being a complete shut-in by the end of her life, hundreds of people were there. Did my mother really have this many friends and connections from her past?

I observed that my father was in attendance. My grandparents blamed him for my mother's demise, for her drug addiction, and for leaving her in the lurch with two young children. They despised him for it. He sat with his older brother, my Uncle James, who'd flown out from Virginia.

I hadn't seen James since his wedding to Beverly earlier that summer in Virginia. Afterward, they'd taken Esther and me on a weeklong trip to Ocean City. We'd enjoyed the boardwalk and beach together and had gone out to restaurants. Everything that my sister and I had experienced had seemed lavish, and I'd felt deliciously spoiled in those moments.

The memory of those carefree days felt surreal now, as if from another lifetime. As I caught James's eye across the chapel, his solemn nod brought me back to the present and the reason we were all gathered.

The pastor from my grandparents' church gave the eulogy. During the service, my whole family was a mess of sobs, especially my sister. The most emotional moment came when my mother's cousin sang a heartfelt lamentation. I didn't cry. I was still in clouds of cotton.

At the end of the service, each family member went up to the casket to say their goodbyes. When my turn came, I found myself frozen in place in front of my mother's body. I hadn't known what to expect, but she looked peaceful, almost like she was sleeping. As I stood there in disbelief, my eyes fixed on the undeniable proof that my mother was really gone, I felt a hand on my shoulder. I turned to see my father standing behind me, his eyes fixed on my mother's face. My father squeezed my shoulder.

I hadn't seen much of my father, and our relationship had always been complicated. But in that moment, I felt a flicker of connection. A lump rose in my throat. A tear slipped down my cheek. I hadn't cried over my mother's death, but something about my father's presence seemed to crack open the numbness that had enveloped me.

After the burial, our grandparents brought Esther and me back to the group home. It had been four days since I'd learned of my mother's passing. Just like that, it was back to chores, public school buses, and a 16:1 children-to-houseparent ratio. I woke up the following day mortified to find that I'd peed the bed, something I hadn't done since my first night at the ACCH. I raced to wash my sheets and blanket before anyone found out. Paulette Macho noticed me stuffing all my bed coverings into the washing machine, but she had the grace to keep quiet.

At the time, and for a long time afterward, I wondered if my mother had killed herself. I'd somewhat disbelieved the autopsy or perhaps that my grandparents were telling the whole truth about it.

It wouldn't have been the first time they'd protected me from a hard truth with a lie.

Esther and I were given our choice of our mother's belongings. There was a simple black cord necklace with a long piece of clear quartz, which Esther wanted, and a large grouping of amethyst crystals, which I took. There was a hunk of fool's gold and a geode. I didn't know what happened to my mother's piano. I couldn't remember her ever playing it. Not even once.

At the ACCH, Christmas gifts were modest—usually small tokens exchanged between kids or occasional presents from local retirees. Having nothing else to give, Esther and I decided to wrap our mother's keepsakes and give them away as gifts to our friends. We agreed that she would have liked that.

13

Did We Even Say Goodbye?

As the days after my mother's death became weeks, everything blurred together, routine masking the turmoil within. Externally, I was an automaton, but inside, I was unraveling. Words like *dead*, *death*, *mom*, *mother*, or *parent* would send waves of dread crashing over me, dragging me out of the present and momentarily into a void where voices fuzzed and the world seemed to tilt on its axis.

As the weeks turned to months, I went from being a mere loudmouth to an out-and-out troublemaker. Even in class, where I cared about the outcome, I'd act out, especially if the teacher was a woman. I forced my English teacher, Mrs. Haltom, whom I greatly admired, to repeatedly toss me out of class. For a while, I spent more time in lunch detention than at lunch. This tapered off, though, once the principal threatened suspension. In science class that year, we were expected to do a science fair project. I didn't even bother, thereby failing the quarter.

At the group home, my behavior was far worse. I ended up on restrictions more that year than I'd ever been. I started sneaking off the property late at night by myself, wandering around the nearby middle-class neighborhood of Taylor Ranch in search of answers to questions that had no words.

I'd walk the residential streets in the dark, the only sound that of my own footsteps echoing off the pavement. The houses were silent, their inhabitants blissfully unaware of lost boys and dead mothers. Under the soft glow of the streetlights, I'd catch glimpses of lives I could never have: a kid's bike left on a lawn, a skateboard propped against a garage door, hints of childish pictures drawn with colorful chalk on the sidewalk. Everything seemed so goddamned normal. It was beautiful.

"David!" Paulette Macho yelled across the common area. "Phone call!"

I didn't receive phone calls often. Surprised, I hustled over. "Hello?"

"Hi, David. It's your Uncle James."

It had been six months since I'd last seen Uncle James at my mother's funeral. Before that, we'd spent time together during the summer at his wedding with Beverly. That visit had sparked something between us—we'd connected in a way I hadn't expected.

We made small conversation for a few minutes, and then James broached the topic he'd called to talk about. "Hey, listen. Your Aunt Beverly and I were thinking, how would you like to come live with us next year?"

"Oh my gosh! That'd be amazing!" But then a thought hit me. "Wait. You're *allowed* to take me?"

"We talked it over with your dad, and he's agreed to let me become your legal guardian. He said you could live with us as long as we promised to take you to a Church of Christ on Sundays."

"Don't my grandparents have control of us now?"

"No. Your dad has the say."

"Oh." I thought for a minute. "What happens to Esther?"

There was silence, then a deep breath. "Well, as you know, Beverly and I were just married. We're not sure we can take two kids."

His words picked up in pace as he continued, "But there's a plan for Esther! She'll be coming to the East Coast as well."

"She's not going to like that. Are you sure?"

"We want to make sure we do this right."

"Oh. Okay. Well…then, yes, I'd love to live with you! Thank you so much!"

I ran over to Esther's bedroom and knocked on the door. She opened it a crack, saw it was me, and impatiently said, "What?"

"Guess what? James and Beverly are taking me out of the ACCH. Can you believe it?"

Esther was silent for a moment, then she asked, "They didn't say anything about me?"

"They did! You're leaving the ACCH, too. But Uncle James said something about how because they were newlyweds, they could only take one of us at their house."

The blood drained from Esther's face as the implications of my words set in. "Oh my god. They're not taking me, are they?"

"Maybe I could call him back and—"

"They're leaving me." Tears squeezed out of Esther's eyes. "They're leaving me!"

"Just wait and see what the plan for you is."

"Of course they pick my stupid genius baby brother over me." Esther slammed the door in my face.

I knocked on her door again. "Come on, Est. I'm sorry. Can we talk?"

"Go away!"

I opened Esther's door a few inches and looked in. She was lying on her bunk bed, head buried in her pillow.

"Est, I'm really sorry," I said.

"Fuck off, wonder boy," she said through tears.

"Est, come on. Don't be like that."

"Go geek out with your aunt and uncle if they love you so much."

"Est—"

"*GO AWAY!*" she screamed.

"Well, maybe if you weren't such a pain in the butt, people would want to be around you more!" I yelled as I stomped away.

James, my father's tall, blond-haired, fair-skinned older brother, was the eldest of the five siblings. He'd always taken responsibility seriously, stepping up to help his mother raise the family when their father passed away during his boyhood. Later, he joined the navy to serve his country. In the wake of my mother's death, his sense of responsibility kicked in again.

The summer before my mother's passing, James married Beverly, a curly-haired brunette with a lovely smile. She was a natural teacher, and despite her reserved demeanor, when she opened up, she was skilled at spinning colorful yarns or engaging in deep conversation. While it was an incredible gift for James to take me in, that was doubly true for Beverly. It's hard to imagine that a live-in thirteen-year-old nephew was at the top of her wedding registry. A nephew, I might add, who'd spent the last five years in a group home and whose recent behavior was euphemistically called "problematic." Yet Beverly agreed to give it a shot.

I learned later that James and Beverly had seriously considered taking both Esther and me to avoid splitting us up. But the more they thought about it, the more unrealistic the idea seemed. Beverly had finally called it. They were newlyweds, after all, and she had real concerns about jeopardizing their marriage. As my uncle and I had hit it off early on in our summer vacations, it seemed natural to him that I should be the one they fostered. So they chose me.

Esther herself might have had something to do with that decision. By fourteen, she routinely threatened suicide when she didn't get her way—a threat people couldn't dismiss. While I was prone to fits of rage in private, she had difficulty managing her emotions around— and in relation to—other people. It was fire or ice with Esther. If she loved you, she'd do anything for you. But it was a cloying, grasping thing you needed distance from. If she disliked you, she'd bust out some crazy-ass Sun Tzu *Art of War* techniques on you, regardless of personal cost.

Yet Esther's intuitive understanding of others was off the charts. She could walk into a room and take over. Her comprehension of our circumstances was years beyond my own. She had higher expectations of our parents and was the first to point out the injustice of our situation. She wondered aloud why our grandparents had never forced the issue of our adoption or taken us in themselves. And Esther never understood why our aunts and uncles tolerated our steady decline at the ACCH. She even had the moxie to push them on it, and the honest answer, "It's complicated," neither soothed nor sufficed. For all her challenges and because of her gifts, not being invited to live with James and Beverly was a grievous blow.

As it turned out, my Aunt Moira and Uncle Elliot, who'd come out years earlier to check in on us, helped Esther relocate to the East Coast that summer. Like James and Beverly, Moira and Elliot took responsibility for Esther's well-being and did so for years. But they didn't offer to take her in. They now had a two-year-old son, Paul, and doubted that they could also handle Esther full-time. Instead, they placed her at Darrow School, an exclusive boarding school in the Berkshires with rolling hills, historic buildings, and a carefully curated sense of tradition. This was a significant life change Esther was on board with intellectually but not emotionally.

Even though Esther left for the East Coast the same day I did, in her eyes, she'd been abandoned. And in terms of her emotional reality, she had been. For my part, I endured terrible guilt over separating from my sister, despite knowing I was surviving as best I could.

At the end of the school year, James and Beverly purchased round-trip airfare from Albuquerque to Washington, DC. We all agreed that if living with them didn't work out, I'd return to the ACCH at the end of the summer.

I dearly want to tell you that I had a heartfelt farewell with Omar. That we'd hugged it out and tried to hide tears. The truth is, I have no memory of saying goodbye to either Omar or my sister. The coming and going of both children and houseparents was so routine that it held no salience. Hell, maybe Omar and I didn't even say goodbye. Instead, he and Bobby might have chatted for a minute after Paulette Macho informed Bobby he could take my place in Omar's room.

"What happened to David?" Bobby might have asked as he dragged a drawer full of his belongings from his old room to his new one.

"His aunt and uncle took him," Omar might have said while stretched out on his bed.

"For good?"

"Looks that way."

"Nah. He'll be back."

"Maybe." Omar might have paused in thought, smiled, and then said, "Maybe not."

And I'd like to think that, before helping Bobby move into his room, Omar might instead have randomly punched him in the arm and yelled, *"Chingasos!"*—a final send-off to his younger group-home brother.

But we group-home kids didn't think in sentimental gestures and honest goodbyes. When it came to love, we'd been desensitized, rendered numb. By the end of seventh grade, I didn't love anybody. Not a soul.

On the plane to DC, I gazed out the window, watching the familiar desert landscape slowly give way to a patchwork of green fields over the Midwest, then to the dense forest cover of the East Coast. I was too young to realize it at the time, but my perception of reality was about to undergo a seismic shift. Behind me was the ACCH: a complex network I had gradually figured out how to navigate. Ahead lay an entirely new system—a family unit with its own intricate web of expectations and dynamics.

PART 3

ORDER: 1988–1993

Could the thoughts inside your head be an echo of the fundamental organization of reality? As a neuroscientist who began with a fascination for technology, I've discovered that networks—intricate webs of connections between small, component parts—govern everything around us. From the social dynamics of the group home to the design of complex technologies to the neural circuits in our brains, networks operate at every scale. Let's explore how these networks manifest in the most complex object we know: the human brain.

On one level, the brain is composed of many large neural circuits wired together, which communicate constantly rather than functioning in isolation. The visual cortex, a master of light and color, paints the fresco of our vision while the motor cortex, a choreographer of limbs, orchestrates the graceful motion of our bodies. Each of these cortical areas is an immense network composed of billions of neurons, and understanding in precise detail how either circuit functions is a holy grail of neuroscience.

But the brain's complexity doesn't stop there. You'll find other circuits like the thalamus, a hub that not only bustles with sensory and motor signals but also plays a crucial role in regulating sleep and wakefulness. Then there's the prefrontal cortex, the master planner. Zoom way in to the cellular level, and you'll encounter astrocytes, diligent helpers supplying nutrients to the neurons and thereby maintaining the health of this living neural network. Zoom further into a single neuron and observe its subcellular machinery, supporting the synapses connecting it to thousands of other neurons. Finally, at the heart of each neuron lies the nucleus, a Library of Alexandria that houses the blueprints of life, your chromosomes.

Chromosomes—long, physical strands of DNA—are themselves akin to libraries, with genes located all along them, somewhat like books along shelves. Think of it as a dynamic library where specific genes are accessed, copied, and regulated by proteins called *transcription factors*, which themselves are controlled by other genes. This sets off a cascading reaction, one gene influencing the expression of others that influence the expression of still others, ultimately determining a cell's physiology and even its identity. Is it a liver cell? A heart cell? Or will it play a tiny part in the mystery of consciousness, becoming a brain cell? As a neuroscientist, I see echoes of the brain in these gene networks, akin to how a neuron's electrical activity depends on the neurons that connect to it, who in turn respond to their own network of input signals.

Let's skip the chemical level and jump from the molecular down to the atomic. Picture a refrigerator magnet—an everyday object with hidden complexity. The magnet, atomically, is a lattice, a brickwork where each atom uses its tiny magnetic dipole—its own north and south pole—to hold hands with its nearest neighbors. In perfect harmony, these neighbors all point the same way, creating a unified magnetic field—the reason our magnet clings so faithfully to the refrigerator. But heating the magnet disrupts this delicate structure. While neighboring dipoles remain connected, their orientations loosen, forming smaller, fluctuating clusters like groups of dancers in a ballet losing coordination with one another as the music changes. The once-unified field fragments, and the magnet's grip weakens.

From the bustling metropolis of the brain to the push and pull of gene networks in a single cell to the hidden organization of a magnet, we find networks governing everything around us. Perhaps, instead of turtles all the way down, we should say that it's brains all the way down: networks composed of networks built upon networks, giving rise to the rich tapestry of our conscious experience and the diversity of life around us.

14

Discover

James and Beverly lived in a three-story town house in an upper-middle-class development, the multicolored brick exterior of each row house blending with its neighbors. The community boasted a fitness center, a swimming pool, and a community garden—luxuries that immediately signaled how different my life would be. Plus, it was just a ten-minute walk to the mall, so I could hit up the arcade anytime I wanted.

We parked in the spot outside their town house, and I pulled my suitcase out of the trunk of my aunt and uncle's Volvo, following them into their home. Beverly showed me upstairs to my room—my *own* room—where I put my belongings down and then accompanied her as she showed me around. We finished in the living room and sat down. My eyes were immediately drawn to the coffee table, its surface covered in a sprawl of colorful magazines.

I picked up the copy of *Discover*, its glossy cover cool against my fingers. The cover read: *Quest for Antimatter*. "What the heck is antimatter?" I asked, holding up the magazine.

"Imagine everything in the universe has an opposite version of itself. That's antimatter."

I frowned in confusion.

"I don't fully grasp it, either," admitted Beverly. "But my understanding of the article is that for every type of atomic particle, like a neutron or an electron, there's an antimatter version of it." As Beverly explained her understanding of the topic, I found myself leaning in, fascinated.

"Dang, Aunt Beverly," I said after she'd finished. "You know a lot."

My aunt chuckled. "I might've been a scientist in another life. Anyway, read it for yourself and we can discuss it later."

I looked at the stack of magazines, then back at Beverly. For the first time since my mother's death, I felt a flicker of curiosity.

Before long, my two favorite magazines became *Scientific American* and *Discover*. While I enjoyed *Scientific American* and would make sure to read a couple of articles from each issue, for the most part, the prerequisites required to grasp the material were beyond my eighth-grade education. *Discover*, on the other hand, was just right. I'd read each issue front to back and then back to front as soon as it arrived in the mail.

One article that blew my mind described a simulation called the *Game of Life*, invented by mathematician John Conway. Conway was interested in understanding how simple systems could demonstrate complex behavior, what we now call *emergent* behavior. Rather than contending with the overwhelming complexity of the physical world, Conway's Game of Life demonstrates this principle using a so-called *cellular automaton*, which simulates emergence with simple rules.

Imagine a huge grid of squares on the computer screen, exactly like you see on grid paper. Each square represents a cell that has two possible states, living or dead. A cell has eight neighbors: up, down, left, and right, plus the four diagonals. In the Game of Life, a cell is either alive or dead depending on the state of its eight neighbors, changing from living to dead or vice versa according to the following three rules:

Birth: A cell changes from dead to living if it has exactly three living neighbors. Any three of its eight neighbors are fine.

Death: If a cell is alive and it has only one or no living neighbors, the cell dies—from loneliness, I guess. If it has four or more neighbors, it also dies, presumably from starvation due to resource competition.

Staying alive: If a living cell has two or three neighbors, it stays alive, a sort-of Goldilocks effect.

While it's called the *Game of Life*, it should really be called the *Simulation of Life*, because to play it, all you do is set up whatever fun, random pattern of living and dead cells on the 2D grid you can imagine—the *initial condition* of the simulation—then you let 'er rip. Many programs allow you to "paint in" living cells using your computer mouse. Then you hit Go, and the rules iterate over and over

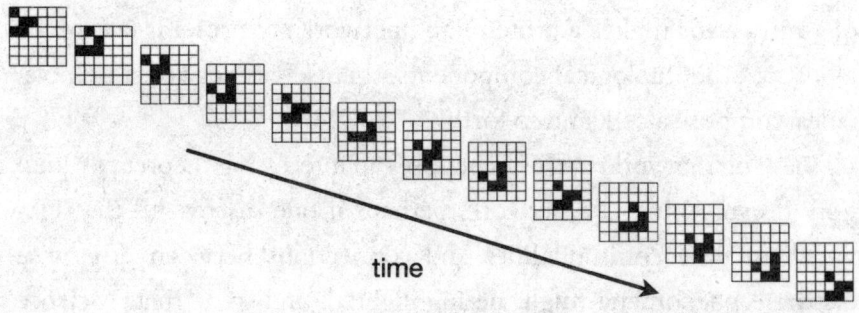

Caption: A lone glider drifts across the grid, a long-lived arrangement of cells obeying the rules of the Game of Life. With each step, it advances, square by square, a tiny explorer in Conway's ever-evolving universe.

without any further input or intervention, allowing you to sit back and watch the simulation evolve.

What unfolds is nothing less than an astounding array of ever-changing, long-lived, complex patterns, with such evocative names as gliders, blinkers, pulsars, and spaceships. Some patterns, like the gliders and spaceships, look like pixelated bugs moving across the computer screen. Some patterns can even replicate.

The Game of Life, and cellular automata more generally, are a bit like brains. In the case of the Game of Life, the state of each cell depends on its eight neighbors and produces patterns according to the rules just outlined. In the case of the brain, each neuron connects to many thousands of other neurons, most nearby but many far away. And just like the cellular automata, the neurons fire their electrical action potentials depending on the inputs they receive from other neurons. So both cellular automata and brains are networks of simple components, and both give rise to complex, emergent behavior.

Broadening out even further, the physical world, and especially the living world, seems to be composed of stacked networks: A network of atoms makes a glycine molecule, a kind of amino acid. A network of amino acids makes a protein, and networks of proteins (alongside a host of other biological components, themselves networks of molecules) compose a cell, and so forth.

Viewing the world in this light poses an interesting theoretical question. If everything is a network, perhaps if one discovered the right viewpoint, the commonalities and connections between otherwise disparate phenomena might be highlighted, and so a "meta" science of networks might be created that explains nearly everything. To use a ridiculous example to make the point, is there any scientific advantage in comparing how human societies organize themselves and how an animal's immune system fights off an infection? At first blush, this seems preposterous; conjuring Gary Larson–esque cartoonish cells organized as a defensive phalanx to fight off the bacterial hordes is a one-way ticket to being laughed out of academia. On the other hand, societies are organizations of people with different roles that, at least in one function of society, fight off intruders. Meanwhile, the immune system is comprised of different cell types with dedicated roles that must fight off the bacteria and viruses that constantly attack the body. Is there some mathematical model or conceptual framework that would shed light on both scenarios? In short, viewing disparate phenomena as networks of networks implicitly asks whether *nonlinear* systems at different levels of organization share fundamentally similar properties.

To understand nonlinearity, let's begin by understanding a simple linear process. For example, when you add sugar to your coffee, more sugar means more sweetness. Even if you dumped way too much sugar in your coffee and it became unpalatable, it would be so because it was way too sweet, not because it somehow became bitter or salty. It's linear because adding a bit more leads to a bit more of the effect.

Conversely, with nonlinear systems, adding more does not result in more of the same outcome. Anyone who has ever had too much to drink will immediately understand nonlinearity. One drink is great, two drinks are fabulous, and depending on one's tolerance, three drinks can be a rocking good time. But sooner or later, consuming too much booze leads to misery.

As it turns out, nonlinear systems are the rule in nature, far more common than linear systems, from the equations Lorenz used to understand the weather, to Conway's Game of Life, to brains, to earthquakes. These systems are also exceptionally difficult to understand and are often chaotic, meaning that their incredible sensitivity to initial conditions virtually guarantees that they never behave exactly the same way twice.

In the 1980s, a group of physicists from Los Alamos National Laboratory had been thinking broadly about nonlinear systems and potential commonalities across different types and scales of physical matter, from interacting particles to molecular biology to stock markets. These scientists, influenced by ideas about emergent complexity that Conway's Game of Life had helped popularize, were big shots in the heyday of physics and were ideally placed to observe the limitations of the scientific method and the shortcomings of constructionism in science. So they founded a think tank in Santa Fe, New Mexico, called the Santa Fe Institute (SFI) to tackle this question head-on.

The goal of SFI was to identify and characterize commonalities between nonlinear systems, such as the mind and the weather, to establish a new physics that studied the complex interaction of how parts create the whole, in the abstract. Thanks to the advent of modern computers, researchers at SFI could write down the equations for a system of interest and use simulations to study its behavior, much as Lorenz had done in the study of meteorology, or legions of scientists and amateurs have done with the Game of Life. Researchers at SFI studied equations of, for example, the weather rather than taking measurements of the weather itself. This allowed them to disentangle the mathematics and algorithmic concepts from the experimental aspects of physics, chemistry, and biology.

Studying networks this way and with these approaches became known as *complex systems*, or simply *complexity*, research. This new field concerned itself with how pieces interact to create an entirely new whole. There was something new to understand, something *emergent*, just as long-lived gliders and spaceships emerge from the Game of Life's simple rules.

The magazine article about Conway's Game of Life was my first introduction to complexity, and I was enthralled. Many of the magazine's stories highlighted not only the researchers but the universities where they worked, such as Caltech, Stanford, and MIT. The mystique surrounding MIT in particular caught my fancy, a place where the high priests of mathematics and physics worked hidden forces to produce all manner of scientific and technological marvels. I decided MIT was a place I might aspire to, if only I worked hard and was clever enough.

Clearly, living with James and Beverly gave me a significantly broader exposure to culture, engineering, and science (though I still attended that weekly Church of Christ service my father insisted upon). I started taking piano lessons, something I'd always wanted to do but could never afford. I hopped on the metro to visit the Smithsonian museums. I went to George H. W. Bush's inauguration in 1989. Astonishingly, I periodically dropped into the Hirshhorn Museum, a museum of modern art—by myself, of my own volition, at the age of thirteen.

When I was at the group home, I couldn't escape religion. It was daily devotionals and Bible study, prayers before every meal, church three times a week, and Bible camp in the summer. We rarely discussed science. When we did, it was always me asking the questions. Popular rebuttals included the missing link in evolution, how a recently discovered cache of early hominid bones was really just the remains of a deformed human child, or how radiocarbon dating was an outright lie to fool the sheeple.

I was a product of these contrasting systems—moving from the religious network of the group home that emphasized faith and tradition to the intellectual network of James and Beverly's household that valued curiosity and scientific inquiry. Though I had been inclined toward the profession of a preacher in seventh grade, by the end of my eighth-grade year, I was seriously considering becoming a physicist or mathematician thanks to the enriched intellectual life I enjoyed with Beverly and James.

15

Ninety-Nine Problems

Looking back, my aunt and uncle's intellectual curiosity was very real—but so was the emotional distance I was too young to notice, a gap that would become unbridgeable once the strain of raising a wounded kid began to outweigh their good intentions.

I was not used to life as a single child. My aunt and uncle both worked, and James was getting a master's degree at night. I was frequently alone and lonely; I simply needed more attention than James or Beverly could provide.

As my eighth-grade academic year began, a serious problem arose. I completed all my homework in class and didn't have any remaining assignments to finish later in the evening. I know; you're thinking, *How the heck is that a problem?* James was a go-getter who dutifully attended the parent-teacher meetings, and my teachers had explicitly told him that I should have twenty minutes of homework per class every night. As my uncle was literal to a fault, his expectation was that I should have no less than two hours of nightly homework.

When James brought up this discrepancy with me, I told him the truth. There was nothing to worry about, because I had more than enough time to do my homework during the class in which it was assigned. My uncle went so far as to visit the principal to discuss the inconsistency. In some straight-up, cover-your-ass bullshit, the principal and teachers all agreed I should have twenty minutes of homework per class. After that, James accused me of telling a bald-faced lie. He settled on the idea that I needed to sit at the dinner table for an hour every single night to give me time to do the homework he believed I was lying about.

When my first report card came in the fall, I received A's for all my classes. You'd think that would have been the end of it. Nope. James insisted on me sitting at that table for the entirety of my eighth-grade year, presumably based on the notion that this dedicated homework time had been the cause of the excellent report card. So I stared at the popcorn ceiling for an hour every night, bearing my uncle ill will the entire time.

As for Beverly, fostering me was a tremendous ask; she wasn't even related to me by blood. And yet—given the primary role a mother plays in a child's life and the additional complexities of my own mother's tragic death just a year before—I was far needier for Beverly's attention. Though we'd go on walks or go to the movies together, she was introverted and mainly enjoyed being alone with her dogs, Nugget and Bean. She just wasn't up for the day-in, day-out challenges of raising me.

Still, all three of us—*especially I*—knew that an imperfect life together was infinitely superior to what my life had been at the ACCH. You could say we were giving it a middle school try.

As the year continued into spring, my relationship with Beverly really began to degrade. I could be a mouthy fuck, and she had a short temper. Most of our fights centered around me being stuck around the dinner table for an hour each night. We got into frequent shouting matches that turned into a contest of wills so common between teenagers and parents. A couple of times, they escalated even further. I'd say something rude, and she'd slap me. Then I'd repeat my comment or state that she couldn't hurt me, so she'd slap me again. This would go on until one of us regained our calm. James rarely got involved in these fights, but when he did, he always took Beverly's side. Always.

So James and Beverly sent me to a therapist specializing in troubled children. I made a stink of it, but it was a charade. I loved this female therapist's company and attention. She was intelligent and engaging, she wore nicely fitting pencil skirts, and the session was all about me. But I viewed the problems I was having with James and Beverly as squarely belonging to them; they were sending me to a shrink to avoid facing their own shortcomings as parents. It wasn't like we were participating in family sessions together, nor was I aware of any therapy they were attending on their own. As a result, I was uncooperative during my sessions, and I went out of my way to sabotage them by playing stupid mind games and avoiding any meaningful conversation about my relationship with my aunt and uncle.

Just after my sessions with the therapist had ended, a grave problem arose, one so serious that I never discussed it with Beverly, James, or the therapist. For no reason I could explain, I found myself constantly furious—and I mean *seething* with anger. Back at the ACCH, I'd flown into rages, but I'd never hit anyone. Early on, I'd punched a few walls but had rapidly discovered solid brick had its own way of punching back. Instead, I'd walk around outside squashing insects or burning them with a magnifying glass and kicking at the dirt. Just as often, I'd retreat to my room and destroy my own shit. One time, I grabbed my alarm clock by the cord and swung it over and over into the floor until it was smashed into smithereens. All the while, I cursed the vilest curses my eleven-year-old brain could muster. The release had been nothing short of euphoric.

My acting out at the ACCH hadn't been a result of any intellectualized notion of rebellion. It was from the gut. I was mad as hell, and if I didn't express it right then, I'd explode and take the whole goddamned world with me.

Life at the group home was manifestly unfair, and the application of justice was often arbitrary. Many houseparents were unconcerned with getting to the bottom of an issue before meting out draconian punishments. I'll never forget the joker-ass houseparents who grounded me for *three weeks* for entering their son's room *with his* permission. It was crazy-making!

Another source of fury had been the complete lack of agency at the ACCH. We had to jump when the houseparents said jump. One housefather, Mr. Texiera, actually made me jump for twenty minutes when he erroneously blamed me for disrespecting his wife. When he learned he had the wrong kid, he walked away without apology, leaving me to wonder if it was okay to stop jumping.

And outside of hikes through the bosque, we couldn't ever leave the compound without supervision. That meant no planned playdates, no organized sports, and no school-related extracurricular activities of any kind. At first, this confinement was merely frustrating. After five years, you wanted to kill a motherfucker.

And then, of course, there were the ass-kickings. The many times I'd been wrestled to the ground, face pressed into the sand, as someone twisted my arm until I hollered with pain or actually cried. The times I'd been slapped, manhandled, beaten up, or dragged out to the common room with only my underwear on. Knocked the fuck out in front of a girl I had crush on. Never once landing a blow. The shame of never, ever feeling like I'd made a good showing.

The ACCH was no safe space, and getting kicked out or running away meant life on the street or as a state ward. All I could do was open wide as the shit was shoveled my way. Yes, boy, you may have some more. So I broke my own stuff, burned bugs, and learned to curse like my life depended on it. Perhaps it did.

And I'd brought all that unprocessed, dormant rage with me to Virginia.

James and Beverly had two black Labs, Nugget and Bean. As a rule, Nugget and Bean stayed down in the basement when we were out of the house, mainly to keep Bean from destroying furniture. She stayed in a kennel, and though full grown, she was still young enough to chew her way to China if left unsupervised. I had my Nintendo set up in the basement, so I was down there with them often.

One afternoon, I got home from school around three o'clock, alone as usual. It was my responsibility to let the dogs out, so I went downstairs into the basement and walked over to Bean's kennel. Bean had vomited up her breakfast all over herself and all over her metal crate. I let her out, grabbed a towel, and got to cleaning.

In Bean's sweet doggy mind, whatever had caused her to become sick was ancient history. Being stoked to see me, she came back over to her kennel and sniffed around curiously to see how I was doing. In the process, she got her vomit all over me.

"Gross! Go away, Bean," I said gruffly, shoving her aside as I finished cleaning.

Once I stood up, she came back over to me again. "Beat it, you nasty fucking dog!" I yelled. I looked down at the vomit smeared across my jeans and shirt, then back at Bean.

Her tail was wagging, and she looked up at me with that friendly dog smile.

I looked back down at the mess on my clothes, and a pure, unadulterated rage came over me. It was faster than I could process, a lightning strike. Zero to ten in the blink of an eye. I was five years of pent-up fury, looking for any target.

Fuck this. I walked the two steps to Bean and kicked her.

She yelped and backed away. I walked toward her and kicked her again, harder. And again. Bean started whining and ran to the corner, cowering. She peed a little on the cream-colored carpet.

Come here, you fucking bitch.

Nugget started barking and growling.

I looked over at him. "You want some, too?" I shouted.

His hackles were raised; he was growling, his teeth bared. He wasn't messing around, either.

No, too dangerous.

The violence in me demanded release; it had to go somewhere. Bean was going to catch a beating, even if she had retreated to the corner. I walked over to her, readying myself for another kick.

Breathe, David, breathe! What are you doing?

The rush faded, and I dropped down on the carpet, head between my knees, in complete shock at my own behavior. Bean, bless her heart, stood up and comforted me, licking my face. Overwhelming shame washed over me.

So it began that about once a week, I'd bring home anger from school. I'd go downstairs to let the dogs out, and the next thing I knew, I was kicking Bean. It wasn't something I planned; it just happened. In the blink of an eye, I went from relative calm to unbridled fury. Afterward, I'd feel rotten about what I'd done. Yet something about the context and the electric release of pent-up anger was strong enough that I'd lose control again.

After four of these beatings, Bean became reluctant to leave her kennel when I returned home from school. Later in the evening, she'd hesitate to come down into the basement with me when I played Nintendo or when it was time to put her and Nugget to bed.

Thank god for that! I was no idiot, and neither were my aunt and uncle. They might easily pick up on Bean's reluctance to be alone with me. I most definitely did not want to end up back at the ACCH. I know that sounds self-serving. But make no mistake, I hated kicking Bean, and I loathed myself for it. That's how I learned that one can despise one's own behavior and yet continue it.

After a month, I resolved to stop, and I *did* stop. I'd come to my fucking senses, and I never hit her again or mistreated her in any way. After another month, I regained Bean's trust and—I hope—her love.

That spring, James and I took a weekend camping trip together. We drove out to a county park near Strasburg, Virginia, in the Shenandoah Valley. It was a chilly weekend, but the forest knew spring had arrived; everywhere I looked, there were delicate splashes of light green across hardwood tree trunks. Camping was something James and I had never done together, and I figured he was giving Beverly a weekend's break from parenting. That evening, we set up our tent under a grove of walnut trees and chatted around a fire, making pleasant, easy conversation.

The next morning, while hiking through the woods, James said, "I was thinking: How would you feel about going to a boarding school next year?"

"What?" I was walking ahead of him, thinking about a girl in my class. "No way."

"Well, there are some awesome schools out there," James persisted, his voice overly cheery. "Wouldn't it be great to check one of them out?"

I paused, balancing on a particularly large boulder. "You mean, like the boarding school in *Dead Poets Society*? That one was cool." The movie had just come out in theaters, and James, Beverly, and I had seen it together.

James nodded. "Well, maybe like that one. I was wondering if you might like to go. It could be fun!"

Something in his voice made me nervous. I turned to face him, my eyes narrowing. "Uncle James, are you messing with me?"

He held up his hands in a placating gesture. "No, no, of course not. It's just that Aunt Beverly and I have been talking—"

Realization dawned on me. "Holy crap! You're sending me away! That's it, isn't it? That's why we're here this weekend!"

"The last year hasn't been the easiest....We don't know if it's really been working out."

"Been working out? Uncle James, I try to be *perfect* for you guys."

Back on the path, a new thought hit me, and a wave of dread came over me. *Oh god, no.* I stopped in the middle of the path and turned around to face James, forcing him to stop. "You're sending me back to the ACCH, aren't you?"

"No, not that. We just thought it might be fun to find a local boarding school."

"Please don't send me back there," I pleaded. "Please. I'll do anything. Anything you ask."

"David, relax. We're not sending you back there," James said.

"Promise me."

"David, we aren't sending you back to the ACCH. Like I said, we were thinking of a local boarding school."

We continued our hike, the crunch of dead leaves beneath our feet and the distant chirping of birds the only sounds that broke the silence. With each step, my initial relief that I wasn't returning to the ACCH ebbed away until nothing remained but the cold certainty of what was coming. After a while, I said, "So I don't really have a choice, do I?"

"We'd really like you to want to go."

As we continued walking, my mind began racing with questions. Where would I end up? Would it be like the ACCH? How long would it take to make friends in yet another new environment? As long as the ACCH was off the table, I'd play along like it didn't hurt. I'd play it cool. But the time of working with James and Beverly was over. No more relaxing. It was time to take care of myself again, manipulate the direction if at all possible, and plan for my own future.

Eventually, I found a way to say the words, "Well, okay, Uncle James, if you think it's best."

My knowledge of boarding schools was minimal, just a few stereotypes from the movies. These involved rich white boys playing lacrosse on well-manicured fields or rowing in long, skinny boats in some river in New England. It was eternally autumn, and groups of boys walked together through the gothic architecture and made lighthearted japes, saying shit like "Just so, chap. Just so."

Financially, James and Beverly got by just fine, but they were by no means wealthy. I had trouble imagining just which Dead Poets boarding school James thought we'd find together. He must have done his research, though.

One night, about a month after our camping trip, with Beverly out with friends, James and I sat alone at the kitchen table. The town house was unusually quiet as he set down two plates of his garlic pasta and took his seat across from me. Steam rose between us as we began to eat, neither of us quite looking at the other.

"So I found this one place that seems perfect," he said. "It's called Milton Hershey School."

I froze, my fork hovering above my plate. But then I remembered my strategy of studied nonchalance. "What about that one in Maryland that we looked at together? That place was awesome," I said, consciously bringing the food to my mouth.

"I know, I know." James held up a hand. "That one was too expensive. But this other school, it's amazing. It's huge, for one thing—over a thousand students. And the best part is that it's specifically for kids like you!"

"Like me, *how*?" For the briefest of moments, I allowed myself the fantasy that Uncle James had found a magnet school for math and science.

"From economically disadvantaged backgrounds. Milton Hershey School is completely free!"

The blood in my faced drained completely, and I struggled to find words. "Uncle James," I said slowly, fighting to keep my voice steady. "You promised you wouldn't send me back to a group home."

James put his fork down. "Now, David, I said we wouldn't send you back to Albuquerque. This is different. It's a great opportunity, and I really think—"

But there was no way I could pay attention. My mind was reeling—being sent back to prison: visions of uncaring houseparents, cleaning up Thanksgiving dinner three times a day, jockeying for status with aggressive boys. I pushed my chair back from the table. "May I be excused?"

James looked like he wanted to argue, but he just nodded. I made myself walk to my room, fighting the urge to scream bloody fucking murder. I knew I didn't have a choice in this decision. But that didn't make the prospect of starting over any less terrifying.

Later that summer, James drove me to Hershey, where I was tested for admittance. This included an IQ test, a physical, and a behavioral exam. Somehow the topic of kicking dogs never surfaced. Milton Hershey School admitted me. The school timed new arrivals to coincide with report cards, so I was to stay with James and Beverly for the first quarter of my freshman year and then move up to Hershey.

* * *

James was a fastidious man. He'd converted their guest bedroom into an informal office, repurposing the unused bed as a massive clearinghouse for the many dozens of yellow Post-it notes he used to manage the details of his life. He applied this same care to structuring my life.

Due to James's attentiveness, I had more conversations with my father during my eighth-grade year than I'd ever had before. I didn't much like my father or these prearranged phone calls, so I never worked at making them meaningful. We'd talk about nothing for ten minutes, the pitch of his voice wavering in accordance with whatever drug he was on, while I was trying to hang up as quickly as possible.

But about a month before I was set to leave for Milton Hershey School, I was on a call with him, griping about James and Beverly. I viewed my father as a total wastoid, so I must have been truly hacked off to disclose anything about my personal life. I remember saying, "I'm half-assing my chores right now. It's my way of punishing them." No sooner had I uttered the words when Beverly marched into the kitchen where I was talking, pulled the phone jack out of the wall, and yanked the receiver from me by pulling on the cord. The receiver bounced along the kitchen floor as she reclaimed it.

"This conversation is over," Beverly hissed. "Go to bed. We'll talk in the morning."

The following day, we most certainly talked. I sat down at the kitchen table with James and Beverly and felt my stomach twist, awaiting my sentence. The clink of Beverly's coffee cup against the saucer seemed to echo in the tense silence.

Beverly finally spoke, her voice cold. "There's going to be some changes around here. As the Native American tribes used to do, you'll be a ghost in our household. You can remain here, eat here, sleep here, but James and I are never going to speak to you again."

I wasn't leaving for MHS for another month.

"You're a ghost," she continued. "You're to remain in your room until you leave for boarding school. From this moment on, you're dead to us."

Beverly's words hit me like a slap in the face. I glanced at James, but his expression was stony. "Wait, you're *serious?*" I asked.

Beverly coolly took another sip of her coffee.

After a few moments of silence, James spoke up. "Yes, David. You betrayed us with that phone call."

I jumped up, my chair scraping against the floor. "This is nuts! I didn't do anything!"

"You're actively attempting to undo our parenting," James continued. "I took a semester's break from my master's degree to spend more time with you!"

Emotions finally overpowered my shock and confusion. I found myself growing furious and began shouting. "All I said is that sometimes I skimp on my chores to get back at you!"

But as usual, James had sided with Beverly. "Go to your room." His tone was final.

I had no idea what my aunt and uncle were on about. There hadn't been any indication in the time we lived together that they'd ever resort to something like this. Yes, we'd had fights, and our relationship was strained—but surely nothing I'd said could've warranted this extreme form of rejection. My classes were going great; I was keeping my commitment to myself about my grades. I wasn't drinking or using drugs. I hadn't ever threatened to hurt myself or to hit either my aunt or uncle; anything physical flowed downstream: Beverly had felt free to slap me, and I'd taken my rage out on the dog. But I hadn't touched Bean in six months, so that crisis was long in the past, not that I'd ever admitted it to my aunt and uncle.

I got to thinking that perhaps James and Beverly didn't quite appreciate just how hard I was working at this whole thing. As far as I could tell, I'd been excommunicated for a bit of sass during a conversation that I'd believed to be private.

Then I remembered a conversation I'd had with Beverly not a week before. She and I had been eating dinner together at Pizza Hut while Uncle James was attending night classes. The discussion had started amicably enough with talk of the day and school. One way or another, it had spiraled downward, perhaps at some mention of my impending departure for Milton Hershey School.

"What do you care about how I'm doing in biology?" I asked. "It's obvious you don't care about me."

"So what's the whole last year been about, then, David?" Beverly countered.

"I don't know."

Beverly took a sip of her Diet Pepsi. "You know we love you, right?"

I just looked down at my plate.

"You know *I* love you, right?"

"No."

Beverly threw her soda in my face right there in our booth.

I'd answered truthfully, though I'd known it would hurt. It was projection, of course. I didn't love anybody, so could anyone possibly love me? I'd lived in a group home devoid of love since I was eight years old. But that single word must have sawed through bone. As a newlywed, Beverly had taken me in for over a year, the fucked-up son of her husband's heroin-addicted brother.

So they iced me out completely. After about two weeks of being ghosted, James must have realized that they'd grossly overreacted and started speaking to me again. But not Beverly; I remained a pariah in her eyes. When I left for MHS, there were no long goodbyes.

Beverly could have said anything else, insulted my parents, told me I was worthless, called me an ingrate who would never amount to anything. But by not communicating with me for over a month, to deny my right to be acknowledged as a human being, to deny my place in their family as a kid who'd spent five years in an orphanage—all in advance of my expulsion from their home—that was as cruel a betrayal as I'd ever experienced.

16

The Milt

Milton Hershey School (MHS) is located in rural southeastern Pennsylvania. Take a Sunday drive on the back roads and you'll wind through rolling green hills, cornfields, and dairy farms. The area is thickly settled, though, with one small town bumping into the next or separated by just a few miles of trees and farm acreage. The grain silos stand sentinel along the way, their rhythmic passing marking the distance like the steady ticking of a clock.

If your drive took you east of Harrisburg, you'd come across the town of Hershey. It's a quaint town with streetlights ensconced in giant Hershey's Kisses; you can smell the chocolate cooking. You've come upon a great power: This is the home of the Hershey Company, producer of everything from York Peppermint Patties to Twizzlers to the many varieties of their namesake chocolate. Milton Hershey, the famous chocolatier and company father, founded the town over a hundred years ago to provide a wholesome living environment and community for his factory workers. Apparently, all those dairy farms made the region ideal for the mass production of milk chocolate.

There's more to Hershey than just chocolate, though, and the town's charm conceals something of a secret. Hershey is also the home of Milton Hershey School, a stupendously wealthy boarding school for economically disadvantaged children. Last I checked, the school's endowment was north of $17 *billion*, allowing MHS to proudly stand shoulder to shoulder with the Ivy League universities in terms of the resources at its disposal.

How did this small town come to be home to one of the wealthiest schools on the planet? A mixture of cocoa beans and philanthropy. As the story goes, Milton Hershey and his wife, Catherine Sweeney Hershey, discovered they couldn't have children. So in 1909, they created an orphanage called the Hershey Industrial School. The couple signed a deed of trust establishing this orphanage as a beneficiary of their wealth. Milton Hershey took it a step further, transferring his controlling stake in the Hershey Company to the school's trust, ensuring its long-term financial security. All of which means that every time you've ever eaten a Hershey Bar, thrown back a handful of Good & Plenty, or marveled at the perfect balance of chocolate and peanut butter in a Reese's Peanut Butter Cup, you were helping fund one of the world's largest children's homes.

The school evolved significantly from its orphanage roots in the decades before my arrival. What began as the Hershey Industrial School—a name eventually abandoned due to its juvenile detention connotations—underwent massive expansion. In 1968, they began admitting boys of all races, and by 1977, girls were welcomed, too. By the time I attended in the early 1990s, the school housed over a thousand kids and operated three separate schools: elementary, middle, and high school, grades K through 12. It even held a nondenominational church service every Sunday and ran an infirmary.

Kids in attendance at MHS hailed from all over the United States, though most students came from Pennsylvania. The kids who attend MHS affectionately call it "the Milt" and call themselves "Milts."

According to the same logic of syllables used by kids at the ACCH, "the Milt" is both efficient and obscure.

When I attended MHS, it was spread across the town of Hershey, covering roughly ten square miles. On the one end of Hershey was the high school building, Senior Hall. On the other end was Founders Hall, a spectacular white-domed building where all the major events, such as prom, graduation, or the weekly Judeo-Christian church service, were held.

The MHS main campus was located near Founders Hall, measuring roughly a square mile. There were grass fields for sports and expansive lawns for roaming. Picturesque streams, fountains, and small pine groves were interspersed throughout. There was no denying that the school grounds were impressive. It was the Shire, but instead of hobbits, it was populated by social orphans.

We called the fundamental living unit at MHS a *student home*, which was basically the same thing as a cottage at the ACCH. Unlike the ACCH, boys and girls were segregated into different student homes, with the boys' and girls' homes located in separate areas of Hershey. There were close to one hundred student homes at MHS, so they had to be more cleverly named than Cottage 1, Cottage 2, and Cottage 3—although "Yes, I live in Cottage 84" would have been right on the money for the systematized living practiced at MHS. Instead, the school gave the student homes names such as Forkroot, Bonnyglen, Pinegrove, and Ripplepond, meant to evoke the pastoral setting of southeast Pennsylvania.

Like the ACCH, MHS was a racial melting pot. For the most part, white kids from the rural counties of Pennsylvania and suburbs of Philadelphia mixed with Black and Latino kids from the inner cities, primarily Philadelphia, New York, and DC.

This diversity brought with it a range of perspectives completely different from my own. Sharice, a Black girl in my homeroom, has always stuck in my mind for refusing to stand during the Pledge of Allegiance. Her behavior was alien to anything I'd ever experienced. My faith in the American dream was so unquestioning, so unconscious and deep-seated, that I'd made an educational commitment to myself at the ACCH subtly predicated upon it. Get good grades, get a scholarship—all of it based on a ten-year-old boy's implicit assumption of a system that viewed his plight through benevolent eyes. Until I met Sharice, it'd never crossed my mind that others couldn't depend on that dream or build upon it.

The social dynamics at MHS reflected a complex relationship with race that shifted depending on context. During unstructured time, the student body largely self-segregated along racial lines—white and Black students especially kept to themselves at dances and recreation periods, while Latinos moved more fluidly between groups. Black culture dominated these spaces, from basketball courts to music choices at dances. Yet in structured settings—classrooms, sports teams, choir—these divisions disappeared. Most striking was life in the student homes, where boys of all backgrounds would laugh together at racially charged comedy like *In Living Color*, trade slang and fashion influences, and engage in friendly insult competitions after lights-out. The moment we stepped out for social events, though, we'd act like strangers, only to pick up where we left off once back in our shared living space—though occasional tensions did flare up. This code-switching between worlds seemed both natural and entirely unremarkable.

The constellation of races wasn't the only difference between MHS and the ACCH. The approach to religion was night and day. At

MHS, the entire student body attended a single nondenominational Judeo-Christian church service on Sunday morning at Founders Hall. We high school boys would dress up in our cheap suits and clip-on ties and put on our beige trench coats. I've no idea how the high school girls managed Sunday clothing, but they always looked lovely as they made their way to service, a vibrant rainbow of dresses fluttering in the morning breeze occasionally revealing a tantalizing glimpse of what lay beneath.

The high school choir instructor would play the organ before the service began, often getting into complex material such as Bach organ fugues. He, along with the primarily Black gospel choir, were my favorite parts of church.

The MHS Sunday service was about as far away from a Bible-thumping Church of Christ service as I could imagine. There was no Communion in the MHS service, and musical instruments were allowed during worship. They'd string together a few platitudes to compose a prayer, and we most certainly did *not* end our prayers by invoking the name of Jesus Christ. Typically, the sermon didn't involve any scripture whatsoever! Instead, it was standard for an invited speaker to give an inspirational message devoid of any obvious theological underpinnings. Another song or two and a final Jesus-less prayer, and it'd be a wrap. We'd put our trench coats back on, sneak a kiss from our girlfriends as we filed out of the building, and climb back into our group-home vans.

The ACCH had weaved Christianity and Jesus into every part of our lives. Having spent five formative years there, my initial reaction to the MHS church service was, "What in the ever-loving fuck is this?" After the shock wore off, I simply looked down on all of it. Church service at MHS was like a failed fusion cuisine. In attempting to blend mellow flavors to satisfy everyone, the daily bread was bland

and so pleased no one. I choked down this watery religious broth once a week for the duration of my stay at MHS, all the while feeling my faith realigning away from my doomsday interpretation of born-again Christianity and toward a spirituality grounded in a physical world that could be understood through science.

It was Monday, October 16, 1989, when James dropped me off at MHS. The two of us drove up from Virginia to Pennsylvania in relative silence. I mostly looked out the window at the fall colors as we crossed the Potomac River while James concerned himself with driving. He was speaking to me again, but neither of us was much in the mood for conversation. Instead, we negotiated our differences through careful interactions around the car radio. James liked the oldies channel, while I preferred the contemporary rock station. We traded off, each getting three songs in a row before the other would take over. We even instituted a veto rule for the two-and-a-half-hour drive, in case one of us thought a song really sucked. If only our time together in Virginia had been so thoughtful.

When I arrived at MHS, I was sent to central facilities to get outfitted in school-issued clothing. They dressed me up in the most busted 1950s outfits you could imagine: gray pleated slacks, an assortment of cheap button-ups, and corny dress shoes. Back in the sixth grade, I may have had some confusion about whether I was supposed to dress like a cholo or a skater, but now as a freshman, even I knew that dressing like a grandpa was right out. I was issued a fifty-dollar suit for Sunday church, a clip-on tie, and a trench coat. I thought the trench coat was cool, though, because I imagined myself as a detective in a pulp novel.

After getting outfitted with my Mr. Rogers gear, I was driven to Forkroot, my new student home. The housefather, Mr. Clodfelter, was waiting for me. He was a short, stocky man in his mid-forties wearing a white T-shirt with a Ford F-150 emblazoned on it.

After introductions, Mr. Clodfelter guided me to the student home office, one of those rooms in large houses that are seldom occupied. He motioned for me to sit on the couch while he took a seat in a chair. The first thing I noticed was that Mr. Clodfelter had a lazy eye that wandered away as he talked to you.

"Here at MHS, you refer to the houseparents by their last names, or as *sir* and *ma'am*. Is that clear?"

"Yes." I paused. "Yes, sir."

"Are you a Christian?" asked Mr. Clodfelter.

"Yes, sir."

"Great." He pointed to the bookshelf. "We keep a copy of the Bible in every student home. You're welcome to read it whenever you like." Mr. Clodfelter lowered his arm, and his demeanor soured. "I'm required to tell you we keep a copy of the Quran as well. I can't stop you from reading that book, but if I hear you reading it out loud, I'll give you five and five."

"Five and five?" I asked.

"Five days' detention and five hours of work. That's how we punish kids who misbehave."

Mr. Clodfelter continued, outlining the rigid rules and regulations that would govern my life at MHS. He explained that Mrs. Clodfelter inspected the house every morning after the boys went to school, handing out four merits a day for attitude, room cleanliness, daily chore, and kitchen chore.

As he droned on, a sinking feeling grew in the pit of my stomach. It seemed that while the details of MHS might differ from the ACCH, underneath the private school veneer lay the same depressing group-home life.

The Milt

Mr. Clodfelter pressed on, explaining that if you earned your merits each week, you kept your privileges and got to go into Hershey on Friday night unsupervised—so-called town privilege. During this orientation, one of his eyes wandered off. Curious, I glanced over at the part of the wall that seemed to have captured its interest.

"David, are you listening to me?" Mr. Clodfelter asked, his voice sharp.

"Yes, sir," I replied, snapping my attention back.

"Okay then. You also have daily chores and after-dinner chores," and off he went. Over the next few minutes, I gave over part of my mind to nodding at all the proper moments.

"One last thing. Only boys with good attitudes in Forkroot. If you display a good attitude, we'll get along. You don't, we won't. You have a good attitude, don't you?" Mr. Clodfelter asked.

"Oh yes, sir," I responded.

"Well, that's reassuring. Because I've heard different." Mr. Clodfelter continued, "I can't abide boys with bad attitudes. I get them straightened out quick, though."

I nodded, unsure how to respond to what seemed like a veiled threat.

Mr. Clodfelter took a deep breath. "That's pretty much that. There's the student handbook over there." He pointed to a three-inch-thick tome collecting dust on the office desk. "Boys who avoid trouble know what's in that book."

I nodded again. *Sure thing, boss.*

I did once thumb through the student handbook for shits and giggles. It covered the basics, such as prohibitions on bullying and fighting. It also included guidance on such minutiae as the correct way to eat an olive with a pit in it or how to use one's fist to correctly measure the mandated three inches a boy should sit from the table.

Mr. Clodfelter walked me back to the student bedroom hallway, which was about sixty feet long, with four bedrooms on each side. Once at my room, he introduced me to my roommate, Bob, who was reading a paperback on his bed. Mr. Clodfelter told Bob to instruct me on proper bed making, and left.

I stood there, staring at my bed, and then at my suitcase. I turned to my closet and back to my suitcase. As the reality of my situation set in, a deep depression swept over me. *I'm back.*

Just then, Bob looked up from his paperback and said, "Hey, fuckwad. Just leave me alone and I won't hurt you." He went back to reading.

I unpacked my belongings and took a walk around the student home. Most boys were at sports practice or after-school tutoring, apparently. There were two boys prepping food in the kitchen, and a couple were watching TV in the living room. They all ignored me. I went downstairs into the basement, where the bathrooms were. There were no doors on the toilet stalls, and none of the shower stalls had curtains. The cinder block hallways were poorly lit and smelled of bleach. It was a cold and empty walk through the length of the basement.

That night, just before lights-out at nine forty-five, my clothing arrived from central facilities. Every piece had a name tag on it with my full name and student home: *David C. Sussillo, Forkroot.* When I asked Bob about this, he explained that a lot of stuff was stolen, so the tags helped establish ownership. Also, laundry for all sixteen boys plus the houseparents was done by a single person as one of the chores. That person needed to know what belonged to whom. My mind battled between the obvious necessity of such a system and the overwhelming sense of depersonalization it induced in me.

Later that night, after lights-out, I lay in bed thinking about Mr. Clodfelter's assertion that I had a bad attitude. My aunt and uncle certainly thought that. Had they set this guy against me? Perhaps the assistant principal, Mr. Silo, had called Mr. Clodfelter? Earlier that day, I'd been sent up to Senior Hall to introduce myself. When we'd sat down for a chat, he'd asked me what my favorite subject was, and I'd honestly responded that I liked them all. He'd pressed, replying that surely there must be one subject I preferred above others. I'd assured him that I was interested in *all* knowledge. After we'd batted around what I thought to be a stupid topic that only served to pigeonhole me, I'd finally snapped, "Why don't you just pick a subject that *you* think I like."

Probably just a misunderstanding, I thought as I nodded off.

The next morning, after completing our chores, Mr. Clodfelter drove us boys up to Senior Hall. The building sat atop a large hill on the north side of town, casting its long, imposing shadow across the town of Hershey. Its front face was about three football fields long, with two stories of smooth brownstone and long rows of dark windows. Art deco meets medieval fortress meets Hometown, USA.

That first day, I rolled into Senior Hall looking like I'd won a shopping spree at the local JCPenney and had made the peculiar but bold fashion choice to clean out the senior citizens' apparel section. As if this wasn't humiliating enough, nobody else was wearing MHS-issued clothing! The other students were dressed like typical teenagers. It turns out that you *could* wear contemporary, store-bought apparel. You just had to bring it in slowly, purchasing only one or two garments at a time, so the housemother could sew in the student's name tags. She also inspected the items to make sure they weren't banned—for example, skimpy women's clothing or gang-related paraphernalia.

In my first couple of classes, I discovered that courses at MHS had no differentiation by academic ability, aside from separating vocational trades, business prep, and college prep. With about 150 students in each grade, this guaranteed that I would ace my courses without putting any effort into them. For the next four years, my classes weren't even a secondary concern.

Finding myself yet again surrounded by a new set of faces in a new school, I decided to reinvent myself; I'd be super friendly. For months, I made a pitiable effort to smile at every single kid during breaks as I passed back and forth through the hallway. I was entirely ignored.

There was one exception to my social isolation, a Puerto Rican kid from the Bronx named Carmelo who'd started at MHS the same day as I had. He was in my social studies class, and we became fast friends. I really liked Carmelo; though a little slow, he was as sweet a boy as I'd met in years. His warmth and easy friendship reminded me of my second-grade buddy, Shiloh, a bittersweet memory I hadn't revisited in a while. For about a month, Carmelo and I hung out nonstop at school and at recreation periods on the weekends. Then one day, he didn't show up to class. When I asked around to find out what had happened, a kid from Carmelo's student home explained that he'd brandished a knife and had verbally threatened his housefather. Carmelo got the boot, and I never saw him again.

My next meaningful interaction happened a few months into my stay at MHS, at one of the home basketball games held at Senior Hall in the evenings. Senior Hall had a large indoor basketball court in the back of the building, with plenty of bleachers and even balcony seating. The other kids in Forkroot wanted nothing to do with me, so I'd kick it up in the balcony as far away from anybody as I could get. I figured it was better to be alone and *feel* like a loser than to hang with boys who took pleasure in removing all doubt.

At these games, the school ran a snack concession operated by some of the seniors. We could use our allowance of about $1.35 per week to purchase candy and whatnot. I'd buy Mentos or Twizzlers.

The Milt

One such night, a tall Black girl with straightened hair down to her shoulders was holding things down at the register. It was just the two of us: I in line and she behind the counter. I ordered my Mentos.

She rang me up and said, "You know, when you get older, you're gonna get all the girls."

I was stunned. It was the first kind thing anyone had said to me in three months, and I swear to god I damn near cried in front of her.

"With that baby face, though"—she thought for a second—"not until you're about twenty-five. But you're gonna be real cute. You just wait. I can tell these things."

I have no memory of what I said in reply, but I hope it was something nice.

17

The Blob and the Brown Zebra

MHS was divided into three sections based on the age of the students. The kids in elementary and middle school lived in dedicated student homes and attended school in different buildings. This division by age had enormous social consequences. While a twelve-year-old will follow the direction of a seventeen-year-old without question in a setting unsupervised by adults, a fourteen-year-old boy won't give a fifteen-year-old boy the time of day. So what happens when you put sixteen boys, ages fourteen through eighteen, in a student home with a single set of houseparents? Fights happen, each a riff, reharmonization, or inspired improvisation on the infamous Stanford Prison Experiment.

At MHS, the boys made fun of one another mercilessly, relentlessly. Everyone did it, including me. There was a "big fish eats the little fish" aspect to this, with the upperclassmen laying into the sophomores, who ridiculed the freshmen. We were a troop of baboons that, having had our caloric needs met, spent the remainder of the day entertaining ourselves by tormenting one another.

I've already introduced you to Bob, my roommate. Well, Bob is what the houseparents and teachers called him. Everyone else called him Blob, or *the* Blob. Yes, like the sci-fi horror movie monster.

The Blob and the Brown Zebra

The Blob was six foot three, weighing in at close to three hundred pounds. His weight was in all the wrong places, and strangely so. For example, he had enormous, symmetric fat bladders, one on each shoulder blade. And as a cherry on top, he had a shock of bright red hair with tight, kinky curls. The hair was just barely under control, and, as a big fuck-you to the world, the Blob kept it long, which resulted in a red, white-boy Afro.

The Blob's coping strategy for his nickname was to embrace it, which worked for the most part, as it made him notorious. If he ever did anything noteworthy, boys would yell, "The Blob!" or "The Bloooooob!" or even *"The Blooooooooooooob!"* The length of extra "ooooo" was in direct proportion to the craziness of whatever stunt the Blob had just pulled.

Putting up with that nickname for four years must have been hell on earth. But I'll be honest, I didn't like the Blob from the outset. Our relationship was shaped by the unwritten rules of our environment; he felt compelled to assert his dominance, however petty it might seem. He never physically bullied me; his preferred verbal technique was to barrage me with nonstop corny taunts—"Hey, butt munch" or "Get the lights, loser" each and every time he spoke to me. Easily tolerated in the short term but grating in the extreme over longer periods.

The Blob had no chance of competing in the popularity game, so he simply didn't try. His approach was noble, and I respected him for it, though I never admitted it. Yet the Blob was not immune to peer pressure, either. Especially pressure from the poisonous upperclassmen we were unlucky enough to share a student home with. Take Liam, for example, a senior who had a feathered mullet at least five years out of style.

Liam was notable because he taught me the power of intimidation. I was hanging out with him and another freshman, Luther, one day.

Liam was a small, thin white guy, five six, 120 pounds, tops. Luther, a Latino, was a large, doughy freshman, who I sensed was extremely strong under that layer of fat.

One day, the three of us were in Luther's room, and Liam asked me, "David, who do you think would win in a fight between Luther and me?"

I looked them both up and down and said, "Luther, for sure."

Liam responded, "No way. I'll show you."

Liam walked over to Luther and slapped him across the face. And I don't mean a little slap; I mean he wound his shit way back, using a 180-degree full-upper-body turn, waited for a second or two, and uncorked it like Sammy motherfucking Sosa.

Luther had to have seen this coming, but he just stood there as Liam slapped him with every bit of force he could muster. *Whaaap!* Luther stumbled sideways and then backward, but he stayed on his feet. Then, slowly, he regained his balance. The Weeble wobbles, but he don't fall down.

Liam slapped him again. And again. Each time was as hard as the first. Liam screamed, "Come on, Luther, hit me!"

Luther just stood there as tears began streaming down his face. He had no idea what to do. Neither Liam nor Luther was laughing; I sure as hell wasn't.

Then Liam stuck his face within inches of Luther's and screamed at the top of his lungs, "Come on! Hit me, Luther! Hit me, you fucking pussy!"

Luther just stood there, crying.

And then, as if nothing had gone amiss, Liam turned to me and, in a completely normal voice and demeanor, said, "You see? I'd win that fight."

I nodded in agreement and got the hell out of there.

The Blob and the Brown Zebra

Luther left MHS shortly thereafter, and I never saw him again.

Just as Liam had engineered the bullying incident with Luther, with me filling the role of the spectator, he also instigated a fight between the Blob and me. He managed to arrange things such that most of the kids in the student home either watched or participated.

It was nighttime when Liam entered our room and casually said, "Hey, Blob, if you give David a brown zebra, I'll get some guys to hold him down."

What's a brown zebra, you ask? Gentle reader, prepare thyself. That's when someone sits on your face with their bare ass, their pants and underwear pulled down around their ankles.

The Blob said, "Okay, sure."

Years of group-home life had endowed me with a sixth sense for danger. *Oh, hell no.* I darted for the door.

Liam blocked the way and called over a bunch of upperclassmen. Though I fought wildly—skinny arms and legs flailing—about eight kids wrestled me down onto one of the beds and held me there.

Sure enough, the Blob dropped trou, revealing his big, fat, jiggly ass. Apparently, the Blob's shoulder blades weren't the only fat bladders on his body. He walked over to me, took a full breath, and heaved his huge ass onto my face. *Faaawhump!* Face, meet inner ass.

The Blob held this position while gyrating his hips, pulling my neck this way and that. Everyone was chanting, "*THE BLOOOOOOOOOOOOOOOOOOOOOOB!*" Finally, he gathered his weight, stood up, pulled up his tighty-whities over the Mariana Trench that was his ass crack, yanked up his pants, and buttoned up. He took a victory lap around the room, arms raised above his head, fists clenched, a triumphant leer on his face. The other kids finally let go of me, and I went downstairs to the basement bathroom to wash my face.

Not five minutes later, as I climbed the stairs into the hallway, Liam came up to me and said, "Daaaaaaaamn, David, you gonna let the Blob sit on your face like that?"

His buddy Seb, another senior who'd helped hold me down, egged me on further, "If you don't get back at the Blob, you'll never live that down."

As the minutes passed, I began to see their point. A line had been crossed. I would *NEVER* live this down if I didn't do something. I glanced over at our room; the door was closed. The Blob had apparently gone back to whatever he was doing. One and done, I guess.

I stood there in the hallway, considering the fact that I had never once in my life been on the winning side of a fight. I couldn't remember ever landing a successful punch. I knew I couldn't beat the Blob in an even match; he was just too damned large.

So, with pretty much every boy in the student home watching in the hallway, I steeled myself, walked over to our door, and knocked on it. Then I hustled back down the hallway about fifteen feet to get a running start. By the time the Blob opened the door a few inches, I'd already achieved kinetic nirvana. *SHORYUKEN!*

The Blob caught my flying fist of rage right in his goddamned eye. It was a perfect blow, perhaps the greatest single moment of physical coordination I'd ever achieved, and he'd had no warning whatsoever. My dude fell flat on his ass like King Hippo from the classic Nintendo video game *Punch-Out!!*

I yelled down at him, "Don't sit on my face, Blob!" Not that he heard me; he was out cold. I'd broken his glasses, and pieces lay all about the room.

Liam, Seb, and the rest of the upperclassmen cheered in delight, "Daaaaaaaaaaviiiiiid!" Sensing that my revenge had been sated, they egged me on further, "Get on top of him! Beat him! If you don't beat his ass, he's gonna get up!" But I didn't have any fight left in me. Like the Blob, I wasn't really cut out for this.

As predicted, the Blob did get up a minute or two later. He caught up to me in the hallway, where I was now taking my turn strutting my stuff. His eyes were all wonky, like his brain had had a core dump and was attempting a hard reboot.

"You broke my glasses," he rumbled. He grabbed me, threw me to the ground, sat on my chest, and started pummeling my face. It wasn't that bad, though, because the Blob was weak like me. Eventually, he tired and went back to his room. That was that.

The Blob declared both to me, the boys in the student home, and anyone else who would listen that he'd won the fight, which, in a strict sense, was true. But he never fucked with me again. Mr. Clodfelter, however, caught wind of the fight, either from the teachers who noticed my resulting black eye, or perhaps because the Blob ratted me out when he was forced to explain why he needed new glasses.

There was a systematized disciplinary system at Milton Hershey School when I attended. It made sense; the school had been around for nearly eighty years. A housefather wily enough to discover transgressions could conveniently look up a crime in the disciplinary handbook and read off the corresponding punishment, all to help a student understand the error of their ways.

The basic unit of punishment consisted of one part additional work and one part social isolation. Offenders were assigned an extra hour of chores on top of their normal three daily chores, coupled with a full day of social isolation, referred to as "X and X," where X was a number between five and thirty. Awful behavior just increased X. For example, being caught out of bed got you twenty and twenty, while getting busted with alcohol earned you a solid thirty and thirty. Serious offenses that got you booted were actual felonies, sex, repeated theft, selling drugs, or threats of violence toward teachers, houseparents, or their children. Credible threats of violence toward fellow students—bullying, in other words—were routinely ignored.

You'd say, "I'm on fourteen and fourteen," and all the other Milts knew what you meant. Every day for two weeks, you'd do that extra hour of work above and beyond your usual chores and then head into social isolation. You'd still attend school, but after that, you were expected to return promptly to the student home. You'd put on your blue canvas house shoes and go to the laundry room for the remainder of the day.

The Blob and I served fourteen and fourteen together. Liam, Seb, and the rest got off scot-free. In the retelling to Mr. Clodfelter, only the one-on-one fight came out, not the brown zebra, and certainly not the bullying that had enabled it. Losers like the Blob and I knew better than to implicate the upperclassmen in Forkroot. I had ample evidence that crossing these older boys amounted to a free van ride to the MHS infirmary.

Stuck together in the student home's office all day, needlessly cleaning obscure portions of the student home together, then stuck together in our bedroom at night, the Blob and I couldn't stand the sight of each other. So the Blob began reading Stephen King's 1,100-page classic, *The Stand*, and I took on a big programming project.

I decided to program Conway's Game of Life so I could enjoy for myself all the funky spaceships and oscillators that emerged from those simple rules that determined how a cell on the 2D grid lived or died. I was learning the Pascal programming language in class and feeling ever-more confident in my ability to code. Plus, MHS had just that year installed computers in each student home. While not an enormous project, it was a big chunk to bite off as a freshman, and it took me the full two weeks.

Coding up the Game of Life got me thinking about the nature of computation and the emergence of life on Earth, how those simple rules of birth, death, and survival on the grid could lead to such long-sustained, organized patterns of activity. Watching the patterns evolve like LED blips and bleeps on a circuit board, it was hard to avoid the impression that you were looking at something living.

All of this got me to wondering: Could one make a computer using something other than standard computer components? Though I didn't realize it then, this question connects to bigger scientific puzzles about how intelligence might emerge from biological systems. I was unwittingly brushing against ideas that scientists and philosophers have struggled with for decades.

Conway's Game of Life, despite its simple rules, is surprisingly powerful in terms of computing capabilities. We can build what we call a *universal computer*, or a *Turing machine*. Here's how it works: The pattern of living and dead cells in the Game of Life can represent information. Then the rules for how cells live or die can be used to process this information. Think of it like building with LEGO bricks. Just as we can create complex structures from a couple types of LEGO pieces, we can create computer components from these Game of Life patterns. One of the most important kinds of components are logic gates. These are the decision-makers in computers. Three fundamental types are AND, OR, and NOT gates:

- An AND gate is like a picky friend: It only says "yes" when all inputs agree. For example, "I'll be happy if I go to the movies AND eat popcorn" is only true if both conditions are met.
- An OR gate is more flexible: It says "yes" if any condition is true. It's like saying, "I'll be happy if I go to the movies OR eat popcorn"—either one is enough.
- A NOT gate is the simplest: Just do the opposite. "I am happy" becomes "I am NOT happy."

These simple logic gates are crucial because they allow computers to process information and make choices. By combining huge numbers of these gates in just-so arrangements, we can create complex logic that forms the basis of *any* computer operation, from simple arithmetic to sophisticated programs that safely land airplanes.

In the Game of Life, we can arrange gliders and other patterns to interact in ways that mimic these logic gates. So it becomes conceptually straightforward to engineer a computer in the simulation. For example, we might paint in a pattern where a glider only continues if it meets another glider—this would be like an AND gate. In other words, we've *implemented* a logic gate with gliders.

Another important computer component is memory. In a computer, memory chips store information. In the Game of Life, if set up correctly, different patterns of live and dead cells can represent different information, similar to a computer memory chip.

Using these fairly basic components, we could build our Game of Life computer as an engineer would. So basically, you'd first "paint" the computer architecture onto the 2D grid by creating specific arrangements of live cells that function as logic gates and memory systems. Then you'd "paint" the input data as another pattern of cells in the appropriate location where the "computer" can process it. The rules of the Game of Life remain unchanged—it's the specific patterns (of both the computer and data) that create a functioning computational system. This means that, theoretically, anything any computer can compute is also computable by the Game of Life.

If the simplistic Game of Life is sufficient to build a computer, what other media might we use? What about water? Water has rich dynamics, but devising a means to hold memory for longer periods seems challenging. What about ice? Ice can easily store memory; simply stack a bunch of ice cubes just so and there's your memory. But ice lacks the rich dynamics required to move those cubes around, so constructing something complex like logic gates to support arithmetic seems nigh impossible. The critical idea here is that any physical or virtual medium might be used to create a computer so long as it can reliably manipulate and store information.

What other material might support general computation? Clay? DNA? A star? The center of a black hole?

Pursuing this question rigorously led to one of the most important and impactful early contributions to artificial intelligence. In 1943, Warren McCulloch and Walter Pitts wrote a seminal paper entitled "A Logical Calculus of the Ideas Immanent in the Nervous Activity." In it, they performed a similar exercise to the one we just engaged in. But instead of using the Game of Life as the underlying medium, they constructed a theoretical computer using a mathematical abstraction of real, squishy biological neurons found in real, squishy brains. If successful, the implication of the work would be that a computer could be created out of the fundamental units of the brain—brain cells, also called *neurons*—when lots of them are connected in just the right way.

While physical neurons are simple with respect to information processing in the sense that they can't do much besides activate electrically when enough of their inputs activate, they are nevertheless monumentally complex molecular devices. McCulloch and Pitts didn't want to contend with any of this complexity, so they abstracted away all the biological detail, thereby constructing what would become one of the world's first mathematical neuron models, the eponymous *McCulloch–Pitts neuron*. Their simplified model could either be "on" (firing an electrical signal) or "off" (not firing), depending on the inputs it received from other neurons, not dissimilar to a cell being alive or dead based on its neighbors' states in the Game of Life.

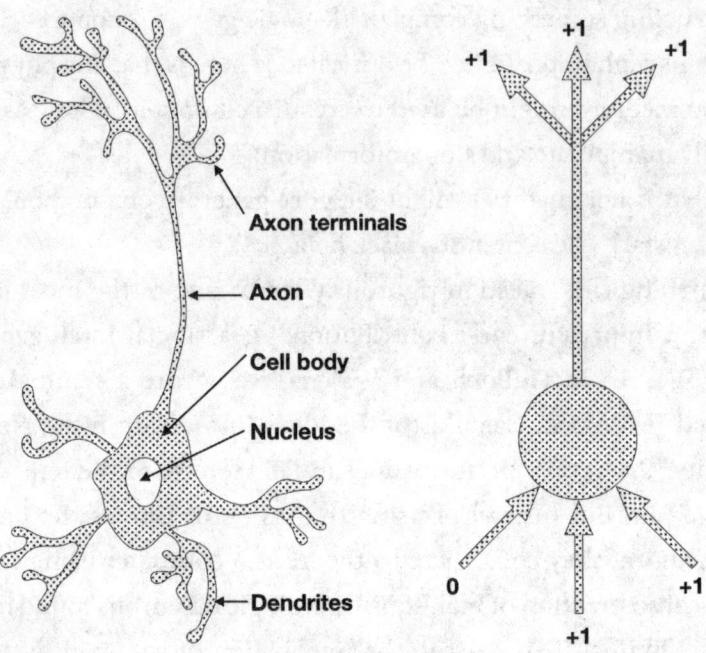

Caption: On the left, a biological neuron, where signals arrive from other neurons through dendrites (bottom). If the inputs are strong enough, an electrical pulse is sent out through the axon (top) to other neurons. On the right, the McCulloch–Pitts neuron—a radical simplification—where inputs (bottom) from connected units add up, and if they reach a threshold (e.g., the inputs sum to two or greater), an output signal is fired to the next layer of units (top). Stripped of biological detail, this artificial neuron captures just enough of the essence of its biological counterpart to power the foundations of computing.

By connecting these simplified neurons in specific ways, McCulloch and Pitts showed mathematically that they could build logic gates like AND, OR, and NOT. More broadly, they demonstrated that by arranging networks of their artificial neurons, they could construct (with some limitations) a complete computer system.

These days, arguing that a brain is a literal computer composed of biological components is considered extremely naive. No practicing neuroscientist believes the brain uses neurons to implement logic gates and a memory tape to build a Turing machine. An engineer didn't construct the brain; it arose from billions of years of evolution, and its secrets are not so easily divulged. Further, we have many decades of empirical measurement of real neurons in humans and animals engaging in complex behaviors. The details don't appear to even remotely resemble a traditional computer.

Regardless, McCulloch and Pitts's work in the 1940s laid the groundwork for the field of artificial neural networks, which would eventually evolve into the powerful AI approaches used today. That's right; artificial neural networks were inspired quite literally by thinking about brains as computers. While McCulloch and Pitts's model was highly simplified, it introduced the key idea that computation could emerge from the interactions of many simple processing units. This idea of *connectionism*—that intelligence arises from the precise structure and strength of connections *between* neurons rather than the complexity *within* individual neurons—remains a central tenet of both modern AI and neuroscience. Of course, today's artificial neural networks are far more complex than McCulloch and Pitts's simple model. But the core insight of connectionism can, in part, be traced back to their pioneering work, which showed that the brain could be studied and understood in terms of computation, a revolutionary idea at the time.

As I sat there in our shared punishment, coding Conway's Game of Life while the Blob escaped into Stephen King's apocalyptic world, I couldn't have known how profoundly these simple cellular automata would shape my thinking. The patterns emerging on my screen—those pulsing gliders and oscillators born from basic rules—felt alive in a way I couldn't articulate. What struck me most was how complexity could arise from simplicity, how order could emerge from chaos. Watching those digital cells live and die according to rigid mathematical rules, I glimpsed something profound about computation and, perhaps, about life itself. In that student home office, serving out my punishment for a fight I never wanted, I'd stumbled upon the question that would eventually define my career.

18

Inhale, Exhale

By day, Mr. Clodfelter worked as a mechanic, boasting on the regular about how little he charged for his services. He said he did it to be generous, and I guess he viewed fixing cars as part of the same ministry as fixing boys.

As an adult, I can imagine that in the houseparents' apartments, kicking back on his couch, he was equally generous with his family. Maybe he'd help his youngest son with his spelling assignment or give his wife a back massage after a challenging day. And I guess there's a world where Mr. Clodfelter got choked up at the end of *Rocky*.

But if he had that side to him, he never showed it to the boys in Forkroot. To us, he was one-dimensional, a cardboard cutout of a colossal penis. Every boy in the student home hated his guts. I hated him, too, and I learned in my first few months at Forkroot that my safety depended on avoiding him.

Clodfelter's favorite form of punishment was to give a kid sole responsibility for kitchen cleanup. Nightly cleanup of the kitchen at MHS was like handling a large Thanksgiving dinner. We collectively called this entire process "dishes," and other boys would joyously proclaim that David "had dishes" that night, knowing that meant they had the evening off. To be crystal clear, "dishes" implied way more than washing plates and silverware. It meant cleaning up *everything*: from clearing the tables to scrubbing the pots, putting everything away, and sweeping and mopping the kitchen floors.

It would be an understatement to say that Mr. Clodfelter took a liberal approach to handing out dishes. It was my dude's favorite pastime, and he'd assign dishes if the kid so much as breathed too loudly. And because it was an informal punishment, Mr. Clodfelter didn't have to disclose it to the school's disciplinary council. This made dishes a versatile tool, the smallest denomination in the currency of punishment at MHS, which had a vibrant and robust disciplinary economy.

Being late for the van was the main reason kids got dishes, and the intellectual part of my mind could relate to this. Imagine trying to corral sixteen preoccupied and preening teenage boys, day in and day out, to get to school on time. How do you manage it? Do you politely remind them? What about the ones that won't listen? Do you browbeat them? What if a few of the boys are being dicks and purposefully coming late? Would you finally get so frustrated that you start meting out punishments? If so, you'd have two tools at your disposal: dishes and loss of Friday-night town privilege. Anything more substantial wouldn't fit the crime, although that didn't stop Mr. Clodfelter on occasion.

But the emotional part of my mind knew that Mr. Clodfelter enjoyed handing out dishes—loved it, in fact. Every morning, at the exact second the digital clock on the van dashboard changed to seven thirty, Mr. Clodfelter would apply a quick spurt of pressure on the gas pedal. Our brown group-home van would jerk backward out of the carport a few feet, and then he'd smash the brakes. Mr. Clodfelter's voice would rise into near-alto territory as he squealed, "Dishes!" every time a tardy boy got in the van. He'd smile as he took down the names on a tiny notepad he kept in his shirt pocket.

* * *

According to the strictest reading of the MHS student home handbook, that inches-thick tome of arcane rules, no students were allowed in anyone else's room. Mr. Clodfelter thought this too strict. He allowed one—and only one—additional person to enter your room, at your discretion.

Four or five months into my stay at MHS, we'd just gotten back from church. I still had my suit on, including my clip-on tie. The boys were farting around in the student room hallway, as was typical while waiting for Sunday dinner to be prepared by the sad sap who had the chore of cooking for all twenty of us. Matt and his roommate, Pete, were bragging about a handle of Jack Daniel's they'd just scored. Another student was already in the room, so I was listening from the doorway.

At just this moment, Mr. Clodfelter walked through the hall. His habit was to walk his beat every hour to make sure the boys weren't fucking up too badly. As a result, students preferred the rooms at the far end of the hall. It'd take Mr. Clodfelter just that much longer to get down there, so you could usually hide whatever illicit shit you were up to before his ugly mug popped up at your door. Seniors and juniors inevitably pulled rank to get those far rooms.

Matt and Pete's room was halfway down the hall, a decent location. Unfortunately, that Sunday morning, Clodfelter didn't walk his usual beat. Instead, he came up from the basement bathroom, whose stairs cut into the middle of the hallway, right by their room.

So it was that Mr. Clodfelter caught me leaning into Matt and Pete's room. I was using the doorjambs to balance myself with my lower body entirely outside the room. Still, my tie and a smidge of my upper body hung a few inches inside. I may have been violating Clodfelter's rule in a technical sense, but I was certainly obeying the spirit of it.

But Clodfelter never wasted an opportunity to lay into a boy. "You do know there is only one guest allowed in each room?" he asked.

"Yes, sir, I know the rule," I replied.

"Are your eyes okay?" he asked.

"Yes, sir. My eyes are working fine," I said.

"Well, did you notice that there was already another person in the room?"

"Yes, Mr. Clodfelter, I did see him."

Mr. Clodfelter built his logically consistent but obvious argument brick by painful brick. "Do you remember that I made an exception from the student handbook so that one person could enter the room?"

"Yes, sir. I remember your exception."

"Don't you appreciate my generosity?"

"Yes, sir. I appreciate it," I replied.

"Well then, David. Why'd I come to find you in the room?"

Then I made a critical mistake. I said, "I'm sorry, sir, but it was only my tie that was in the room."

Mr. Clodfelter's tone changed instantly. "Are you getting smart with me, boy?" his voice rising.

"No, sir," I said.

"Well, I think you are. If you don't appreciate my generosity, I'll take away your room privilege and see how you like that!" He looked up for a minute, thinking. "No, even better. The entire student home loses their room privilege. Starting now!" Mr. Clodfelter raised his voice to carry down the hallway, "Boys! You've all lost your room privilege, thanks to David! If I catch anybody in anybody else's room, that's five and five. Pass it along."

He looked back at me and pointed his finger at my chest, all the while his drifting eye was going wonky. "You have a real attitude problem, David, and I'm going to fix it."

Throughout the day, older—and far larger—boys came to my room and told me off in variations of "What the hell is wrong with you?" and "You'd better go make this right, or you're dead."

That night, Mr. Clodfelter held our usual Sunday-night student home meeting. Life at MHS was one never-ending series of dull routines, but this weekly meeting was the crown jewel of tedium. Clodfelter was boredom's patron saint. These meetings lasted over an hour and involved our housefather picking nits on this or that person's chore performance or droning on about perceived attitude problems.

This particular student home meeting, it was my turn.

"As you know by now, I caught David inside of Matt and Pete's room with another student present. So I've taken away your room privileges," said Mr. Clodfelter. "This could have been avoided, but David has a big mouth and a bad attitude."

My memory of his next words will never fade: "Perhaps you all should teach David a lesson."

I woke up to overwhelming pain in my jaw. Evidently, someone had initiated the beating with a blow to the face while I was sound asleep. Punches rained down all over my body from all sides. It was pitch-black, so I couldn't see anyone or anything, but given the size of a single bed, I guess about half the student home was there.

"Stop! Please! I'm sorry!" I curled up into a ball to protect myself.

Eight or ten teenage boys kicked the ever-living shit out of me. It lasted for about twenty seconds—an eternity when it comes to beatdowns.

One Mississippi.

"Stop...I didn't do anything..." My words were punctuated by another vicious blow to the face.

Two Mississippi.

Someone wrenched my hands away from my body, exposing my midsection to a brutal punch to the gut. I gasped for air, choking out, "It won't happen again…I promise."

Three Mississippi.

"I'm sorry. I'm sorry! Please stop…"

Four Mississippi.

Five Mississippi.

Six Mississippi.

My cries grew less discernible—more of a mewling, a whimper—as the blows continued to land.

…

Afterward, my assailants ran away under the cover of darkness. They hadn't said a single word. But the message was clear: I was a target that could be got to at any time.

I don't remember how long I lay there, trying to catch my breath and calm my racing heart. Even in my senseless state, I noted with some small, bitter pride that I hadn't pissed myself. That night, I hated Mr. Clodfelter as much as a boy could hate anyone or anything. For his cruelty, for his manipulation, for setting the other boys against me. But most of all, I just fucking hated him.

The following day at breakfast, I couldn't eat the pancakes because my jaw hurt too much, though it didn't seem broken. Afterward, I showered, carefully timing things so that no one else was downstairs in the bathroom. One particularly sadistic senior, Seb, would make a point of staring at me from a few feet away when I was on the toilet or showered. I wanted to avoid that kind of thing that morning.

Confident I was alone, I studied my face in the mirror. I had a big black eye and a yellow bruise on my jaw that hurt like hell. I hopped into the shower and took stock of the damage on my body. I had over fifty bruises forming on my feet, legs, chest, and arms. And I mean real bruises, which colored over the next few days into dark purple, green, and yellow hues. The boys had done their job well.

I never figured out who did it, but I had a good idea that it was the upperclassmen. Over the next couple of days, a few of the seniors were actually friendly to me, likely to assuage whatever guilt they were feeling. With that brood of vipers, niceness was a tell. I smiled back at them, but inwardly, I made silent prayers to the Good Lord above that their dicks might fall off.

A couple of days later, Mr. Clodfelter reinstated his ad hoc room privilege. There was never any discussion about the beating, neither with other students nor with my houseparents. Nobody ever commented on my bruised face. I was deeply ashamed of what had happened, so for once, I kept my big trap shut and my head down. Also, it hurt to speak.

I had no idea if Mr. Clodfelter knew about the beating, though I suspected he did. On the surface, it seemed absurd. Mr. Clodfelter was the housefather and was meant to stabilize a student home full of aggressive boys. Yet he had explicitly set up the circumstances for the assault.

I never reported the incident, though at the time, I didn't understand why. I could have shown my body to the disciplinary council at school. I could have just told my thoughtful biology teacher, and she'd have done the rest. It would have turned MHS upside down; there would have been a lawsuit, bad press, all of it. Perhaps they would have broken up Forkroot and fired the Clodfelters. At the very least, I would have been transferred to another student home.

It never even crossed my mind, in part because I was ashamed. But with the perspective of hindsight, perhaps after six years of institutionalized living, I'd internalized that I had no control over my life. About the same amount as a dog, one might say.

* * *

That beating broke me. Forkroot was an environment I couldn't best. So I gave up on being me. Much as you swiftly pull your hand away from a hot flame, I arrived at this decision reflexively, born more out of instinctual self-preservation than considered thought. My housefather held all the power in my world; I needed to lie low and avoid poking the Clod. I'd conform to his expectations, I'd "yes, sir" and "no, sir" him, and maintain a "shiny happy people" attitude, at least to his ugly fucking face.

The more complex question was how to interact with the other boys. Life in a group home can have surprisingly little interaction with adults, but it's impossible to avoid your peers. There was no way I could take the Blob's nobler route of trying not to give a shit. It just wasn't in my personality. That left fitting in, playing the game.

So I decided to move up the rungs of popularity, however slow or unsuccessful I might be. We had a Nintendo in the student home, and early on, I'd play fantasy role-playing games regularly, such as the *Ultima* series, but I put it all down when the upperclassmen started calling me "Wizard." It was not a compliment.

I stopped hanging out with my few loser friends who actually liked me. Instead, I imitated and kissed up to the upperclassmen at Forkroot—the very boys who beat me—falling in line by cultivating the image of a rebel. I became aware of the appearance of being intelligent and actively suppressed it. At lunch, a hot girl I admired questioned my large vocabulary: "Why do you use such big words?" On the spot, I made a silent vow to discontinue my study of class-taught English and instead learn all the slang, curses, and idioms people actually use.

I became an outrageous troublemaker, especially in class, but pretty much everywhere that Mr. Clodfelter wasn't. For almost the entirety of my four years at MHS, I smoked, drank, and got high whenever I could. Say what you will about teenage rebellion, but a junior varsity attempt at self-destruction is nevertheless an act of self-determination.

But that rebel I became wasn't who I was, not underneath. Inside, I was the boy who contemplated the stars, thought about religion and science, and attempted to keep a few close friends. The sensitive boy I'd been took a four-year-long medicated nap starting the night I received that beating.

Keep in mind, I had no one to talk to, which I think is hard for people to truly wrap their heads around. By my freshman year in high school, I was *six years* in institutionalized living with no mentorship whatsoever. I had no regular conversations with my parents, obviously. Houseparents acted as a single unit, so Mrs. Clodfelter was out of the question. I wasn't speaking to a counselor at school or any sort of therapist. I occasionally connected with one of my relatives, but not at nearly the cadence required to navigate my problems. James was my legal guardian, which came with real obligations, and he dutifully visited me once a month. But he and Beverly had given every indication that they were glad to see the back of me. Whenever I thought to call them, I remembered being ghosted for a month and walked past the phone.

Gone were the days at the ACCH when I tried to "be perfect" or considered what life as a preacher might be like. Worst of all, I even forgot about the commitments Omar and I had made together. The only reason I received excellent grades at MHS was that classes were a joke, a combination of circumstance and the pure, privileged luck of a genetic lottery for which I could claim no credit.

Yet amid the darkness and pain of my years at Milton Hershey School, there was always a summer reprieve: my time spent with family on

Masten Lake. When MHS let out for the summer each year, all the kids, regardless of circumstances at home, had to leave. This was something that could have never happened at the Albuquerque Christian Children's Home, since most kids there had no alternatives.

For me, that meant staying with my Aunt Maria and Uncle Brad up in the Catskill Mountains in upstate New York, in a tiny community called Masten Lake. My summers there were the only aspect of my childhood that approached normalcy, and they allowed me to heal and rediscover the parts of myself that had been lost during a year at MHS.

The lake was a little gem about two miles in diameter with a collar of houses and docks, surrounded by forests of maple, birch, and pine. There were always canoes, rowboats, and a few speedboats on the water. It was a deep lake, and I played mind games with myself for years, wondering if there were monsters lurking in the depths. When I grew older, my lake friends and I would row a boat out to the middle, throw out an anchor, and watch it sink into the abyss. Then we'd dare one another to see who could go farthest down the line into the dark, cold water before chickening out and shooting back up to the surface.

In the afternoons, I'd often find a quiet spot on the shore to read. The scent of sunscreen would linger even as the heat of the day was tempered by cool, pine-scented air coming off the lake. As evening fell, the sky would transform into a stunning canvas of oranges, pinks, and purples, the colors reflecting off the lake's surface. At night, the smell of burnt marshmallows and campfire smoke would fill the air as the crickets sang their chorus.

Maria and Brad had two children, my cousins Tomasina and Danny, who were four and ten years younger than I was, respectively. I was so much older than Danny that I remember him being born. The first word I ever heard him say was *strawberry*, and I immediately thought he was brilliant. Danny had been born with spina bifida, a condition that meant he'd spend life in a wheelchair. Considering that they had two children of their own, one of them with special needs, made Maria and Brad's offer to take me in during the summers all the more generous.

Vacation always began in the same strange way, with me arriving in the Catskills only to come down with a mystery illness. I guess my body or immune system was going through some kind of detox. Having been in a defensive position for nine months, it could finally afford to wheeze, groan, and then sputter out.

"But, Aunt Maria, I never get sick. No joke, I've never missed a day of school at MHS or spent a night in the infirmary," I'd say.

She'd just laugh. "Don't worry about it, nephew; we'll get you fixed up."

After a few days, whatever flu or cold I had would pass, and the summer would begin.

Maria was adept with children—and every summer, she was a surrogate mother to me. A ham-and-egg sandwich here, a shoulder rub there, often a casual conversation on the beach. She'd listen to my dreams in the morning, still in her bathrobe. Maria also heard me when I told her just how many chores I had to do at the Milt, so she let me off the hook for the summer.

One evening during the summer after my freshman year, easily my hardest year at MHS, she and I ended up chatting through the evening. Uncle Brad was away for work, and I found myself curled up next to Maria in their bed. As we lay there, our talk turned to the future.

"I just want to make something of myself," I confessed. "I want to go to college, to prove that I'm more than just"—I cut my sentence short but then found the courage to finish—"more than just some reject from a group home."

Maria's arms tightened around me. "You know," she said after a moment, "college is a wonderful thing. And I'll be so proud of you when you get there. But I want you to know something, David. My love for you, it has nothing to do with your achievements. I love you for who you are, not what you do. Even if you didn't go to college, I'd still love you."

I began crying quietly. For my entire childhood, I'd defined myself by my intelligence, using it to garner attention from adults despite the chaos of my circumstances. But here was my aunt, offering me a different kind of validation, one based on nothing more than the inherent worth of my being.

With Maria's love and the support of the entire family bolstering my spirits, I found myself relaxed during those summer months, even diving into new intellectual pursuits, my curiosity and passion for learning reignited. Tomasina and I would play board games, hang out at the lake, and play Nintendo together. Midway through high school, the hot Nintendo title was *Super Mario Bros. 3*, and Tomasina would scream, "Get the free!" whenever we discovered a 1-up green mushroom, which conferred an extra life upon the player. Her sheer joy around video games always reminded me of Shiloh back when the two of us played *Ms. Pac-Man* in the arcade. Danny joined in the fun as soon as he was old enough to manage a Nintendo controller.

Tomasina had a fabulous habit of waking me up by thrusting a Game Boy into my face, first thing in the morning, always excited to watch her "big brother" play. As I grew older, she'd hand me my TI-81 graphing calculator. Both the TI-81 and the Game Boy used processors built on Federico Faggin's Z80 microprocessor architecture, so common in the video games of the early 1980s. Tomasina knew I loved that blue calculator like a pet that I kept on my person no matter the social consequences. It was special to me because it had a simple programming language, not dissimilar from BASIC. So during my last years in high school, I set myself the challenge of automating every single algorithm I learned in my math classes. This meant that after I'd programmed the recipes into my calculator, I could just plug in the inputs and have the TI-81 answer all my homework assignments.

One algorithm eluded me, though, and for an apparently simple—even trivial—problem. How to turn a decimal representation of a number, say, 0.75, into its reduced fraction representation, which is 3/4. I couldn't find the algorithm in any textbook I'd been given. I racked my brain for months, and then one day, just sunning on the beach while messing around on my beloved TI-81, I divided 1 by 0.5 and saw 2 (the three numbers are related by ½ = 0.5). The contours of an algorithm that might work for the general case flashed in my mind, and I immediately set to work. In the process, I discovered continued fractions, a powerful idea used in number theory. The amount of dopamine released in my brain engaging in that project virtually guaranteed that I'd end up making a career in research.

In many ways, those summer months were a photo negative of life in the group home, a counter to my life in the unrelenting Upside Down. My time at the lake also served as something of a control experiment in the science project of life. No matter how nuts things usually were, I learned that I could be—and *feel*—okay. At least under highly idealized conditions with the most supportive of people, I was capable of not fucking things up.

Yet for all the good vibes and happy times, I never once asked to live with Maria and Brad outside of the summertime and holidays, and my aunt and uncle never made the offer. For my part, the ask was too risky, the impact of rejection too enormous. And for theirs, well, they had their own life, complicated and busy, the same as everyone else's.

Amid the peace and normalcy of Masten Lake, there was one single occasion that reminded me of the complexity of my family history: a rare visit from Esther. For the most part, when I visited the Catskills, my sister wasn't around. Initially, at the ages of ten and eleven, she and I would spend a bit of time with Maria and Brad at the lake first and then move around among the rest of our aunts and uncles. By the time I reached my freshman year in high school, I spent my entire summer at the lake house, and Esther stopped coming up altogether, having decided that the lake was a snoozefest compared to Manhattan, where she stayed with Moira and Elliot.

But at the end of my junior year, Esther did come out to Masten Lake once for a family reunion. During the party, she snuck into the kitchen and stole a bottle of vodka while everyone was socializing out on the porch. She and I ducked into a back room and started taking swigs straight from the bottle.

"So do you get wasted with your friends at school?" Esther asked as she tilted the bottle back. Her acne had cleared up completely, and her blond hair had grown out and was no longer permed. I guessed Elliot and Moira financed her wardrobe, because she looked super classy in her long plaid skirt and designer blue poncho.

"Pretty much every chance I get," I said. "But up here, never."

"Why not up here?" Esther gave a devious smile.

"I don't want to fuck up a good thing. I love coming up here."

My sister nodded and handed me the bottle. "So. You have a crush on anyone?"

"This girl named Cathy at school."

"Awww."

"She doesn't know I exist, but still."

"One of those." Esther laughed. "So I guess you haven't done it, then."

"Done what?" I asked as I took another pull.

"It."

I knew what Esther meant, but I didn't really want to talk about *it*. I didn't know Esther well at all; plus, she was my sister. Ick. Instead, I looked away.

Esther smiled. "Okay. I get it. Just wait and see, though." After a moment of quiet, the smile faded. "We never had that, you know. Love."

"Since Mom died?" I asked.

"Since forever. Our entire lives."

I nodded in agreement. But this conversation was beyond me.

"Maybe when you are older," Esther said. "Now pass me that bottle."

We reminisced about the ACCH and told stories about Omar and Bobby. We chatted about some of the girls, like Jess, who'd been my first kiss. We commiserated in our shared hatred of our current living arrangements.

In under an hour, Esther became rip-roaring drunk, ultimately spending the evening hugging the toilet. As Esther stumbled off to the bathroom, I couldn't shake the feeling that something was off. The sneaking away to drink—this I knew well. But the complete disregard for whether she might be caught combined with her extreme intoxication signaled recklessness. Plus, our conversation had depressed me. It all pointed to something deeper, sadder, as if something was missing for my sister.

Miraculously, nobody except me noticed Esther was ill that night.

19

The Utterly Unremarkable Experiences of a Mediocre Swimmer

I glared up at Michelle and pulled a long drag of my cigarette. "I cannot wait to get the fuck outta here."

Michelle was one of the only people I trusted. Not only was she one of the top-three students in high school, but she was also tough as nails. During her freshman year, a group of girls in her student home had tried to kick the shit out of Michelle's roommate, a girl they knew wouldn't fight back. Michelle had blocked their path, saying, "Through me first, bitches." The girls had backed off, and both Michelle and her friend had been left alone for the remainder of high school.

Smoking was, of course, forbidden at MHS. To avoid ten and ten, Michelle and I had snuck off into a pine grove during Saturday recreation period, when kids were allowed to leave their student homes as long as they stayed on campus.

"Heading to college is all I think about," Michelle agreed, exhaling a puff of smoke. "So, how's the whole advanced placement thing working out for you?"

The Utterly Unremarkable Experiences of a Mediocre Swimmer

"All right, I guess. I'm feeling good about biology and calculus." I began chuckling. "But fucking Mr. Kim—he ordered the wrong AP test—literature instead of creative writing. So I wrote a screed against him and the Milt instead of answering the questions. I hope the grader got a couple of yucks out of it."

"That's so petty." Michelle wheezed between laughs. "You failed, I presume?"

"Almost surely. But Mr. Kim's a chill guy, so since the rest of the year's shot, he's been killing time by showing us a PBS series on how brains work. I had no idea brains were that interesting."

"I don't know anything about it," Michelle said.

Smoke stung my throat as I took another drag. "Turns out, some people have epilepsy so bad that they need to remove the part of the brain that's causing the seizure. The doctors put electrodes in their brains to test and see where the epilepsy is coming from."

"God, that sounds awful."

"Totally. But it gets weird, right? When the doctor zaps different parts of the brain with electricity, the patient reports all kinds of weird visions and shit."

"Like, they actually see stuff?"

"Yes! Visions, smells, emotions. All kinds of hallucinations. There was this one woman, whenever the doctors stimulated the electrode—she said it made her feel *sexy*."

"Whoa."

"They even showed how our brains build patterns from light hitting our eyes, how we piece reality together. How crazy is that? Everything…it's all in our heads. Fucking electricity in our heads."

Michelle put her cigarette out. "Maybe Mr. Kim ordering the wrong test wasn't so bad, after all. Come on, let's head back to Rec."

I never gave the whole world of weirdness happening inside our skulls any thought until Mr. Kim started showing us that *NOVA* series. It was my first moment of awareness of the brain or of a thing called *neuroscience*. I couldn't have known it at the time, but some of the studies showcased in that *NOVA* series were seminal.

It wasn't until the mid-twentieth century that neuroscience blossomed into a distinct experimental field. Even then, technical limitations held back progress. First, our skulls are biological safes made of thick bone that protect our brains from injury. Second, even when scientists figured out how to safely get a recording electrode inside a brain, they couldn't effectively measure or record the activity of single neurons—the brain's fundamental building blocks—because the tech was too primitive. Instead, neuroscientists relied on equipment that averaged across huge numbers of neurons, yielding a blurry picture of neural activity that couldn't possibly speak to mechanism. And when neuroscientists finally gained the ability to study individual neurons, they often focused on their isolated cellular properties rather than on how they worked together.

Take vision, for example. Twentieth-century psychologists had long sought to understand how we create a unified image from the world around us, despite our eyes taking in only partial information as they flit around when consuming a visual scene. The first clue came when neuroscientist Stephen Kuffler discovered *ON* and *OFF* cells in the retina (the light-sensitive cells in the back of the eye) in the early 1950s. These cells, serving roughly as tiny camera pixels, fire only when light hits specific spots within the portion of the visual world a retinal cell cares about. ON cells increase their firing when light appears in their receptive field while OFF cells do the opposite, firing more when light disappears. Yet a mystery remained: How does the cortex, the brain region responsible for complex visual processing, transform these representations of points of light into the rich visual world we experience?

McCulloch and Pitts had laid the theoretical foundation, suggesting that such a computation required networks of neurons connected in just the right way; indeed, they showed that artificial neural networks inspired by abstractions of biological neurons are universal Turing machines, capable of computing anything that can possibly be computed. But how did this actually happen for computations such as those that underlie vision? No one knew.

Enter David Hubel and Torsten Wiesel in the late 1950s. They aimed to uncover how neurons in the cat's early visual cortex—just a bit downstream from the retina—reacted to patterns of light projected onto the eye. First, they inserted electrodes into the visual cortex of an anesthetized cat to measure the responses of individual neurons. Then, through a projector, they shone various patterns in front of the cat's eyes. Surprisingly, neurons didn't respond vigorously to spots of light, as one might hypothesize given Kuffler's result, so they tried still other patterns.

Eventually, they stumbled into a serendipitous breakthrough that would change the course of neuroscience. They noticed that neurons responded whenever they adjusted their display equipment. On a hunch, using bars of light they began designing rectangular stimuli that mimicked the switching of slides—for example, a dark rectangle against a light background or a light rectangle against a dark background. When they used these rectangles as stimuli, the neurons in the visual cortex fired like mad. Edges with sharp contrast triggered strong, reliable responses.

Further, Hubel and Wiesel discovered that these neurons only fired when the bar of light was oriented in a particular direction, one neuron focused on bars that were vertical, others focused on horizontal bars, and so forth. They named these edge detectors *simple cells*.

Knowing that the retinal cells in the eye responded only to specific points of light (Kuffler's ON and OFF cells), the two scientists saw a clear connection. They reasoned that the response of a simple cell in the cortex, which cared about an oriented edge, could easily be built by wiring up retinal cells that cared about points that compose that edge.

Hubel and Wiesel went one step further than simple cells, identifying so-called *complex cells* that also responded to oriented bars of light. But complex cells were less concerned with a bar's exact location, exhibiting a useful property for processing images called *location invariance*. This meant complex cells could help identify a shape regardless of small shifts in its position, just as you can identify a picture of your dog regardless of whether it's centered in a photo or over to the side.

By piecing this all together, Hubel and Wiesel proposed a groundbreaking model of how vision might work. Imagine visual processing as a series of feedforward steps, a bit like dominoes set up to fall: First, ON and OFF cells in the retina pinpoint spots of light or darkness. Then, in the early visual cortex, simple cells detect edges by receiving input from these cells in a precise arrangement. Finally, complex cells create shape detectors with location invariance by receiving input from simple cells, again, thanks to carefully arranged connections.

Stop for a moment to consider the impact of this hypothesis. Before Hubel and Wiesel, neuroscience thought of the brain basically as a bag of neurons with mysterious, inscrutable electrical properties. They knew the connections mattered, but they had no idea how. Hubel and Wiesel succeeded in presenting a plausible hypothesis for a straightforward circuit structure. Suddenly, the neuroscience community had a concrete explanation for how layers of neurons lined up in feedforward chains might build an increasingly complex visual understanding.

The impact of Hubel and Wiesel's work was enormous—the ideas revolutionary—and they would go on to receive the Nobel Prize. More

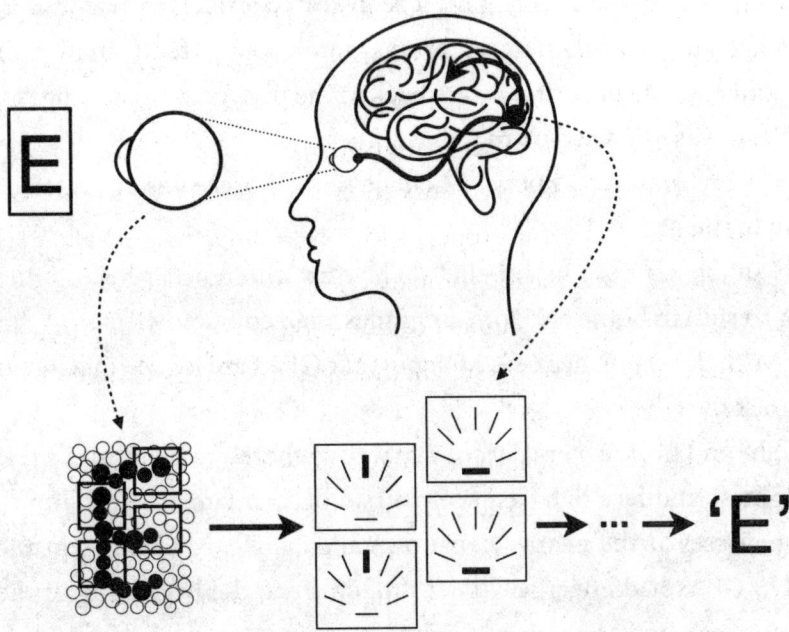

Caption: In the top row, a human looks at the letter E. Light is processed by the eye, which sends signals to the visual cortex (black dot) and further processing areas to recognize the letter. In the bottom row, retinal cells in the eye (left) detect individual points of light, passing their signals to simple cells of the visual cortex (boxes in the middle), which fire only when they detect edges in specific parts of the visual field with specific orientations. Though many simple cells exist (4×8 in this diagram), only four fire in this example (bold lines in middle boxes), highlighting how the brain extracts meaningful structure (e.g., by picking out the edges of the letter E). Layer by layer, neurons in the visual system build up an increasingly complex representation, culminating in recognition (of the letter E on the right).

than just a theory, this idea was backed by experimental evidence—backed by the actual response properties of neurons in the cortex. For perhaps the first time ever, we saw how real, squishy neurons might cooperate to perform complex computations.

* * *

That *NOVA* series planted in me a deep-seated interest in brains. But in springtime of my senior year, brains were about as far from my mind as could be. Michelle and I were back in the pine grove, smoking. This time, it was Michelle's turn to have a beef.

"We're toast, you know," Michelle said. "Borace has got valedictorian in the bag."

I shook my head in disbelief. "The only difference is his A in fucking freshman home ec. Do your grades even count now?"

Michelle shook her head. "Nope. Our GPAs are locked in. Gig's up; game's over."

She and Borace were part of a trial run whereby a handful of MHS's brightest and best-behaved seniors had been invited to enroll in college classes at the nearby Lebanon Valley College. This meant their MHS GPAs had effectively been frozen since the beginning of their senior year, and Michelle had just found out.

I hadn't been invited to participate in this trial program. I'd gained a school-wide reputation for trouble my junior year, thanks mainly to events surrounding "that weed incident," whereby the school authorities had brought down a drug ring—well, a weed ring; it was high school, after all—that had resulted in one boy's expulsion. I'd bought a dime bag from this guy, and everyone who'd done so had been busted along with him.

Frankly, the MHS authorities would have been derelict in their duties if they'd allowed me to wander off to some random college. I'd certainly have abused the privilege. But not being invited cut deep. I'd had four years of Milton Hershey's panoptic eye on my punk ass, and I was counting down the days until parole. More than anything in the world, I wanted to be set free.

"This impacts you, too, you know," said Michelle. "If you're still thinking about MIT, it wouldn't hurt to have been valedictorian."

"I'm sure I'll get in. Why wouldn't I?" I did a quick jig, complete with jazz hands and a spin. "Anyway, it's a done deal. I sent in my application months ago."

"There are lots of smart people applying, that's why," Michelle answered. "People who haven't been huffing Air Duster or hitting whip-its nonstop for four years." She took another drag. "So what did you write about for your essay?"

"Fuck this place," I said.

"Yep."

I'd had no guidance during any part of the college application process. I had no parents to ride me. Nor did I have any idea that many other kids applying to top-tier schools—my competition—would likely have received assistance. There was no one to hire a coach to help me organize my efforts or provide application templates. The guidance counselors at Senior Hall were completely missing in action.

So I'd winged it. Throughout the application process, there were signs that things weren't going well. First, I bungled the SAT. I didn't prepare for the test as I didn't even know that preparation was a thing. I just walked in on the appointed day, sat down with my handy-dandy No. 2 pencil, and started filling in tidy little circles. I scored 1,310 out of 1,600, receiving a 700 in math and 610 in verbal—excellent scores but nowhere near the stratospheric numbers required for acceptance at MIT.

Second, MIT required an in-person interview. I interviewed with an MIT alumnus in his forties, and we spent most of the time talking about fantasy novels. While a lovely way to spend an evening, shooting the breeze about the relative merits of elvish weapons versus dwarvish armor isn't the most direct way to get accepted into what is arguably the world's most prestigious technical university.

Finally, the application contained an essay section on what aspects of my life might make me an outstanding candidate. After reading the instructions, I started writing directly on the application page with my black ballpoint pen right there in AP Bio. No drafts, no reviews, no revisions—just the first thing that came to mind. And that was about my love-hate, well, hate-hate relationship with competitive swimming:

My Most Significant Challenge by David Sussillo

I think that I will be able to utilize my ~~skills~~ mental abilities at MIT regardless of how challenging the coursework is. One place that I've been ^able to do this already in my life is through competitive swimming. Even though swimming isn't something that I ~~like enjoy relish lap up~~ luxuriate in, I am able to realize that keeping body fit is a prerequisite for all the ~~classes~~ herculean ~~mental~~ tasks I desire to undertake.

And it went on in that uninspired vein. I guess I'd have failed that AP Creative Writing test even if Mr. Kim had ordered it correctly.

The truth was that I'd been ten years in the habit of *hiding* my childhood story, not sharing it. It was beyond my comprehension that an essay that meaningfully engaged in the real challenges I'd faced might reflect well on me and indicate what I might be capable of, given the right balance of challenge and support.

"What happened to your hand?" Michelle asked a month later, graduation now quickly approaching.

"Oh, I put it through a window. Just a scratch, luckily. I kinda lost it after reading the rejection letter from MIT." I looked down at my bandaged hand. "But fucking Clodfelter gave me five and five for it."

"Did the letter deviate from the standard form letter?"

"Not really. Blah blah, lots of qualified applicants...blah blah.... Most students who don't get in end up at excellent universities. Eat shit and die."

"That sucks, Dave. I'm sorry. But they're probably right. You'll get in somewhere great."

In the end, the higher minds at MIT had the right idea. Michelle was accepted to the University of Pennsylvania, and I was accepted to several terrific schools, including Carnegie Mellon University (CMU), in Pittsburgh, which had world-class drama and computer science departments. I decided to go there and began deliberating on which major.

Chemistry was out of the question thanks to my recklessness in the laboratory—I'd nearly busted my head open when I'd passed out after inhaling the fumes of some clear liquid in a stoppered glass jar. As for biology or medicine, my squeamishness kept me away. Physics was the obvious choice, given my love of math and my fascination with chaos and Conway's Game of Life. Plus, I remembered the promises I'd read in *Discover* and *Scientific American*—that by mastering such a fearsome magic, one might produce great works. Physics also resonated with my religious side, instilled by the ACCH. I yearned to get to "the heart of the matter," to discover the nature of things as they really were.

But for a long time, I had a massive chip on my shoulder about getting rejected from MIT. What hurt even worse was admitting that I hadn't earned admittance.

My uncle and legal guardian, James, helped me out with the applications' financial side. Most importantly, he made sure I had "independent status," which meant that the universities and the federal government would accurately view me as someone with no financial resources whatsoever. And that meant I would receive the maximum amount of financial aid.

Penn State was among several schools I'd been accepted to, and so James took me to State College to visit. While there, we met with a financial aid officer who had some broad authority. James explained my life circumstances to him—deceased mother, drug-addicted father, yada, yada, yada. I sat there in embarrassed silence as a total stranger went dumpster-diving through my childhood.

But the humiliation was worth it. The officer checked the appropriate box in the computer software. That single bit of information passed at light speed through the plumbing of the pre-interwebs and navigated its way onto the correct government server. *Poof!* I magically had independent status. Including some help from MHS and a combination of private grants and federal support, I received a full ride to CMU—though I'd be totally broke until I got a real job.

Later that spring, on a warm, sun-filled day, I graduated from Milton Hershey School. All my aunts and uncles headed to Hershey to celebrate with me, including James and Beverly, Maria and Brad, and Moira and Elliot. Even my father's aging mother made it. They had a merry time as they watched Michelle and me share salutatorian honors (indeed, we ended up tying for second place behind Borace, the valedictorian). They cheered us on as we walked down the aisle to receive our diplomas. Even I, as jaded as I was, had to admit it was a big deal.

Neither Esther nor my father came. Esther had found her way back to New Mexico, and it didn't seem financially realistic for her to attend. As for my father, after twenty-five years of nonstop illicit, drug-related nonsense, the cops had finally made him. He was serving time for impersonating a pharmacist and writing himself and others fake opioid prescriptions. I was certain I'd never speak with him again.

PART 4

THE EDGE OF CHAOS: 1993–1998

Brains are, without a doubt, the most complex material known to humankind. Though we've gleaned some rudimentary insights from stimulating specific neural circuits, the mystery of how thought and emotion—our very selves—spring forth from the physical matter and electrical signaling inside our heads remains largely unknown. Yet every act, every dream, every nuance of consciousness emerges from the patterned electrical activity of neurons. Even the songs of our past, the bittersweet soundtrack scoring the movie of our lives, are mere patterns stored in synapses.

We *do* know some particulars, many of which are compelling and beautiful. Take the inner ear: We know that fifteen thousand so-called hair cells transduce vibrations in the air into electrical signals that your brain interprets as sound. You will be awed by the gorgeous details of this system, I promise. But while molecular pathways and single-cell physiology are worthy of our understanding, narrow biology doesn't satisfy our broader curiosity about how eighty-six billion neurons give rise to thoughts, emotions, and ultimately consciousness. It's as if we can only study the bark of a single tree while the forest of mind fades behind an impenetrable fog across a thousand different dimensions.

We are missing the forest, not because we always prefer to study bark but because it's all we can currently comprehend. Perhaps the neuroscientist's desire to dissect the *how* of the brain is a fool's errand, like analyzing individual lines in the source code for *Ms. Pac-Man* to understand why it's beloved by generations of gamers.

With the caveat that it's a gross oversimplification, it's helpful to understand the brain as a kind of biological computer, one forged through the survival and death of our forebears over a thousand thousand generations. When you decided to wolf down that bacon double cheeseburger last night instead of picking at the leftover chicken breast, there was a calculation underlying that choice. It was the same when you navigated through traffic on your way to work this morning. Even emotions are a computation of a sort. Indeed, many mental illnesses, like dysregulation of anxiety or anger, are diseases of miscalibration. Though the lived experience belongs to all of us, there's no denying the rattle of enigmatic computational processes just beneath the surface.

Humans are not unique in having computing brains. Imagine you're driving down a country road one day, and you spot a raven in the distance picking at some bit of bloody roadkill. The raven looks up at the metal monster bearing down on its tiny frame. Unconcerned, it pecks another bite. Then another. It looks up again, watching, head cocked, beady-eyed and unblinking, then, with a calculation as precise as any stopwatch, hops twice—not one hop and not three—exactly two hops, finding safety in the opposite lane. The raven's walnut-size brain, brimming with computational might, has just orchestrated its own survival.

And here is where language and metaphors falter. "Computer" isn't right; it's woefully inadequate. This isn't the sterile silicon of your office laptop. This is a swirling, dynamic tornado of computation, a living Turing machine capable of composing symphonies. One that can do math, follow instructions, and hold a best friend's secrets close, all within the confines of limited biological resources.

This computational capacity of brains, from the raven's walnut-size organ to our own intricate neural networks, raises profound questions about the nature of information processing in biological systems. How do these organic computers manage to be both stable enough to maintain memories and fluid enough to adapt to new situations? To understand this, we must look beyond neuroscience to other fields that grapple with complex systems.

Physicists have long considered the dance between order and disorder in dynamical systems, of the interplay between the forces of contraction and those of expansion. Take, for example, ice and water. Ice, rigid and crystalline, resists change, demanding power to shatter its frozen structures. Water, fluid and yielding, submits quickly to external forces, yet can erupt in unpredictable turbulence, like milk swirling in a steaming cup of coffee.

Have you ever considered how strange it is that water exists as ice at all temperatures below zero degrees Celsius, and then *right* at zero, suddenly it transitions to water? Physicists term this a *phase transition*, a qualitative change in the material resulting from a tiny temperature change. A smidgeon below zero, you have ice. A smidgeon above, you have water.

Neural networks such as biological brains also exhibit a phase transition, termed *the edge of chaos*. It is a magical realm that supports the emergence of rich electrical structures that support computation, where memories solidify like ice and then flow like water for thought to sculpt anew. Too much rigidity, and we become crystalline, unable to learn or adapt. Too much chaos, and neural patterns disintegrate, rendered purposeless.

My early childhood was downright chaotic, but life in group homes had forced a rigidity perhaps more damaging. Still, as I approached college, I began to see my life as a cauldron of possibilities. One where my future teetered on the edge of chaos.

20

Serious Decision Number 3

At some point before high school graduation, my French teacher, Ms. Dahlia, had pulled me aside after a class period in which she'd grown irritated with me for my general lack of *concentrer*.

"You could be crème de la crème, David," she said. "If only you would apply yourself!"

It was the first time, in all my classes with her over the years, that Ms. Dahlia had switched from French to English. Like the Zen master that, at the last, sparks enlightenment in the dim-witted pupil by hitting them upside the head with a shoe, her language switch had made me strangely receptive to both her rebuke and her compliment.

Before heading to college, in the tranquility of my summer life at Masten Lake, I took stock of my situation. I was no longer a minion in the orphan-to-productive-citizen factory that was MHS. More broadly, I'd survived my childhood. Sure, I had a whole mess of scars and a broken rib, and there was that back injury that acted up sometimes…But goddammit, I was going to college! My educational commitment to myself, dormant for years and barely held together with twice-used duct tape and half-remembered dreams, resurfaced with surprising vigor.

I arrived at two serious decisions.

Serious Decision Number 1: It was time to grow the fuck up and drop my loudmouthed rebel routine.

Serious Decision Number 2: Put up or shut up. I'd be earnest and—god forbid—follow Ms. Dahlia's advice.

It's hard to describe all my impressions that first day in late August when I showed up in Pittsburgh for freshman orientation. Standing there alone, looking over the CMU campus from the dorm's rooftop lounge, I saw a new life before me. Professors walked with grad students on perfectly manicured lawns while groups of students sat in circles under lush trees, played volleyball, or kicked a hacky sack around. I studied the buildings. The engineering quad held Wean Hall, with its brutalist concrete architecture, home of the vaunted School of Computer Science. A couple of hundred yards back into the main campus, I spotted the College of Fine Arts building, with its marble niches and nearby sculpture gardens. I could hardly help but notice the so-bad-it's-good university administrative building that looked for all the world like a one-hundred-foot flashcube from a '70s-era camera.

This was a far cry from the War Zone in Albuquerque when my mother hadn't bothered to enroll Esther and me in elementary school. There were no crumbling stucco apartment buildings, no lengthy cracks running through the building facades. Real care had been taken to create an environment so the people working and studying could thrive.

As I stood there, looking over the campus, excitement and anxiety—two sides of the same coin—battled within me. For the first time in my life, I was free to do whatever I pleased. I had no idea if I belonged here, but I was determined to find out. I felt laughter bubbling up; perhaps a sob of relief trying to escape. If I had jumped off that roof, I would have flown.

Serious Decision Number 3

In a word, the classes at CMU were...blistering. Where do I even begin? In my programming classes, I learned how to handle pointers to pointers to pointers in the C programming language. In math, we proved zero doesn't equal one, and I contended with the mathematical mindfuck that there are actually different sizes of infinity. I spent my junior year in an all-out, no-holds-barred death match with the philosopher Heidegger. My mind expanded into seventeen different dimensions. All at once. At warp speed. Scottie beamed my shit straight up.

But that first semester, my classes were standard fare for a physics first-year. While paging through the registration guide, I noticed a series of two math classes called Analysis 1 and 2. The classes were a replacement for Calculus 1 and 2, and the description promised to teach the topic's theoretical foundations. I loved calc in high school and thought some theory was just what I needed. Plus, when I read that Analysis was to be offered to only the most advanced incoming students, the siren song of infinite series and delta-epsilon proofs proved impossible to resist.

I used this new communication tool called email to arrange a meeting with the mathematics department chair to discuss enrolling. He was a tall, skeletal man with large facial features and wild hair. After introductions, the first thing he did was look my SAT scores up and down.

"David," he said, looking at his computer monitor, "it appears you scored a 700 in math."

"Yes, sir. That's my memory."

He spread his huge hands apologetically. "Unfortunately, that score isn't indicative of the prerequisites we hope an Analysis student comes in with."

"Why not?" I asked.

"Well—and this is a bit awkward—most of the students going into Analysis scored a perfect 800."

I'd always been disappointed in my score and knew damned well it wasn't elite. Internally, I'd rationalized my performance. Those math whizzes likely hadn't been getting their asses handed to them for ten years straight. But the time for excuses was over. Instead, with visions of the beautiful Ms. Dahlia standing behind me, whispering *crème de la crème* into my ear, I countered, "Well, sir, do you happen to have my AP test scores?"

"Let me see." The chair tapped on his keyboard.

"If so, you'll see I aced the Calculus B/C section."

The chair rubbed his chin. "So you did."

"That was through self-study. My high school teacher only covered the A/B material."

The chair was convinced. "All right, I'll allow it! Welcome to Analysis, David!"

I grinned and shook the fucker's hand like he'd just sold me a new car.

In Analysis, I met a couple of fantastically nerdy friends. I'd grown up apologizing for being smart and suppressing my geekiness, preferring an attenuation of self over ridicule. Now, I wanted to explore this side of me, this idea of intellect and nerdiness as culture.

But for you to understand just how far down the rabbit hole I went, I need to recalibrate you to the CMU nerd scale. CMU was the kind of school that handed out computer floppy disks at football games to increase attendance. By conventional standards, even my jock and frat friends were nerds. My art friends were nerds. Basically, every undergrad at CMU could recite the Constitution of the United Federation of Planets—in Klingon.

I need to introduce you to the *ultra nerd*. When I say *ultra*, I'm talking about that next-level geek who'd absorbed the culture into their bones and likely had never known anything different. I'm talking about those

Serious Decision Number 3

lute-playing, *Dungeons & Dragons* dice-rolling, live-action role-playing, *Magic: The Gathering* spell-casting, *Galaxy Quest* "Hadn't even gotten to the relevant conundrum"–quoting mofos. I regularly hung out with these dudes. And they were actually all dudes; more's the pity.

Two such ultras in my Analysis class were Jeremy and Josh, each fascinating in their own ways. Jeremy was a trivia god with a thick crop of dark brown hair and a near-photographic memory. He'd absorbed decades of pop culture and so had turned himself into a trivia-spewing fountain of useless knowledge. Ask him anything about national politics or popular music of the last fifty years, and he'd rattle off the answer without looking up from his class notes.

Josh taught me what it meant to master pinball by taking me to the student union to play the all-time pinball classic, Addams Family.

"Are you any good?" he asked.

"Quicksand, fumes, toxic waste! It's all mine!" I recited, repurposing a line from the game and feeling confident.

"Okay then." Josh grinned, rubbing his hands together. "Let the games begin."

We inserted our quarters and battled, and Josh kicked the ever-living shit out of me, completing the circuit of mini-games twice. Then he put one hand behind his back and beat me again using only a single hand for both flippers. In four years of pinball with Josh, I might have won a dozen times.

The professor for Analysis was an old head in his mid-seventies. He had thick white hair, parted to the side and held down with pomade. He wore a blue cardigan and gray slacks, and you could regularly catch him smoking filterless Pall Malls outside Wean Hall. The indie rockers on campus had nothing on my Analysis professor.

In our first lecture, we started engaging in the intricacies of delta-epsilon proofs, the mathematical equivalent of juggling rattlesnakes while blindfolded. Professor Pall Mall didn't use course notes. He just picked up a piece of chalk, rolled up the sleeves of his sweater, and started slaying on the blackboard.

Universes of possibility and beautiful mathematical structures opened in front of my eyes. It was love at first proof. He was so impressive, and we were so green, that if Pall Mall had channeled lightning during that first semester, I would have simply nodded in silent admiration.

After a month of classes, it became obvious that everyone was either seriously smarter than I was or was significantly better prepared. So I joined a study group.

One young woman noticed me struggling, leaned over, and said, "You solve that one by using the Wronskian technique."

"The Wrons-what?" I asked. "That wasn't covered in class."

"Oh, they didn't teach it. I learned it in my differential equations class back in high school."

My mouth went dry. "You took *differential equations* in high school?" This advanced material was typically taught in the junior year of college.

"Didn't everyone?"

Naw, girlfriend, not everyone. This was the first moment in my life I ever really understood the word *privilege*, what *elite* meant in terms that I cared about. But I kept my mouth shut and learned from her.

I followed the lectures easily enough when the professor led us through the material on the blackboard. But back in my dorm room, reading through proofs in the textbook or extending them in the homework, I was stumped. Over the semester, new material built off what had come before, each proof more confusing than the last. With each new assignment, I became more mystified and more concerned.

Serious Decision Number 3

I didn't know how much my classmates were comprehending, but it was clear I was in trouble.

When the midterm results from Analysis came back, my fears were confirmed. I'd bombed it, scoring fifty-nine out of one hundred. I decided to do some sniffing around, so the next class, I sat next to Jeremy.

"How'd you do on your midterm?" I asked.

Jeremy grinned as he looked over at me. "Crushed it. Ninety-three."

"Come the fuck on."

Jeremy pulled his test out, and there at the top, in red ink with a big, happy circle around it, was a ninety-three.

After class, I caught up with the pinball wizard. Josh had aced it. A perfect score.

As I walked back to my dorm, the weight of my situation began to sink in. The midterm grade wasn't just a number; it was a stark reminder of how different I was from my peers. While they had spent their childhoods preparing for this moment, I'd spent mine just trying to survive.

Ironically, when the semester had kicked in, I'd discovered that, in some ways, I was *better* equipped for college life than many of my peers, at least in those areas related to daily routine. Mr. Clodfelter had been an effective drill sergeant, so I got up every day at seven, made my bed, and tidied my room. I arrived at my classes on time and completed all my assignments. Skipping was out of the question.

But there was weird stuff, too. I found I was afraid to enter the buildings where I didn't have a class. Even with the onset of Pittsburgh's miserable winter, I couldn't bring myself to cut through a building to keep warm if I didn't have a scheduled reason to be there.

And then there was money. While I was on a free ride academically, on a day-to-day basis, I was scraping by. The two hundred and fifty bucks James had given me for the semester barely covered essentials, so I ate every meal in the cafeteria, where my food credits counted, and picked up a work-study job as a desk attendant. From 4:00 a.m. to 8:00 a.m. several times a week, I'd throw on A Tribe Called Quest's *Midnight Marauders* and solve math problems in the dead of night.

My fifty-nine on the midterm still burning in my thoughts, I showed my ID card at the dorm entrance and headed upstairs. My entire sense of self-worth was caught up in that test. When I was a kid, the idea of college had never been about knowledge or career opportunities, per se. It'd been about escape; the story I'd told myself *about myself* to survive. Now, for the first time, I was faced with a terrifying possibility: Maybe I didn't have what it took. This idea threatened to destroy the fragile identity I'd pieced together from scraps of approval collected over years of institutional living. It threatened to unravel me entirely.

As I entered my dorm room, my anxiety began to get the better of me. I knew damned well that I had nowhere else to go. I had no parents and no place to call home. Before CMU, there had always been an ACCH or an MHS, something to fall back on, however miserable. Sure, Maria, or James, or Moira would have let me stay with them for a bit. But how long would it take to wear out my welcome if I flunked out and was forced to leave school? A month? Two?

And so, as I sat down at my desk and pulled books out of my backpack, I arrived at Serious Decision Number 3: This moment—right here, right now—was my one shot. I would find a way to succeed, *no matter what*.

I opened my Analysis textbook and got to work.

My math buddies were great to hang with after class, but ever since my first friendship with Shiloh, way back in the second grade, I'd always been on the lookout to fill the hole he left behind—a buddy

I could share all my experiences with. At college, I found two: Sport and Don.

Sport lived down the hall in our all-male dorm. With his ginger-tinged brown hair and Scottish heritage, he was a study in contrasts—quick to irritation but surprisingly tender, and unfailingly loyal to his friends. He'd earned his nickname from his fractious nature on the basketball court, but in a rare feat of self-awareness, he'd actually changed his behavior after realizing why he'd earned the nickname. Still, the name stuck.

Don was one of those guys who appeared to be blessed with everything. He was perhaps the world's hottest ultra nerd. Or, as a female friend once put it when explaining why the women at CMU threw themselves at him, he had "highly refined facial bone structure." Don was enrolled in the world-class computer science program at CMU. He was a nerd's nerd, an ultra, and gave all of zero minutes to his appearance, content to throw on the same green hoodie, ripped jeans, and black shitkickers every day. That he happened to be from Santa Fe—my spiritual hometown—felt like cosmic confirmation that we were meant to be friends.

These two were the first people outside the system that I trusted enough to tell my story to. Not all at once, but in pieces, trading histories as we got closer. By mid-semester, I thought I knew them pretty well. Then I overheard them in the student lounge talking about calling home.

"Wait, you regularly call your parents?" I asked as I came over and sat down.

"Yeah," said Don, smiling. "My mom calls on Sunday evenings."

"So you enjoy talking to your folks? Like, non-ironically?" I asked.

Don and Sport looked at each other and then back at me. Sport said, "Yeah, man, most kids at college are talking to their parents regularly."

"Non-ironically," Don added. "When I first got here, I didn't mind the break. But now I look forward to chatting with them. Especially with my mom."

That word, *mom*, might as well have been from a different language. "So what do you talk about?" I asked.

"Simple stuff. How're things, the family, classes, you know," Don explained.

I didn't know. "Just so I'm one hundred percent clear on this, you both *miss* your family?"

"Yes, that's what we're saying, David. Jesus freaking Christ," said Sport.

I couldn't remember ever missing my mother or my father. As a matter of fact, I couldn't remember actively missing anybody, with the single exception of Shiloh when I'd returned to Albuquerque as a third grader.

At MHS, the telephone itself had been a constant source of tension. The houseparents wielded it as a disciplinary tool; take it away, give it back, take it away, give it back. Plus, there was one phone for sixteen boys, so there was a pecking order to the whole business. Always under scrutiny, the phone's use was fraught with a whole hierarchy of unspoken rules.

But as I became ever-more nervous as the semester unfolded, I resolved to overcome my phone shyness and reach out to someone about how poorly my math class was going. Nobody came to mind. Eventually, I phoned my Uncle Elliot in New York City. He'd always had a way of making difficult conversations feel natural, and he and Moira had come out to visit Esther and me at the ACCH just before I'd started the fifth grade. They'd been the ones to rally the extended family to take us in during the summers. And they were both psychotherapists.

Serious Decision Number 3

"Hey, kiddo, what's up?" Elliot asked when I finally called him.

"Hey! Not much, college stuff...Can't complain. How are things with you and Moira?"

Elliot chuckled. "Something's up, David. I can hear it in your voice."

"Jeez. I guess they pay you for a reason."

"They sure do," agreed Elliot. "Now what's up?"

I told him about bombing the midterm and about the other kids at CMU. "It's like I signed up for checkers and they all brought chessboards. They're all experts at a game I've never played before. They already know everything."

"How about your other classes?" Elliot asked. "How are they going?"

"Lots of B's."

"B's seem just fine to me."

"I'd always...well...I'd always assumed I was the smartest one around."

"Ah. Well, what else, buddy? I don't mind listening."

The dam broke, and I poured out my anxieties, my feeling of inadequacy in the face of the other students' brilliance.

After listening to me a while, Elliot said, "David, college is a huge transition, and you should expect some bumps. But from my perspective, it seems like you're doing all right." He paused for a minute. "Say, how would you feel if we talked regularly for a few months?"

"I'd love that. Thanks so much!"

I hung up the phone and noticed that the pit in my stomach was gone. I shook my head and smiled. "Well, I'll be damned."

21

A Quarter for Your Past

After my disastrous performance on the Analysis midterm, something shifted, likely related to my phone calls with Elliot. I scored ninety-seven on the Analysis final—the highest in the class. It helped that the material moved on from the cursed delta-epsilon proofs, which I never mastered. Maybe it was the additional time I'd devoted to studying. Regardless, you can rest assured that I caught up with both Josh and Jeremy before the winter holiday to flaunt my score in front of them.

Thanks to that score, a *very* hefty curve, and the fact that half the class had dropped out, I received an A-minus for the semester.

Emboldened by my success, I elected to take six classes my spring semester, including Analysis 2, the continuation of the first-year theory class that had given me so many problems.

"What's wrong with five classes?" Sport asked on our way to Formal Logic.

"I just want to push through the core material and get to the fun stuff," I replied.

"Are you sure? We're around a lot of smart people, David. Everyone else is just fine taking five classes."

"I'm set on six," I said. "What's wrong with that?"

"Nothing, man," he said, shaking his head.

When I ran my plans by Josh, he grinned and extended his hand. "I've opted for six as well. May the best man win."

Experimental Physics—one of the core classes for my major—was a total grind. Tape a marble to a piece of yarn, watch it swing for a bit, and take a few laughably imprecise measurements with a ruler and a stopwatch. Then spend the entire weekend propagating errors in quadrature for twenty fucking pages. Even worse, my hope that I would "get to the heart of the matter" by learning physics turned out to be grossly naive. Everything was an approximation! Complex shapes became circles. Living systems reduced to point masses. If that's what physics was, I wanted no part of it.

In contrast, my computer science classes were mind-bending. They rekindled the thrill I used to get when I programmed my TI-81 calculator up on Masten Lake. Here was a field where theory met reality head-on, where abstract ideas could be transformed into something concrete and useful. I dropped Experimental Physics midway through the semester and switched to a double major in computer science and mathematics.

One spring afternoon, Sport and I were hanging out on Flagstaff Hill, a sloped park with a huge lawn right next to Carnegie Mellon. We were returning from our usual walk, chatting about our three favorite subjects—philosophy, complexity, and women—when Sport pointed at something on the road. "Dude, check out that truck!"

Some kind of rectangular military vehicle was heading our way. While there was someone behind the wheel, he seemed utterly disinterested in driving, instead looking out the driver's-side window.

"Wait," asked Sport, "is he waving at us?" He was, and with both hands.

"Okay," I laughed. "Now he's just fucking with us."

The camouflaged truck passed us directly, and the guy continued staring out the driver's-side window, waving both hands and smiling. Yet the truck took the curve just fine.

Later that afternoon, we asked Don about it.

"Oh, that's the NAVLAB. It's a project from one of the robotics groups in computer science. They're researching how to automate driving."

Remember Hubel and Wiesel's groundbreaking discovery about how the visual cortex processes information? They found evidence that visual processing in the brain is hierarchical, whereby cells in the retina sample circles of light, not dissimilar from pixels in a camera. This information is sent to neurons in the visual cortex that detect edges, which then feed into yet other neurons that recognize more sophisticated patterns. These initial *layers* of processing are thought to be among the first in a series of steps that turn light into representations of the external world that underlie visual understanding.

Their discovery helped inspire computer scientists to create *artificial neural networks*. Just as your brain is hypothesized to process visual information in steps, artificial neural networks are constructed to process information similarly. They start with raw data (like images from the cameras in a self-driving car) and process it through layers of artificial neurons, each layer building on the previous layer's work to ultimately produce a useful computation (like steering directions).

Artificial neurons in artificial neural networks are dramatically simplified versions of real brain cells. Like their biological cousins, they receive information from multiple sources and, if enough signal comes in at once, they fire off their own signal. The connections between these artificial neurons, called *synaptic weights* (or just *weights*), are the tunable parameters of the network, akin to the dial on an old car radio used to find a particular station. Increase the connection strength on important connections, reduce it on less useful ones, and gradually the network learns to perform complex tasks—like keeping NAVLAB between the yellow lines.

While far simpler than a real brain, artificial neural networks can be *trained* to perform complex tasks, such as visual recognition or driving a vehicle. And that's exactly what powered the NAVLAB.

NAVLAB (NAVigation LABoratory) cruised the streets of Pittsburgh powered by an artificial neural network called ALVINN (Autonomous Land Vehicle In a Neural Network). The system used a video camera and laser range finder, feeding images into ALVINN, which outputted driving commands. Imagine how ALVINN processed the information about the road coming from the cameras: First, edges pop out, then curves in the next network layer, then yellow lines, maybe a crosswalk, then, "Hey, is that dog off its leash?!" Finally, an output layer integrates all this information to make a final determination: Turn the steering wheel left fifty degrees.

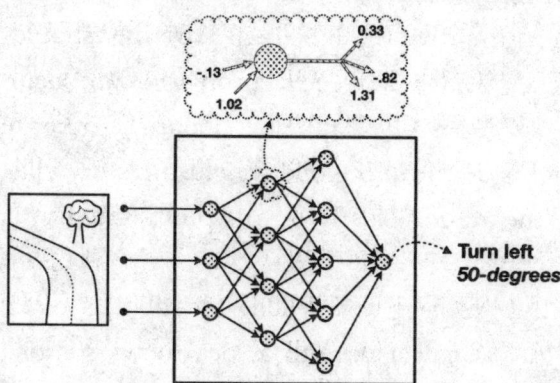

Caption: A feedforward neural network processes an image of the road, transforming raw pixels into a steering command. Each layer extracts increasingly complex features—edges, curves, lane markings—until the final layer outputs a decision: Turn left fifty degrees. Within each layer, artificial neurons compute weighted sums of their inputs, activating only if the total crosses a threshold—flipping like a relay switch when it contributes to the network's learned behavior.

Today's neural networks are built layer upon layer, like a towering stack of specialized processors—which is why they're now called *deep* networks. Deep networks are the workhorses of modern AI, powering everything from the voice assistant on your phone to language translation apps. So if you understand something about neural networks, then you have a pretty clear idea of what's happening behind the scenes in today's AI. But neural networks don't just process information; they can create, too. Submit a text prompt like "a storm lit across her face" to an image-generation system and it will create original artwork that can be so striking and sophisticated, you might think it was made by a human artist.

A modern neural network with tens of layers from input to output and thousands to millions of artificial neurons will have billions to trillions of synaptic weights connecting those neurons (the puny but pioneering ALVINN had a miniscule thirty-five thousand weights). So getting an artificial neural network to function correctly can be quite a challenge. To improve the NAVLAB's driving, should the magnitude of weight #23,632 between neuron #143 and neuron #172 be tuned up 0.6 or down 1.19? And what about the other tens of thousands of weights? Will tuning one weight mess up what were good values for all the others? Clearly, setting these values by hand is a lost cause.

The ALVINN project was headed by robotics researcher Dean Pomerleau. In an interview with a local news station, Pomerleau explained how they got ALVINN to work correctly: "We don't tell it anything, except *steer like I do*. Learn to steer *the way I'm steering right now*."

Pomerleau's point was that the team never wrote ALVINN a driving manual. Instead, they taught ALVINN by example. They *trained* ALVINN using an algorithm called *error backpropagation* or simply *backprop*, which is akin to how a novice driver might learn by closely watching and imitating an experienced instructor's every move at the wheel.

ALVINN's synapse weights were initially set to random values, so it began as a *very* poor driver—your toddler could do better. To improve ALVINN's driving, the team first painstakingly collected data to train the neural network (e.g., thousands of hours of postdoctoral researchers manually driving the NAVLAB truck through Pittsburgh while the camera and laser range finder were active). The postdoc's steering served as the example ALVINN should mimic, given the driving circumstances captured by the sensors. Then the team fed these high-quality human driving examples—paired with the recorded sensor readouts—to ALVINN *while running backprop*, which changed the weights to make ALVINN's driving ever-more similar to the postdoc's.

Backpropagation is a learning algorithm that allows the network to compare its proposed output with the correct target and adjust its internal weights to reduce the difference. In this case, the proposed output is ALVINN's steering decisions, and the correct target is the human's. Backprop works by propagating these performance differences backward through the layers of the neural network so that every single weight gets a tiny responsibility for any mistakes that happen. "Nope, wrong turn; rewind, adjust synapse #724 just a smidge upward.... There you go!" Slowly, through millions of these tiny nudges as assessed across the enormous training dataset of human driving examples, ALVINN's random guesses morph into decent driving. With even more data, a neural network can yield near-human-quality driving.

While the mathematical details of the backpropagation algorithm can be overwhelmingly complex, the intuition is simple. Imagine what you'd like to have changed in your life today: *I sure wish I had a*

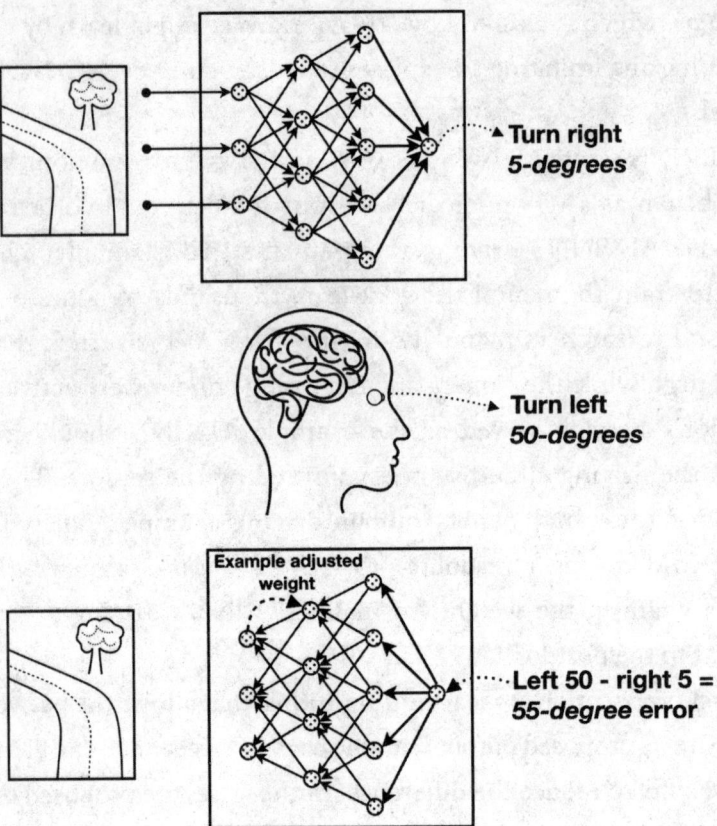

Caption: The neural network ALVINN (top) initially erroneously predicts "Turn right five degrees" when the human, manually driving the NAVLAB (middle), correctly steers "Turn left fifty degrees," resulting in a fifty-five-degree error for ALVINN. The backpropagation algorithm (bottom) calculates this error and propagates it backward through the network (note reversed arrows), adjusting synaptic weights to improve future predictions (e.g., arrow with dashed line). With enough training on human driving examples, ALVINN's synapse weights gradually change such that its initial random guesses transform into reliable driving decisions.

million bucks in my bank account. Then work backward to think about all the tiny changes in the past that might have added up to achieving today's desired outcome: *I should have invested that money in a killer tech stock five years ago* works backward to *I'm going to start saving money so I can invest,* all the way back to *If I really wanted a million in the bank today, I shoulda kept that bad job ten years ago that paid really well.* In essence, the backprop algorithm is like working with an anal-retentive accountant, one who takes note of every small detail that might make a difference in your finances. They compel you to make changes—eat out only one night a week, take a red-eye flight—all slowly building toward that million bucks in the bank.

ALVINN might seem like a rusty relic now, but Pomerleau's group's application of neural networks to autonomous driving was decades ahead of its time. Given that artificial neural networks are ubiquitous in today's technology, one might think that ALVINN would have led to huge academic and commercial interest in the technology, but that's not what happened. While Pomerleau's work was well known in the AI community, the overall perspective on neural networks remained largely negative during the '90s.

The truth is that researchers in the late '80s had begun to sour on neural networks. Computers were slowpokes compared to today's computers, and neural nets were resource hogs in terms of computational requirements. Further, while we know now that neural networks excel at extremely difficult problems, they didn't compare favorably to other approaches on the smaller problems researchers studied at the time. So neural networks' slowness, lackluster performance on simple problems, and difficulty in training effectively with available hardware made them unappealing. Finally, it was well known that neural nets often yielded imperfect solutions. This deeply bothered many AI researchers, many of whom were looking for hard, mathematical proof that they'd taken the correct approach to a problem.

Nearly everyone ditched neural networks for other approaches, such as expert systems or, later, support vector machines. The rest is history: Through the AI winter of the '90s, neural network research came to be viewed as something of a backwater. Except for a few brave souls, the community just sort of moved on.

The revival of neural networks would require a technological breakthrough—one that would come from an unlikely source. While AI researchers were abandoning neural networks, gamers across the world were unwittingly paving the way for AI's future as they pumped quarters into arcade machines.

Finals came and went, and my freshman spring semester ended. I received two A's and three B's. In an era before grade inflation, at a university known for its brutal grading, these were marks to be proud of—especially considering how poorly I'd started in the fall.

As the year wrapped up, Sport, Don, and I discussed what we were going to do for the summer. I was preparing myself for a boring couple of months tucked up in a dorm room on an empty college campus.

"Why don't you come stay with me in Santa Fe?" Don asked me. Don knew I'd grown up in Albuquerque.

"I haven't been back to Santa Fe since I was in second grade. Your family's cool with this?"

"Oh yeah. I've kind of told them about you," he replied.

I wasn't sure what to make of that comment, but I said, "Don, I'd love to go."

A couple of weeks later, Don, Sport, and I drove out to New Mexico, with Sport continuing to his parents' place in Phoenix. We made it to Santa Fe in the middle of the night and pulled off the highway. It was dry and cool out, and the scent of juniper was in the air. There was no light pollution, so we stood outside and smoked a joint as we gawked at the Milky Way, admiring its majestic complexity. I'd forgotten what seven thousand feet of elevation did for a night sky. I breathed in the fresh air and sighed. It felt great to be home.

To earn dough over the summer, I scooped ice cream at the Häagen-Dazs right on the Plaza, the historic old town in Santa Fe. The Plaza is a large square with a park in the middle and adjoining brown adobe buildings on all four sides. Bordered by stores of all kinds, the Plaza is a huge tourist destination; everyone ends up there sooner or later.

Sure enough, I soon ran into my sister. Don and I were at a coffee shop just down the street, and Esther strolled in. She'd blossomed into a blond-haired Amazon topping out at six feet. Esther had a high forehead, as all Sussillos do, a perfectly sculpted nose, and fair skin. Her lips were colored with bright red lipstick. While I looked like my mother, with her soft nose and large lips, it seemed that Esther had taken after my father.

We hadn't seen or talked to each other in two years. She recognized me first and burst into tears on the spot. After I introduced her to Don, we excused ourselves to catch up.

Esther filled me in on the last few years of her life. How she'd left her boarding school in the Berkshires as an independent minor and moved back to New Mexico to live with our father, before he'd been arrested. She'd completed her GED and was now working toward a bachelor's in archaeology at the University of New Mexico down in Albuquerque.

"So, how was it living with our father?" I asked.

"Awful," she said. "He told me he wished he'd never had me. That he should have jerked off into the gutter instead."

"Damn. He was that bad?"

"He was, and I had to put up with it, not you." She was looking down, spinning her coffee cup around in the saucer. "You always had the easy way out."

I thought back to that night I'd woken up to being beaten by half the student home. "I don't know if I'd put it that way," I responded.

"Oh, whatever. The family always liked you best."

"Here we go with the guilt trip," I said.

"James and Beverly took you *in*. Moira and Elliot dumped me in that insane asylum and forgot about me."

"It was a boarding school, Esther," I said.

"I was the one who was there," she retorted, her voice tight with anger.

Just like that, we'd picked up our unfinished fight from the Albuquerque Christian Children's Home. I took a deep breath and got up to refill my coffee. When I got back, the conversation shifted to our childhood.

"Esther, what else do you remember from the early days?"

My sister hesitated. "I don't think you're ready for it. I'll tell you when you're older."

"Older? Esther, I'm in college."

"I remember the early stuff, and I protected you from it."

"Then share it with me. It's my history, too."

Esther took out her lipstick. "No," she said as she reapplied it with deliberate care.

"Dammit, Esther. I'm not a child anymore!"

But Esther refused to go further, insisting her memories were hers alone. I knew next to nothing about my mother despite having lived with her for eight years, so it burned me up that Esther wouldn't confide in me. But I never doubted her claims of remembering terrible things about which I could only guess.

That summer, I also bumped into Jake and Tania Lovato, my second set of houseparents at the ACCH. Tania had introduced me to the library and had had me tested for the gifted and talented program. Jake had taken us inner tubing on the slopes of the desert hills after a big snowstorm. They'd been my favorite houseparents ever.

A Quarter for Your Past

They strolled in for ice cream during the Santa Fe Indian Market. I took my break, and we caught up on the Plaza. They had aged ten years, but Tania still had her blond curls, and Jake was rocking a cowboy hat and a handlebar mustache.

"You both look terrific!" I said.

"Our thirties aren't so bad after all," Jake said.

"Wait...*what*? So you were how old when we were at the ACCH together?" I asked.

"Our early twenties," said Tania.

"Motherfu— Gosh!" My brain nearly broke with the effort of not cursing in front of my old houseparents. "In another couple of years, I'll be the age you were then."

Tania explained that they'd been introduced to the ACCH by their pastor, who'd described it as "a once-in-a-lifetime experience."

Jake nodded. "So we decided to give it a shot."

"Well," I said, suddenly and unexpectedly teary-eyed, "thank you for that." After a moment, I asked about Omar.

Jake looked down and kicked at the grass with one of his cowboy boots. "He's not doing so hot, David."

"Why not?" I asked.

"He's in trouble with the law," he replied.

Omar had been arrested for gang-related activities. He'd been involved in a shooting or a drive-by or some such and was now contending with lawyers and court dates. He had always only ever been one or two steps away from a street tough. That had been his survival strategy. Even if he didn't do time, I gathered Omar's chances of succeeding in life were slim.

"We're praying for him, as we do for all you kids the Lord entrusted us with," Tania said.

* * *

One early evening, after finishing my shift at the Häagen-Dazs, I sat on a bench in the Plaza, relaxing and smoking a cigarette. I noticed a homeless guy right near the Five & Dime General Store. He had a thousand-yard stare going and was absentmindedly panhandling.

The young man looked to the tourists on his left. "Got a quarter?"

Nothing.

A middle-aged couple came in from the right. "How about you? Spare a quarter?"

Ignored again.

As his gaze swept over the Plaza, he looked my way, and his eyes focused. This guy picked himself up off the sidewalk and headed straight toward me, making eye contact the entire time. I watched him approach, wondering what was about to go down.

Upon reaching me, he said, "Hey, was your mother Norma Sussillo?"

The man looked to be in his mid-twenties. He had a spotty beard and that gritty look that comes with hard living. His clothes were filthy, his shoelaces untied.

Oh my god! I know this person! Underneath the grime, it was Shiloh, my best friend from second grade.

"Yes, that's my mother's name. You're Shiloh, aren't you?"

"Yes. You're David."

I nodded.

Dumbfounded, we both just stared at each other for a few moments. Despite a rush of nostalgia, I couldn't bring myself to ask Shiloh how he was doing. It was clear how he was doing—obviously fucking poorly.

Shiloh spoke up first. "I heard a few years ago your mother died. I'm sorry."

"Thanks," I said. "How's your family?"

"They're all out of their fucking minds."

We made awkward conversation for a minute, trying to connect a few dots from our past. It was evident to me, and I assume to Shiloh, that the gulf was unbridgeable. We said goodbye, and that was that. He went back to his spot near the Five and Dime, gathered up his few belongings, and left the Plaza. I watched him go, and he glanced back a couple of times himself.

Eleven years earlier, just before we both left Santa Fe as eight-year-olds, we'd buried our plans and predictions of the future behind his trailer. We'd promised each other with the solemn oaths only children can make that we'd return on our golden birthdays to dig them up together. Providence had allowed us to keep a part of that promise.

In the second grade, we'd been a team, sharing the same desperate circumstances. We'd sweet-talk the ladies at the laundromat for quarters. We'd been thieves at the Kmart and had regularly gone dumpster-diving searching for food.

Watching Shiloh walk away, I couldn't help but feel like I was watching another version of myself. Eleven years. That's how long it'd taken for our lives to diverge. I was finishing my first year in the top-ranked computer science department at Carnegie Mellon. And here was Shiloh looking haggard at nineteen years of age, apparently living on the street, begging for quarters.

However much I'd hated living at the ACCH and all that had followed, it'd apparently been better in the long run than whatever Shiloh had endured. I was forced to conclude that the world was indeed an unknowable, chaotic place.

22

Complex Variables

I thought about Shiloh a lot when I returned to CMU, aware of the distance between our lives and more determined than ever to make the most of my opportunities. My freshman year had been about proving to myself that I had a place at a university like Carnegie Mellon. After a rocky start, positive evidence started rolling in; I belonged. I even got over my fear of entering the buildings.

But when I returned from Santa Fe to begin my fall sophomore semester, those head games from my childhood were very much with me. I still needed to prove that I was special, one of a kind, the greatest. So, on top of my computer science classes, I enrolled in the most demanding math courses I could find, a set of classes called Math Studies. They were effectively four graduate-level theory courses taught to ambitious sophomore undergrads with a death wish. But unlike grad students, we actually gave a shit about our grades; we defined ourselves by them.

Fifteen students enrolled: fourteen young men, including Jeremy and Josh, and a single young woman. Together, this group constituted the Brain Trust, as Sport and Don were now calling us. Childhood aside, these math classes were the hardest undertaking I'd ever attempted, and they just about broke me.

At the beginning of each class, we'd receive theorems we'd have to prove by the end of the following week. Each homework was a new foray into the arcane, a magic carpet ride through the scaffolding of pure mathematics. When I first scanned a homework assignment, I literally didn't understand the symbols on the page. Sometimes I wasn't sure if I was holding the page right side up.

Professor Marvin was one of our three Math Studies professors. He was an odd guy in his late thirties with a shaggy mop of brown curls and glasses on his wide face. He wore Milt house shoes, of all things, those blue canvas slippers with brown rubber soles. Apparently, Professor Marvin didn't care to clip his toenails, though, so the gnarly toenail on each big toe sliced through the canvas, a claw that stuck out of each of his shoes. Once an ultra, always an ultra.

Early on, I took a somewhat adversarial approach to Professor Marvin, perhaps because of his shoes' association to MHS or maybe because I'd concluded he was a jerk. During the midterm that first semester, he passed back the tests. I'd done okay, not stellar but not awful.

As Professor Marvin made his way through the aisles, he passed by the desk of this one young man, Yi-Shin, and dropped the graded test off. He looked at Yi-Shin and said, "You were supposed to take a test, not make par on nine holes of golf."

While the Math Studies homework scared me half to death, the classes were a source of strength and inspiration. I'd always shone brightest in a group setting, and Math Studies was no different. I made a conscious effort to enliven the classes by asking hopefully brilliant but half-mad questions, the hardest ones I could think of while still staying on topic. I actively sought to trip up my genius professor. Maybe if I could ask a clever enough question, I'd get back at our profs for fucking with our heads so hard, and we'd all learn something in the process.

One time, I asked, "How do we know if mathematics is consistent? Will we ever find a contradiction, like discovering a proof that $1 + 1 = 3$?"

Professor Marvin didn't miss a beat. "Most mathematicians think math is consistent. But you'll have to wait for the more complicated answer till we learn about Gödel's incompleteness theorems."

No luck that time.

A few weeks later, I looked over at Jeremy, grinned, and raised my hand way up high.

"Yes, David?"

"Why do some functions have closed-form integrals while others do not?"

Professor Marvin paced back and forth in front of the class, head forward, arms behind his back. He came to a stop and hemmed and hawed for a few seconds. Finally, he said, "This relates to Complex Analysis, which you'll be learning next semester."

Closer.

A month later, I finally got him. "How does a computer have a sense of number?" I asked. This question had been bothering me ever since reading that book on the Pascal programming language that Dana had given me at the ACCH way back in fifth grade.

Professor Marvin stood dead still. Fifteen seconds went by, then thirty. Both his hands found their way to his brown locks in an attempt to massage an answer out of his outsized cerebrum. A minute went by.

Jeremy looked over at me and gave a subtle nod.

Two minutes passed. The students in the class started looking at one another and back at Professor Marvin. Had this guy's brain just gone blue-screen-of-death?

Finally, Professor Marvin said, "That's an interesting question, David. I could answer it"—he looked up at the clock; there were just under five minutes left in class—"but it'd take more time than we have. I'll see you all on Friday."

I didn't know it at the time, but it was a bit of a trick question. Computers don't have a sense of anything; they just have logic circuits that mindlessly implement arithmetic. But that's easy to forget because of modern programming languages, where the details of the hardware have been completely abstracted away.

But like Analysis, Math Studies meant much more to me than just a set of math classes should have. I loved math! But psychologically, the math was incidental.

I would have been just fine if Professor Marvin had said, "Well, students, sorry, but this class isn't really about math. It's about levitation. By the end of your sophomore year, we expect you to know how to float in the air."

Yes. If I'd been required to levitate by the end of the year to pass the course, I would have spent the year trying. It was my mission to prove I was special. It mattered more to me than anything else I'd ever done. It infused my life with meaning.

Both Don and Sport knew I'd enrolled in some crazy math classes and that I was "going through some things." I saw them at the frat house, where we all shared a room that year. They'd inquire about Brain Trust gossip, who'd proved which theorem or who'd finally cracked and dropped out. On Saturday nights, Don, Sport, and I would get hammered. Otherwise, I was cloistered away in some library cubby or at a coffee shop doing math.

And out of nowhere, with the force of a meteor obliterating a snowy Siberian village, I fell in love. Smack in the middle of the mental Ironman of Math Studies.

Just as I hadn't taken my classwork seriously until college, so it was with women. Sure, I'd gone out with a few girls in high school. But at MHS, I was still very much a boy, and the few girls I kissed were still girls, though light-years more mature than I'd been.

By my sophomore year at CMU, a series of events forced me to fess up to an embarrassing truth. When it came to women, I was chickenshit. Thanks to Shiloh and Omar, I was comfortable with intimate friendships, and that crossed gender; indeed, some of my closest friends in high school were girls. But whenever I thought about a physical connection and what that might mean, I'd find excuses to not pick up the phone. At the age of nineteen, I would have never been able to articulate it, but after an institutionalized childhood devoid of physical attention, and the separation from my mother and her untimely death, physical intimacy was just too risky.

Compounding my fears into an outright complex was the fact that I'd never had sex. I'd had a couple of opportunities, but I'd felt vulnerable in the moment and had slowed things down before the critical mass could go nuclear. I knew I was in serious trouble because of a mortifying romantic failure early my sophomore year with a student named Inaya. I'd daydreamed about her for months.

So imagine my surprise when, early in my sophomore year, at a basement party at the frat, Inaya cornered me. We'd been introduced maybe once. I had no idea what to do. Over the next few weeks, we dated, and though I was drawn to her, I was increasingly intimidated by her, strung out on impossibly difficult math and overwhelmed at facing my own limitations. I ghosted her in pure terror.

Midway through the fall semester, I asked Don for advice. My best friend was an absolute chick magnet. We'd be sitting there in the student union café, trying to figure out how a spinning top didn't fall over. Hottie after hottie would drop by, somehow riveted by Don's musings on the conservation of angular momentum.

After making sure the door to our room was closed, I asked, "How do you do it, man? Get with all the ladies, I mean."

"It's easy. I just keep things moving forward."

"Don't you have doubts or worries?" I asked. "Any of that?"

"I try to turn that part of my mind off."

"Just like that, huh?" I asked.

"Dave, you're overthinking it. The crush-from-afar thing doesn't work. Knock it off and take a risk."

This was my state of mind when I met Serra.

Don and I had no plans one Saturday night, so we huffed it up to Squirrel Hill, a residential neighborhood about a mile away from the university, where our friend Bree said a party was going down.

Amid circles of friends chatting and nerds perpetrating a fraud on a makeshift dance floor, I saw her. Full lips and a laugh—damned near a cackle—that I could hear from across the room. Dark, curly hair framing a pale, pretty face. She held court by the keg, gesturing like mad, clearly caught up in some deep conversation with a girlfriend. Then she looked over. She put up a hand, halting our approach. "Who the hell are you two, and how did you get into my party?" she demanded with a playful smile.

"We're friends of Bree," I said, smiling back. After introductions, we got to chatting. Serra had been at the University of Pennsylvania studying chemistry for two years but hadn't enjoyed it. She'd grown up in Connecticut, and—

Another friend of Serra's interrupted our conversation. Don and I wandered off to find Bree.

About a week later, I was at the Coffee Bean, a café halfway between Carnegie Mellon and Pitt. I was deep into a proof concerning the duality of column and row spaces in a linear functional:

```
There exists f: V→F, with F a field such as the
real numbers and V a vector space. Assume that
(f+g)(v) = f(v) + g(v), with v in V...
```

"Hi, David!"

I looked up, and there was Serra.

"Mind if I sit down with you?" she asked, looking around. "The rest of the tables are taken."

I smiled. "Be my guest."

She took her bag off her shoulder and plopped down onto a seat.

We made some light conversation, catching up on the party and figuring out exactly how we knew each other. This line played itself out, so I went back to my proof. Serra got up to buy a latte and, after returning, cracked open a book. The front of it read *The Origins of Totalitarianism* by Hannah Arendt.

"Some light reading there?" I asked.

She glanced over to my page filled with equations. "I might comment along similar lines. Whatcha working on?"

"Oh, I'm trying to prove a theorem from some insane math class I probably shouldn't have enrolled in," I replied.

With that inroad, our conversation turned a bit more personal. Serra was studying English at Pitt but was really focused on women's studies. She was getting a minor in history, thus the Arendt title. I looked at my watch; an hour had passed in a heartbeat. I hadn't made much progress on the proof, but it was time for me to go.

As I made it through the exit, I glanced back at Serra. She was watching me leave.

A couple of days later, about the same time, I headed back to the Coffee Bean to work on the same cursed proof. Who was there but Serra! There were plenty of free tables, but I asked if I could sit down at hers.

So it came to be that Serra and I started hanging out at the Coffee Bean in the afternoons. We studied some and chatted. I learned that Serra's mother was a big-time biomedical researcher at Yale. Her family had moved to New Haven from Seattle when Serra was a young girl.

I shared with Serra my ongoing struggles with my math classes. I spoke of my love of New Mexico, and I gave a couple of hints that my family background was atypical. Over a couple of weeks, I noticed I was studying less and less, and we were conversing more and more. One day, Serra looked up from her book and asked, "Tell me something, David."

"Yes?"

"Are you into women?" she asked.

The question caught me so off guard I could only stare.

"We've been meeting here for three weeks," Serra continued. "What do you think we've been doing? Surely, there's some chemistry between us, or am I missing something?"

"Well—"

"So I'm legitimately curious. Are you into women, or are you above all that?"

I took a breath. "Yes. I'm definitely into women. And yeah, I see what you mean. So, should we go on a date or something?" *God, I'm a dolt.*

"Listen, sweetie," she said. "Here's my phone number." She wrote it down on scrap paper torn out of her journal. She glanced over at my math scribbling. "About the only number, I'll note, that you don't seem to use. Give me a call when you get a break from all that, all right?"

Serra picked up her things, waved goodbye, and departed.

My mistake was ignorance, not paralysis. It hadn't crossed my mind to ask Serra for her number. Thanks to the insanity of my classes, I hadn't allowed myself a moment to think over the last couple of weeks. When a beautiful woman asks to sit down next to you, you say yes. If it happens over and over, you continue saying yes. For once in my goddamned life, I'd done what had come naturally without overthinking it. It just hadn't been enough.

The more I thought about Serra, the more obvious it became that I was wildly attracted to her. I decided I *was* available. I gave her a ring and stumbled all over myself while managing to convey that, no, I wasn't gay. Neither was I about to transcend to the next plane of existence. Yes, I was a moron. Of course I was interested in her, and I'd be honored if she'd find time for me.

Placated, she suggested I go over to her place. For our first official date, Serra made enchiladas, thoughtfully choosing a dish that spoke to my New Mexican roots. But her oven picked that very night to stop working, so she begged a neighbor to use theirs. I'd brought over a cheap bottle of merlot, and we got tipsy waiting for the food.

When the enchiladas were served fully an hour and a half later, they were utterly inedible. Bless her heart, Serra had gone to the trouble of blending up dried red chiles to make her own red sauce from scratch. But it was her first time, so she hadn't seasoned it to taste. As a result, the enchiladas were too spicy. Now, I don't mean slightly too hot for the delicate palate of some milquetoast from Rhode Island. I mean, throw it in the trash and start over, 'cuz you done fucked up, and a single bite will put you in the emergency room, to say nothing of the following morning.

"It's not bad if you drown it in sour cream," Serra said.

"No. Not so bad at all. Can you pass the wine?"

Serra passed the bottle; it was almost empty.

"David, can I ask you a question?" Serra was using her fork to ensure another bite of enchilada went to a sour-creamy grave.

"Sure. Anything," I responded.

"Have you had sex before?" she asked.

I considered my options and went with honesty. "No."

"You're a virgin? A fucking frat boy?" Then she smacked her forehead. "No wonder! It all makes sense now."

"Damn, Serra," I said, pretending I was enjoying her disastrous meal.

"Okay, okay," she said, chuckling. "An honest-to-goodness virgin."

"I'm glad you're finding this funny."

"Meh." She smiled as she shrugged. "We all go through it once."

I could see how Serra had gotten her signals crossed. I'd been introduced to her with Don at my side, that Fabio "I can't believe it's not butter"–looking motherfucker. He'd already managed to hook up with one of her friends. Evidently, Serra assumed I came from the same stock.

We finished up in the kitchen and headed out to the living room. Serra sat down on one side of the couch, and I sat on the other. We lit up cigarettes.

"So," I said.

"So," she replied.

I could reach over and take Serra's hand or kiss her if I wanted to. I did want to. *Now's the time to make a move, dumbass.*

I finished my smoke. "I should get going."

"You can stay here tonight if you want," she said.

"Well..."

"Holy hell, David, are you into me or not?"

Fuck it. I bent over and kissed her.

I started hanging out with Serra *a lot*, and much of our time together was spent in her bedroom. It was a small space occupied primarily by a futon lying low to the floor, with orange tapestries on the walls and candles scattered around the room. We'd listen to Tim Buckley, Leonard Cohen, and Tom Waits. We made love constantly.

One night a couple of months into our relationship, we were lazing about in bed. Serra had just turned on the University of Pittsburgh radio station to catch *Blues Before Sunrise* when she asked why I never talked about my family or my past.

"I can talk about it," I said. "I'm not ashamed or afraid or anything. I just wanted you to know me better before you knew my story. It can throw people."

She put on a naughty smile. "Should I be excited or frightened?"

I laughed.

Then I shared my story with Serra: my drug-addicted parents, the five years at the ACCH, the high school years at MHS. She talked about the complexities of her family life. We lay there for a while, enjoying the music and each other.

Finally, I said, "Serra, I'm falling in love with you."

More time passed. Eventually, Serra said, "Because I asked you about your past?"

"No. Well. That might have greased the gears of conversation. But no, it's been on my mind for a while."

"Are you sure?" Serra asked.

"I'll be honest; I wasn't sure I was capable of it. But yeah, it's kind of hard to miss."

Serra and I often walked the length of Shenley Park down past Flagstaff Hill and CMU and into the neighborhood of Oakland, where we'd hang out with her friends around the University of Pittsburgh. One such time, we went down to Atwood Street. Serra had introduced me to a friend of hers, a guy who called himself the Paladin of Chaos, who owned a secondhand shop filled with curios and geek-chic clothing. By normal standards, I was nerdy as hell, but this dude's nickname was a bridge *way* too far. I couldn't bring myself to do it, so I called him by his real name, Gary, and nerdom be damned.

That day, Gary was playing a game on his computer in the back office. A couple of his friends were standing around, watching. Gary was navigating a marine-looking dude through an incredible rendering of what appeared to be a research facility. Hordes of demons were coming in from all sides, and Gary was doing his damnedest to bust some ass. The marine guy pumped his shotgun and filled demon after demon full of buckshot.

"Get some, hellspawn!" Gary yelled.

"Holy shit!" I said. "This looks amazing!"

Serra smiled. "I thought you might wanna see this."

"Gary, what are you playing?" I asked.

"*Doom!*" he responded, not bothering to look up. "Came out about a year ago—id Software. Best game any of us ever played."

"Can I try?" I asked.

"Hey, get in line!" said one of the guys standing around.

Later that afternoon, I had my first date with a Big Fucking Gun—the BFG9000, to be precise—*Doom*'s most powerful weapon. The game absolutely slayed. Demon guts, shotguns, rockets, and adrenaline-pumping action. No video game I'd ever played was even close to the thrill I experienced that afternoon. The first-person graphics put you right in the action, and you could hook up multiple computers for a death match or enjoy a cooperative campaign with a friend.

Just like *Pac-Man*, *Super Mario Bros.*, or *Street Fighter 2*, *Doom* irrevocably altered the course of gaming history. It's the undisputed father of modern first-person video games, from *Halo* to *Half-Life 2*, and a guaranteed entry on any "greatest games of all time" list. No major first-person title since has existed without echoes of *Doom*'s groundbreaking achievements.

But the gaming revolution set off by *Doom* had deeper implications than any of us realized at the time. I venture a bolder claim: *Doom*, with its mind-blowing graphics, might have inadvertently set the stage for the end of the 1990s AI winter. While artificial neural networks wouldn't fully showcase their potential for another fifteen years, I think *Doom* was the prologue. Of course, it wasn't a straight shot from the BFG9000 to the backpropagation algorithm used to train neural networks.

By the early '90s, artificial intelligence research had hit a wall. Neural networks had shown promise for decades, and by the '80s, researchers had even figured out how to train them using backprop. But there was a fundamental problem: Neural networks were computational beasts that required massive processing power, and the computers of the day were just too slow. Training even simple networks took forever and often failed. Frustrated, most AI researchers abandoned neural networks entirely, moving on to other approaches that seemed more practical. The field entered what became known as the "'90s AI winter"—a period where neural network research was mostly viewed as a dead end.

Enter *Doom*. Released late in 1993—the same year that the NAVLAB piloted by the neural network ALVINN was cruising around Pittsburgh—*Doom* revolutionized computer graphics with its immersive first-person perspective. Rendering this visually accurate world at playable speeds required unprecedented processing power. As the first-person video games that *Doom* inspired pushed hardware limits, a new technology emerged to meet the demand: graphics processing units (GPUs). Though GPUs wouldn't fully take off until the late 1990s, their design for massively parallel matrix-matrix multiplications[1]—operations critical for efficient graphics rendering—would later prove invaluable for neural network research. That's because artificial neural networks feast on the same mathematical operations as flashy graphics, so they could benefit from all the acceleration that GPUs provided.[2]

And so I argue that *Doom*, this blood-soaked game no mother could condone, became an unexpected catalyst to the technological ecosystem that would eventually enable AI's resurgence. Inadvertently, it fostered the technological advancements that would solve a major bottleneck in neural network research of the '90s—slow execution speed. Of course, GPUs alone weren't enough—it would take another decade before researchers fully realized what they had, and even longer before the pieces came together: massive datasets from the early web, algorithmic breakthroughs, and finally the computing power to make it all work. When they did, neural networks' triumphant return in the 2010s and beyond would reshape everything from self-driving cars to language translation to intelligent chatbots.

23

The Oracle Hive Mind

By the time my junior year at CMU rolled around, I'd learned to implicitly trust both my creativity and intellect. I'd successfully run the gauntlet of Math Studies, so I viewed the rest of my coursework as little more than absorbing material—still important and challenging, but not the test of mettle that those math classes had been. Although much of my time was occupied with Serra, I found myself somewhat aimless. So when a professor approached me with a new research idea, I was ready to rock and roll.

Professor Barrett Fingo and I met in line for coffee in the lobby of Wean Hall. Our conversation turned to the internet; we both were fascinated by how it was going to change society. I mentioned I was in the computer science department and had taken the Math Studies classes, which were infamous in the nerdier hallways of CMU. Professor Fingo invited me back to his office for further conversation.

Once there, the professor bounced in his chair with a youthful energy that contrasted with his buttoned-up appearance: perfectly groomed beard and horn-rimmed glasses. "I've got something cooking that I think you could make a valuable contribution to. It's an idea for information retrieval revolving around one's network of friends and colleagues. Basically, it'll let anyone answer almost any question for a nominal fee. You'd be the primary research programmer. Any interest?"

"When do I start?"

Professor Fingo—who insisted on being called Barrett—was something of a computer science hotshot. He'd been a kick-ass database theorist back in the day, and by the time I met him, he was conceiving ways that humans would interact with software and one another once everyone on the planet was connected via the internet.

His idea was an information retrieval system called OracleHiveMind (OHM). If you had a question you'd pay to have answered, you could submit it to the OHM website. You'd be able to discover the solution to anything so long as someone on the planet already knew the answer. Nowadays, we'd use a search engine or ask an AI chatbot if we had a question, but this was the earliest of early days on the internet.

It was the first social networking idea I'd ever heard of. Keep in mind, this was 1995; Mark Zuckerberg was eleven years old. Though Barrett turned out to be dead wrong about folks' willingness to part with their money for information, he was at least ten years ahead of the curve in appreciating the social potential of software. The guy was a walking, talking Facebook advertisement eight years before the company existed.

Our arrangement was that in my spare time I'd build the OHM software from soup to nuts, and I'd draw a salary for my efforts. So I put down my pencil and paper, closed my math textbooks, and started spending way more time in the computer lab.

Barrett took me under his wing. He taught me how to think in pairs, give space to another mind, and visualize concepts using a whiteboard. We became friends, spending time in the office together and in his Volvo driving to and from campus. Together, we watched the AI Deep Blue beat Garry Kasparov in chess, pondering the implications for mankind afterward. He commented once on the philosophy class I was taking, saying, "I just don't know what to think of philosophy that existed before computers." I was speechless, seeing his point at once.

A few months into our collaboration, I attended Shabbat at Barrett's place and met his wife and children. Later that night, he asked me if I'd be interested in tutoring his kids in math. Barrett had a way of making me feel special. I began to look up to him as a father figure, and I felt he saw me as more than just an employee.

By the time my junior academic year wound down, I'd made so much progress on the software that Barrett transformed the project into a company, also called OHM. Initially, I was the only employee, but I ended up hiring a bunch of friends from my CS and Math Studies classes, including Josh, Jeremy, and Don.

As more and more of my friends realized I was the source of money and exciting work, I became something of a big man on the CMU campus, a welcome and novel feeling. It was the first time in my life I wasn't broke. In fact, I was sleeping on a mountain of Benjamins. I was a college senior in dirt-cheap Pittsburgh, making $40,000 a year. I know that sounds like peanuts these days, but I had five roommates in a row house apartment that cost me no more than two hundred bucks a month, and my classes were covered. This money was transformative—and not just for my lifestyle. It gave me a wonderful sense of security I'd never experienced before.

When my senior year rolled around, I began to wonder how to manage a full load of classes while keeping the momentum going at the start-up. We'd grown to twenty people, most of them programmers, and I was the technical lead. I'd become so busy overseeing everything that I decided to go to school part-time and finish my degree in two years instead of one. Barrett didn't encourage this choice, but neither did he discourage it.

It was in this period of expansiveness, early my senior year, that I received an email from Esther from out of the blue:

Hi David,

It's your sis! It was great to see you in Santa Fe a few years ago! I just broke up with my boyfriend and need a place to land. Can you help me out with some money? Maybe I can hang with you in Pittsburgh?
Let me know, k?

XOXO,
Esther

After a bit of thought, I figured, *Sure, why not?* I hardly knew my sister, our chance encounter in Santa Fe notwithstanding. I had some trepidation, but I was curious, too.

My thoughts turned to Serra. By my senior year, we'd broken up, but we'd remained good friends, so I arranged a meetup to see if she could put Esther up in her apartment, as I knew there was a spare room. Serra pulled some strings, and just like that, Esther had a place to stay.

I picked my sister up at the airport when she arrived in Pittsburgh. She came out of the gate, we hugged, and she took me by the shoulders, sizing me up. She grimaced. "Dear brother, did you go on a shopping spree at the mall? We'll have to get you cleaned up."

I was miffed, having pretty much recently gone on a shopping spree at the mall. But if there was one thing my sister knew well, it was beauty and fashion. After some cajoling, I acquiesced to a visit to a hair salon that saw the end of my long hair. We rummaged all over town through consignment shops, and the next thing you know, I was looking like an indie-rock hipster. Yet one more makeover in a life full of them. I had to admit, it was a significant improvement.

Esther and I met up three weeks later for coffee to see how she was settling in.

"So…you dated Serra."

"Yep." I smiled.

"She's…well…a little mousy, don't you think?"

"Serra? She's as far away from mousy as you can get. A real firecracker!"

"It takes all kinds, I guess," she said, studying her nails.

My jaw clenched. "That 'mouse' was kind enough to take you in on short notice."

"Fine, but she's not all that, you know."

"Esther, am I missing something here?" I asked. "Are you two not getting along?"

"Whatever." She crossed her arms. "I don't want to discuss it."

Two months later, Serra asked to talk, so we met at the local dive, ordered a couple of beers, and sat down at a booth.

"Esther's got to go." Serra's face was serious. "She's a nightmare."

"Okay. But can I ask, what's the problem?"

"Everything! She insults me and my roommates constantly. She refuses to put on a sweater in the middle of winter in Pittsburgh and then won't shut up about being cold."

Serra was nothing if not levelheaded, and I began to wonder how well I knew my sister. Already in her brief stay in Pittsburgh, she'd established a bad habit of calling me up to ask for money. My mind returned to Serra, and I said, "I'm sorry. I never should've asked you to—"

"So, we've come to a decision. Esther has been making noises about returning to Portland. The girls and I are just going to"—Serra made a pushing motion—"give her a little help."

"How's that?"

"You know how she's always broke?"

I took a big swig of my beer and gave a vigorous nod.

"We're going to buy her a plane ticket." Serra smiled. "Then present it to her as a gift."

"Holy shit. Are you that desperate to see the back of her?"

"Yes! We all are. And it'll be great. No fuss, no muss," she gestured as if wiping dust off her hands.

A couple of weeks after the conversation with Serra, Esther showed up at the OHM office unannounced in the middle of the workday. Everyone was there: Barrett, the admin staff, Jeremy and Josh from the Brain Trust, and Don.

My sister burst through the door, her eyes wild and makeup smeared. As she made her way toward me in the middle of the open office space, she blurted out, "David, I don't know what I'm going to do! I don't have any money in my bank account."

Esther had never once come to visit me at the office, and I was instantly nervous. "Let's talk outside, Esther." I made my way toward her.

"David, you aren't listening! I'm broke, and our parents never helped us!"

I glanced over at my coworkers. They were statue stiff, heads pointed toward monitors. But the clickety-clacking of the keyboards had stopped.

"Come on, let's take this outside, Esther. Please." I reached for her arm, trying to guide her toward the door.

She wrenched away from me. "You just want to get rid of me!" she said, raising her voice to a near scream. "You sit here in your little company, writing your little programs. Aren't you just the king of your little world? What about *me*, David?"

Jeremy and Josh exchanged uncomfortable glances even as they pretended to work. Esther stood there crying, dark runnels of mascara-darkened tears cutting through her base makeup. I grabbed a tissue from a nearby desk and handed it to her, desperate to end this scene.

"Maybe you could give me some money?" Esther asked. "Keep me going, you know, just a little bit longer until I get back on my feet?"

"Well, Esther, I don't know," I hedged.

"I have nothing, David! *Nothing!*"

Don abruptly stood up and left the office.

"Okay, Esther. Let's go to the MAC machine; there's one at the corner."

With this, Esther agreed to be led out of the office. When we got to the ATM, I took out two hundred bucks and gave it to her, and she took off.

I returned to the office, my face burning with embarrassment. Don pulled me aside. "Everything okay?" he asked. I nodded, not sure how to even begin explaining.

A month later, Esther left on a plane bound for Portland. Her stay had lasted just four months, and she'd managed to anger or alienate every person in Pittsburgh who'd shown her a modicum of kindness. Frankly, I was glad to see her gone. She could roll from crisis to crisis on someone else's emotional and financial tab. As I watched her plane take off, I couldn't help but wonder how she could possibly land on her feet.

Fall led into spring, and I deprioritized my studies even further to build Barrett's business. But as my responsibilities and stress at the office had mounted over the last year, I'd seen less and less of Barrett.

He was at Carnegie Mellon, focused on his professorship, while I was down in the trenches, with my bachelor's degree very much a secondary concern. It was thanks to *my* recruiting efforts that Barrett had managed to siphon off extraordinary talent from the senior year computer science class.

My discontent became so strong that I broached the topic with another programmer at OHM, Eve. She'd been a top student in the Math Studies program, so I'd interviewed and ultimately hired her.

"Oh yeah. Exactly my experience," Eve said. "I initially thought I had a special mentorship with Barrett. But then I took the job, and he just disappeared. I guess I wasn't so special in his eyes after all."

With the realization that I hadn't understood the nature of our relationship—that I wasn't even unique in my misunderstanding—my discontent metastasized into full-blown disaffection. I'd seen Barrett as a father figure, something I craved, whereas he saw me as a worker, a gifted kid who could get shit done.

I knew trouble was brewing, because I'd become a total bore, bitching about OHM to anyone who would listen. In late March, I used the spring break to visit Sport in Phoenix, who'd had to leave CMU after a scholarship fell through. We were hiking South Mountain, and I should've been enjoying the tranquility of the desert landscape, but instead, I chewed Sport's ear off.

"You're burned out, Dave," Sport said after listening for the better part of an hour. "It's obvious to everyone. Except for you and Barrett, it seems."

"I guess so," I replied.

"You *guess* so? David, you've been racing at a hundred miles an hour since the very first day I met you. First Analysis, then Math Studies, and now you're building a freaking start-up, and you haven't even finished college!"

"It's one of my superpowers from group-home life," I said as I kicked a loose rock. "A pathologically strong work ethic."

The source of my stress at OHM wasn't the tech; it was the people and managing a million tiny details under deadlines. You may be thinking, *Welcome to life, kid.* Okay, fine. But a displeased housefather lived in the back of my mind, checking over every unimportant item on my to-do list. If my work wasn't perfect, it was a failure. And black and white ruled the day with interpersonal conflict as well. With limited resources and time, there was always someone who was disgruntled or an argument I couldn't smooth over. My emotional system told me I was at war when everyone else thought we were having a minor disagreement. I'd grown up in group homes where a claustrophobic unison among all people all the time was essential for my emotional well-being and often my physical safety.

I had to face the facts: Group-home life had turned me into a high-end amplifier. Within a narrow range of stress or conflict, I was as attuned as they came, easily able to read the room and sort things out. But push me just a little bit further, and I'd hit the rails with all manner of accompanying emotional distortion. It seemed the only difference between Esther and me was how fast saturation occurred.

Barrett must have finally picked up on the signs, because he arranged a meeting outside of the office at a local park. When we met, it was just the two of us.

Barrett began, "I know we've been swamped lately. You've been on my mind, though."

I just looked at him.

"I wanted you to know how important you are to OHM. So I bought you something."

Barrett walked around to the back of his white Volvo station wagon, opened the hatch, and rummaged around for a minute. He brought out a box and gave it to me. The side read *Palm Pilot*.

A goddamned personal organizer? I tried to muster a smile as I accepted the box. "Thank you, Barrett," I said. "It looks cool."

It was actually a lovely gift, and I got about a zillion hours of pleasure playing *Dope Wars* on that thing. But an electronic gadget designed to improve my professional productivity couldn't possibly bridge the rift that had grown between us.

I finally cracked later that summer after my senior year. I gave no notice. I just quit OHM and fuck everyone and their mothers as I slammed the office door on the way out.

But at that point, I needed money. My financial aid had run out at the end of my senior year. When I'd been earning a steady paycheck from OHM, I could swing those last four classes myself. But without that job, the numbers didn't add up. In a rash decision, I decided to move to Boston to work at a video game / AI start-up.

The student adviser for the School of Computer Science, Mike Dino, caught wind of my withdrawal from school and called me in for a check-in. After offering me a seat, he looked down at his notes. "It's not every day that a highly regarded senior walks away with four classes left, David. What's up?"

"Well, I've always loved video games, so I'm excited about this opportunity with Lifesource. And they're starting up in Boston," I replied.

"What happened with OHM?" he asked.

"I guess I was kind of done with that place. I think the opportunity at Lifesource is better," I said.

"Mm-hmm." Mike took his glasses off and rubbed the bridge of his nose. He gave me a penetrating stare and then looked back at his notes. "With the internet going mainstream, there's a lot of dollar signs in people's eyes right now."

"I'm mostly interested in the opportunity to learn about artificial intelligence," I said.

Mike looked back up at me. "I thought this was about video games."

"Oh...well, AI and video games," I said.

"I'll level with you, David. I'm not sure what's going on here. Care to tell me?"

I shifted in my seat, wanting badly to avoid Mike's penetrating stare. How could I level with this guy? How could I tell him that I'd stupidly looked up to Barrett as a father figure? That I'd poured my life's blood into his company under the never-spoken assumption that part of my compensation was the warm attention and benevolent mentorship I'd missed my entire childhood? I'd been a goddamned idiot. "Nothing's going on, sir," I finally said.

"If that's how you want to play it, fine. But it's my responsibility to tell you that most students who do what you're about to do never finish their degree. They don't come back."

"Oh, no, sir. I have every expectation of finishing," I said.

"I hope so," he responded.

As I left Mike Dino's office, his words echoed in my mind. He'd as good as told me I was making a mistake.

24

Boston Shakers

Imagine a pile of rice—the Platonic ideal of a cone—rising to a single, perfect peak. Now imagine individual grains of rice falling, one by one, on top of this pile. The first grain lands softly and rolls to a stop without any visible impact. Grains continue to fall; now and again, a tiny avalanche occurs—just a few grains moving down the pile. Less frequently, a grain of rice falling on the pile induces a larger avalanche. And once in a great while, a single grain falls and *boom*! There's a full-scale avalanche that changes the entire structure of the rice pile.

The rice pile demonstrates a concept in physics called *self-organized criticality*—a phenomenon where complex systems naturally evolve to a critical state. In this state, even small perturbations can trigger large-scale events. And it's not just rice; this principle extends to various natural phenomena, from avalanches in mountainous terrains to the sudden release of tectonic stress in earthquakes.

It also applies to biological structures, including the human brain. Networks of neurons in the cerebral cortex—the outer layer of our brains—exhibit patterns of electrical activity known as *neural avalanches* hypothesized as a potential signaling mechanism, where small inputs might trigger spreading waves of activity that help distribute information across the brain.

While neural avalanches are well documented, the concept of self-organized criticality might extend further. It's conceivable that this principle governs more complex brain dynamics, including those underlying our emotional states. If so, our psychological resilience might operate much like our rice pile, accumulating stress until it reaches a critical point.

In my first twenty-two years, I'd stockpiled a lifetime of stressors, tiny shifts in the earth under my feet. Most were no more significant than a grain of rice. But it was a magnificent emotional pile, and by the time I moved to Boston, it had achieved self-organized criticality. The Big One was about to hit.

Lifesource was out in a dull suburb of Boston called Newtonville, right next to that overpass above the Mass Pike with the Star Market on it. The only redeeming aspect of my new workplace was the daily interaction with the attractive young women at the Dunkin' Donuts counter that I patronized every morning. My breakfast included a french cruller, a coffee regular, and a "How are you this morning, David?" The accompanying smiles were the most nourishing part of the meal.

My job at Lifesource was, yet again, the hardest thing I'd ever attempted. The company was developing a specialized programming language for video game AI, along with a compiler to make it run on a computer. Lifesource had hired a PhD named Linus to write the first pass of the compiler. He was a true genius, and I don't use the word lightly. In my CS classes at CMU, which aggregated exceptional talent from across the planet, I'd met one or two real-life geniuses. People about whom I'd say, "They weren't like most students at CMU, and their abilities would scare the bejesus out of you."

Linus was one such dude, a wizard of compilers and programming languages.

A compiler is like a magical translator. Briefly, it takes human instructions, like this simple BASIC program:

```
> 10 PRINT "David is cool"
> 20 GOTO 10
> RUN
```

and turns them into the language of 0s and 1s that a computer can execute.

First, it considers the vocabulary: Yep, *PRINT* and *GOTO* are recognized words. Next comes the grammar; yes, a number follows GOTO, so we're cool. The compiler then slowly lowers those human-level ideas down into the binary code that can be run on the computer hardware. This happens layer by precise layer, chopping, slicing, dicing, and reorganizing until all interpretability is lost and only meaning is preserved. By the end, the compiler lays out the program as a thousand tiny, specific instructions, like "take the number 0x153753 from memory slot M15 and the number 0x935793 from slot M89, add them together, and put the result into the register R37." Only then can the central processing unit mindlessly execute the program at billions of instructions per second—and, zooming all the way back out to the human level, create magic for a young boy as he sees his name spill all over the monitor of a Trash-80 computer.

As you might imagine, writing a compiler is no joke. In fact, it's considered one of the most challenging programs to write or reason about. But that was my job—to understand the compiler that insane genius-with-a-pulsating-brain Linus had written. I had no clue how his mind worked, yet I had to master and then innovate upon what he'd built. He was moving on to an assistant professorship, which meant he'd be around for only a few months. To make matters worse,

Linus had never moved to Boston, so the best I could do was get him on the phone.

My work routine was as follows: Drive out to Newtonville through the snow and ice of the busted Boston winter in my ancient 1988 Toyota Camry, grab my breakfast from Dunkin' Donuts, flash a grin, and head into the office.

I'd park myself at my desk and get to work. Then began a contest of wills, a battle royale that could have been on pay-per-view, *David vs. the Compiler*. After getting worked over for five hours straight, the Olympics of the mind transitioned to a marathon of emotions. Sometime after lunch, overwhelming frustration kicked in. So back to the doughnut shop for a double chocolate, coffee regular, and another smile. Then I'd finish out the afternoon swearing under my breath. By five or six, I'd be cursing up a storm so loud I could be heard two rooms over. *How the fuck had I been talked into taking this fucking job?* Barely contained rage was my cue to go home. I'd get back in my blue Camry, turn on a classic rock station, and belt out the tunes while concentrating on the icy roads.

Boston was the first place I'd ever lived alone. Ever since I was eight years old, I'd lived in large groups. In college, it was a snug set of four or five. My roommates, while great guys, had been a wild bunch, so I figured, *What the hell, let's give this solo thing a shot.*

I managed to land a one-bedroom apartment in Brighton, just off the Chestnut Hill reservoir. I kept my pad sparse, almost like a monk's quarters. I hung no art or posters on the wall, though I did place my indestructible philodendron near the window that overlooked a playground. My queen-size mattress lay on the bedroom floor, and an outdoor plastic patio set served as my kitchen table and chairs.

I had one, maybe two, friends from Lifesource. My college buddies Sport and Don had taken jobs in other parts of the country. I had no dating prospects whatsoever. Thanks to my time with Serra, I no longer wilted around women; I was merely cautious. But I had no one to talk to and no support structure. I hadn't been in regular contact with my Uncle Elliot since those phone calls my first year at CMU. Nor had I been in touch with my Aunt Maria from Masten Lake. My relationship with James and Beverly had never recovered from our ill-fated year together.

I quickly realized that I had too much time on my hands. Lonely, quiet time. At first, I played online chess to pass the hours but finally gave it up after realizing it was indistinguishable from work. I always lost, it hurt my head, and I wanted to punch babies by the end. I tried my hand at jazz piano, but the lessons only served to confirm my long-held suspicion that I was a musical no-talent. Even going out to a bar for a couple of beers and pinball wasn't much fun without any drinking buddies.

My weekends stretched out to an eternity. A typical Saturday looked something like this: Get up at 8:00 a.m. and drink coffee. Futz. Look at the clock. It's 10:00 a.m.; I'll go for a walk. Okay, it's noon. Now what? I'll cook something. Look up at the clock; it's 2:00 p.m. Drive around! Contend with Boston traffic for an hour and a half, say screw it, turn around, and be back in the apartment by 4:30 p.m. Now what? *Tick. Tick. Tick. Tick.*

I realized I hated Boston. Even locals who lovingly sing her praises—all the while sitting outside in the snow for hours to fend off would-be interlopers from *their* cleared parking spot—will agree that Boston can be unfriendly to newcomers. If you grew up there, you were happy as a clam. If you were nestled in one of the many colleges in and around the metro area, you were in like Flynn. Otherwise, Boston was an ice pick to the lonely soul.

To kill time, I started reading the Russian classics. I read *The Brothers Karamazov, Crime and Punishment, Anna Karenina*, and *The Death of Ivan Ilyich*. After plowing through those chucklefests, I moved on to religious texts. In no particular order, I read the *Tao Te Ching*, started up on the Bible again, read parts of the Quran, all of the Bhagavad Gita, and not a few Zen Buddhist texts.

I began to wonder about the absolute limits of the human experience. What did it mean to be perfect, and what was enlightenment? What was a saint? Why was I here, and why the hell was I working? I started meditating, not having a clue but giving it a try anyway.

So that was my routine for six months. Drive to work each day and bang away on the compiler. Head home, make some dinner, and endure the brutality of unending silence. When I couldn't stand it any longer, I'd crack open a religious text to try to make some headway, wondering what it meant for me.

In hindsight, it's clear that I was lost. Most people's lives begin in their early twenties; psychologically, mine was ending. My ten-year commitment to educate myself was essentially complete. With no long-term objective to focus on and no smaller distractions, the solitude of my first year in Boston triggered emotions and thought patterns that I'd managed to ignore for years. I found myself coping in ways similar to when I first entered the Albuquerque Christian Children's Home: becoming inwardly focused, studying religion with renewed intensity, and indulging in a bit of grandiosity. These things had nourished me as a child, providing a sense of control in an uncontrollable environment. But now, it was simply maladaptive behavior.

The first sign that I might be having problems came over the Christmas holiday. A bunch of my fraternity brothers had returned home to Boston, and we all agreed to go out to the bars on Newbury Street. As the bartender shouted last call, George Thorogood came on the jukebox, "One bourbon, one scotch, and one beer." On impulse, I offered to buy this trio of drinks for anyone on the stipulation that they had to knock back all three at once.

Pandemonium broke out immediately afterward. The next thing I knew, a pack of drunk frat boys were jousting with discarded Christmas trees in the middle of Commonwealth Avenue into oncoming traffic, and then removing furniture from the lobby of a random apartment building. Call it luck or grace that the lot of us weren't arrested and thrown into the drunk tank.

The next day, I recovered from my raging hangover while watching TV. There was this one newscaster who wouldn't shut up, and it seemed to me that the guy's face was being controlled by his mustache, which might be an alien. I told myself the thought was silly, but I couldn't get the idea out of my head. Weeks later, I was still perseverating on that guy's mustache for no reason whatsoever.

I started having nightmares. If you're ever in a dream playing piano duets with a benevolent female poltergeist, and she tells you to stay focused on the keyboard and not to look back, for the love of all that is good, do not look back! I woke up screaming at the top of my lungs.

Then came the day that I'll remember for the rest of my life. I discovered a new fact of the lived human experience. You can simultaneously feel a thing and not be aware of it. I know this sounds nuts; the verb *to feel* implies that you're aware of your feelings. But it's not always true. There must be a gate in your head that separates the conscious from the unconscious. That day, the gate opened slowly enough that I observed it happening.

I was sitting at my desk at Lifesource, writing a debugger for our godforsaken compiler. A coworker of mine was whistling, as was his irritating habit. I asked him to knock it off, and he did. Yet still, I couldn't focus. After a few minutes of reading the same line of code over and over, I took a break and took stock. What was going on?

I noticed my heart rate was elevated. *That's strange; I've been sitting at my desk for a while.*

I was freezing, yet my head was sweating. *Why would I be sweating? Dana keeps the office at a cool temperature.*

Then I felt it. *I'm kinda fidgety. Well, no, more like nervous. No, that's not right, either. Am I frightened? It's more than that. I'm freaking out! For no reason at all!*

I sat there for over a half hour with this new awareness, wigging the fuck out. *Is this a heart attack? Am I dying? Am I going crazy?* I had no idea what to do, so I sat completely rigid, hands flat on the desk, eyes all bugged out, glancing left and right. Attempting to program only made things worse.

The feeling finally dissipated, and I became exhausted. It was as if I had partied all night and then ran ten miles first thing in the morning. I went home and collapsed on my mattress.

What I experienced that day goes by many names—terror, dread, panic. A panic attack is, by definition, the most potent fear you can experience and has the prominence of overwhelming pain. Whatever you were doing beforehand loses all importance. When a panic attack takes you, you can't knock it off, you can't tell it to stop, and if some ignoramus tells you to "just snap out of it," you'll want to punch the motherfucker; I promise.

Imagine the most frightening thing that's ever happened to you—you'd do everything in your power to avoid it. But with panic attacks, you have all the fear but no sense of agency. Did *you* cause it? Or was it Bob Dylan's voice as he sang "Lay Lady Lay" on your car ride home? Who the hell knows? No agency means no calm.

So between the intensity and the lack of control, you worry about it happening again—a lot. It's a new and separate anxiety from the panic itself. You can even induce a panic attack by worrying about having one.

Before that first panic attack hit, I hadn't noticed my anxiety, though in hindsight, it had been there for at least a month. But once it was front and center in my consciousness, the floodgates of terror were thrown open. These attacks started occurring on a near-daily basis, with breaks in between that consisted of exhaustion and low-level chronic worry about when the next one would come. It was hard to believe that not a year before, I'd been very much on top of my game (if somewhat burned out from four intense years at college) and helping to start up OHM.

There was a bit of relief. I became friendly with my next-door neighbor. He was a Berklee College of Music graduate and introduced me to jazz and John Coltrane. Art stopped being a foreign concept to me as I understood the relief it could provide. Listening to Coltrane and Eric Dolphy's strangely melodic screaming to the gods became my nightly medicine.

As late winter turned to early spring, I found myself avoiding work. The last thing I could handle was losing my shit at the office. I lost the desire to eat. Then depression set in. I just couldn't be bothered anymore. My favorite new pastime became turning on the shower and sitting in the tub for long stretches. I stopped getting out of bed. What was the point? My life had been reduced to its two bare essences—terror and waiting for terror. Letting the drama play out on the comfort of my mattress seemed as fine an idea as any.

The first time I didn't get out of bed, it was a weekend. Saturday passed. Then Sunday. Then Monday rolled around, and I couldn't find a way to get up and go to work. Tuesday was the same. Finally, on

Wednesday, a knock came on the door. I got out of bed, threw on a T-shirt, put on my game face, and answered the door.

It was Craig from Lifesource. Craig had replaced Linus and was my direct partner on the compiler project.

"Hey, Craig," I said from behind a door I'd opened no more than a few inches.

"David, how are you? Jeez, we hadn't seen you in the office, so I told the guys I'd stop by to see if everything was all right."

"I'm fine. I'm sorry for not phoning. I'm just a bit under the weather," I lied.

"Would you like me to get anything for you? Maybe some Tylenol or cough medicine?"

"No, I'm getting better. Thanks for stopping by." I practically shut the door in Craig's face.

When I returned to work the next day, Craig said, "I'm sure glad you're feeling better. Dang, though, I was nervous I'd have to break the door down, and I'd see you hanging from the rafters."

Right then and there, I had a panic attack at the idea that my coworker thought I'd killed myself. I fled the office and finally calmed down when I went over to Dunkin' Donuts and ordered a coffee. I concluded I had to at least get my ass out of bed and into work unless I wanted to find out what a full-scale nervous breakdown really looked like.

It was early summer. I'd been having panic attacks for five months. Outside of work, I'd become something of a shut-in. But the weather was great, so I navigated my way up to the roof of my four-story apartment building. I enjoyed the warmth of the sun and the view, breathing deeply of the scent of trees still in blossom.

Then I walked a bit closer to the edge and looked down. It was asphalt directly below.

I could do it.

A fence divided my building's parking lot from the playground of the adjacent elementary school. It was a Saturday, so no kids were around. But the empty swings swayed in the breeze, and the basketball hoop stood sentinel over the silent court. For a moment, the scene stirred something in me—a faint echo of the past, of promises made long ago.

No way. Not now. But if I can't figure my way out of this shit, there's always this.

I have to be honest; I took incredible relief in knowing that there was an escape from the fear if all else failed. But I wasn't anywhere close to that yet. I went back downstairs to my apartment and my misery.

I resolved to talk to someone. But to whom? I had serious confusion about therapy. On the one hand, there were my Uncle Elliot and Aunt Moira, both psychotherapists, who'd had a positive impact on me throughout my life. On the other, there was the failed therapy from when I lived with James and Beverly. To crystallize the quandary, that year while I lived in Boston, *Good Will Hunting* came out. While I loved the movie, I just didn't buy that six months of conversations with a therapist, no matter how compellingly played by Robin Williams, were going to magically alleviate the serious problems the main character was contending with.

A week after the rooftop, I took a walk around the Chestnut Hill reservoir. Along the way, I sat down on a bench next to a well-dressed man in his late forties. He had one or two missing teeth, was smoking a cigar, and appeared to be enjoying the ducks and geese paddling through the water. I've no memory of how we got to speaking or how we opened up to each other. Still, after twenty minutes, I'd revealed I was dealing with debilitating anxiety, and he'd explained he was a practicing Catholic with a heroin habit. It was as if the universe had summoned my father in a moment of terrible need.

Next, I made an appointment with my doctor, whom I'd never met before. Being a twentysomething and physically healthy, I'd chosen my GP by pointing randomly at the list of names in the insurance pamphlet. When I arrived at his office, people from all walks of life filled the waiting room. Each time someone came out of the back office, they thanked the doctor profusely and hugged him. Clearly, this was a man who garnered respect and was unlike any doctor I'd ever interacted with.

"So what brings you in?" Dr. Subramanian asked when we finally met.

"I'm extremely anxious. It's getting in the way of my life."

"How anxious?"

"I think I'm having panic attacks."

"Ouch! I'll give you a referral to an acupuncturist. That's helped a lot of my patients," he said.

"Does acupuncture work?" I asked.

"Oh yes, it's very effective for anxiety. They put the needles here, here, and here." The doctor pointed to his ears and the top of his head. "It's a peculiar feeling."

The doctor wrote me a referral and handed it to me. "Is there anything else?"

"Ummm...yes. Doctor, my uncle is a psychoanalyst. He's mentioned in the past that psychoanalysis is very beneficial, so I was considering calling him to get a referral. What do you think?"

Dr. Subramanian frowned. "Psychoanalysis? Don't do *that*. That's for rich people, and the underlying theories have largely been discredited."

"Really? But my uncle is an amazing guy," I said.

"I've no doubt he is."

"But you don't think it's a good idea?"

"You should do what you think is best, but just know that there are far more effective ways to deal with mental health problems these days."

I didn't hug the good doctor on the way out of the office, but I smiled earnestly and thanked him. I left feeling encouraged, like I had a lead.

A few days later, the acupuncturist stuck a pin in the top of my head and one in each ear, true to the doctor's words. Over twenty minutes, it was as if a balloon slowly deflated inches above my head, and all my fear leaked out with it. The absence of fear was euphoric, not dissimilar from the pleasure you experience once you finally pee after a five-hour car ride. I nearly cried with relief.

I left the acupuncturist's office on top of the world. I went to work and focused effectively, whistling and strutting my stuff for three solid days. Then I remembered that place in the back of my head where my anxiety lurked. I couldn't leave it alone; I had to go digging. The panic attacks returned as if the acupuncture had never happened.

A week or two later, the shaking began. This new symptom of my panic attacks caused my arms and legs to tremble violently. This was on top of all the other symptoms—the abject terror, the cold sweats, the increased heart rate. I came to call my panic attacks "shakers."

Dr. Subramanian happened to call me right in the middle of a shaker, which I was enduring while lying on my mattress. I crawled on my hands and knees over to the phone and answered, "Hello?"

"Hi, David. It's Dr. Subramanian. I'm calling to see how you're doing."

"I'm fine, Doctor." Never in a life of lying had I told such an outrageous whopper. I was as fine as a cold corpse lying on the side of the road.

"How'd the acupuncture go? Did you find any relief?"

"Yes, the acupuncture went—"

I dropped the phone. I couldn't hold the phone steady because my arms were shaking so badly. I picked up the receiver.

"Sorry, yeah, I'm here. Yes, the acupuncture went well."

"Well, let me know if you want another referral. Good night."

I hung up the receiver and crawled back to my mattress. *Why'd I lie to him?*

As my shaker ended, I wondered if I belonged in a hospital. I thought about my mother and visiting her in the psych ward. I couldn't think of anything more repulsive than ending up like her, years in the loony bin and then found dead, face down on the carpet. She'd have only been four years older than I was when she first went into the hospital herself. *Oh, hell no. I'm not that sick. Not yet.*

Then I remembered her taking Esther and me out of the ACCH on the weekends, and her moving back and forth between the hospital and the War Zone. *She'd tried. At least she'd tried.*

With these images in my head, I resolved to reach out to my lifeline. I called my Uncle Elliot and Aunt Moira, who'd been there for me in fourth grade. Elliot had entertained those talks with me that first year at CMU. After just a few minutes, they could tell I was in a seriously fucked way. They invited me out for the weekend to visit them at their country home in the Berkshires.

That Friday, I drove the two hours west on the Mass Pike, feeling better than I had in months. While we visited over the weekend, Elliot said he had a colleague, Dr. Laquercia, who'd come up through the same school of modern psychoanalysis as he. He wrote the number down and gave it to me, and I put it in my wallet. I didn't mention my doubts about therapy.

I visited with Elliot, Moira, and their twelve-year-old son, Paul, many times through the summer. I felt I called on them too often, worrying that I was making myself a nuisance. I visited anyway; I just didn't want to be in pain anymore. Yet for all my insecurities, they found a way to support me. My aunt and uncle even invited me to go on vacation with them on a houseboat on Lake Powell later that summer. These visits helped structure my week and, together with the vacation plans, gave me something to look forward to.

The last time I visited them, I had a shaker right there in front of Elliot. It was the first time anyone had witnessed one of my full-blown panic attacks. It would have been hard to hide with my arms and legs flailing like mad.

Uncle Elliot held me as my body rebelled.

"Why is this happening to me?" I asked as I sobbed in his arms.

"I don't know for sure. My best guess is you're sitting on a volcano of rage, and it's starting to blow. We'll get through this thing together, though." He paused. "But, David, you need to call Dr. Laquercia."

"I don't know why I haven't called him. You know I'm no good with phones."

"Call him! Let's nip this thing in the bud. But *you* have to make the choice. The choice matters."

"Why?"

"Did I ever tell you the one about psychoanalysts screwing in a light bulb?"

"No."

"Okay. Here goes. How many psychoanalysts does it take to screw in a light bulb?"

"I don't know."

"Just one. But the light bulb has to *want* to be screwed in. Look, the magic of psychoanalysis is in what you and he create *together*. David. Call Dr. Laquercia."

I got back to Boston Sunday night and took from my wallet the scrap of paper that held Dr. Laquercia's number. I placed it right by the phone.

A choice, my uncle had said. What was the choice, really? To pick up the phone and call a therapist? No way. It was much bigger than that.

I got up the next day, went to work, and came home. The phone number was staring at me as I opened the door to my apartment.

A choice. To look myself in the mirror or to remain ignorant. Because that's what it'd be at this point—willful ignorance of emotional problems so acute I was barely functioning. And even if I got better, I'd always know I'd had my moment but had chosen to look the other way.

Tuesday came and went.

Wednesday morning, I walked over to my phone, picked up the scrap of paper, and studied the shape of the numbers as if that might signify something.

A choice. Between life and death. Wasn't that why I was in this mess? All the striving, all the contortions, all the ridiculous shit I'd endured to make it to this very moment? Hadn't it all been a choice for life over death, made in conversations with Omar back at the ACCH when I was ten years old?

I picked up the phone and dialed the number.

"This is Dr. Laquercia."

"Hello, my name is David Sussillo. I've been unwell. I'm wondering if I can schedule an appointment."

PART 5

EMERGENCE: 1998–CURRENT DAY

Imagine a shimmering river, not of water but of scales. A thousand sunlit fish weave and pulse as one, coordinating to avoid predators. Schooling is a dance choreographed by the invisible hand of emergence. It's explained by so-called local rules, just like the process of determining a cell as living or dead in Conway's Game of Life. Each fish swims in lockstep with nearby fish by attending to their movements. If one fish gets too far away, nearby fish accelerate to keep up.

It starts with light bouncing off scales, triggering a chain reaction in a fish's eyes. Like the photosensitive cone cells in our own eyes, a fish's cones support a chemical cascade that converts light into electricity, the lingua franca of the behaving brain. Electrical activity within the cone is passed on via an electrochemical reaction that exchanges salt ions across the cell membrane, reducing the release of glutamate molecules at the cone's terminal end. This drop in glutamate levels signals the next neuron to respond, continuing the electrical propagation further into the fish's brain. Now many neurons amplify and distribute the signal in an ever-increasing cascade across a neural network that accomplishes visual processing. Across millions of neurons, higher-order processing areas receive this electrically encoded visual information. These circuits implement those local rules for how a fish should swim in a school.

Eventually, the brain proceeds toward movement initiation, commencing a motor command. A series of electrical patterns are sent down the spinal cord, where motor neurons release the chemical acetylcholine. Acetylcholine binds to receptors on the muscle fibers, causing channels to open, triggering an electrical signal that causes calcium to be released inside the muscle. This release of calcium activates actin-myosin complexes, inducing contraction. There's a flick of the fish's fin, and an acceleration of the fish's body. Other fish in the school see this as a change in the sun's light reflected off fish scales. And so the schooling of fish continues.

Everything about fishes' schooling behavior can be reduced to the absorption of light and the electrochemical activity of fish biology—chemical and physical processes that drive information processing and, ultimately, movement. In short, fish schooling can be reduced to low-level biology, governed by chemistry and electromagnetism.

When it comes to schooling, a fish is just one part of a multi-node, multilevel network. From the macro-perspective, it's not clear that the concept of a fish is useful in this context. Schooling arises from—and yet is separate, above, or autonomous from—the fish. A group of fish moves this way and that, and no one fish governs the school's movement.

It's natural to wonder: Who's in control—the individual fish or the school? Is the school something more, a tornado or hurricane dynamically woven from the movements of countless fish? Or is schooling simply the epiphenomenal fumes—the smoke but not the fire—of individual fish attempting to escape a predator? You're probably thinking, *Wait, the fish is the obvious entity, and schooling is a transitory phenomenon, clearly caused by fish.*

I'll ask the question in another way.

Does thinking control the neurons in your brain, or do the neurons in your brain cause thinking? Your thoughts come and go, and you sleep for long periods. You can be knocked unconscious or anesthetized. Yet most of us feel that our thoughts, not our neurons, define who we are. We're biased because, well…the *you of right now* is the schooling.

The schooling of fish is an example of emergence—not because it can be traced to its roots, but because what arises from those roots is startlingly new. If we had wanted to, we could have followed the phenomenon all the way down to the exchange of electrons between atoms. And yet, an examination of the behavior of a single fish would never have led us to predict that putting hundreds of these animals together could create the novel phenomenon of schooling. More really is different. Even with perfect equations that describe the fish's brain circuitry, we likely still wouldn't have predicted schooling. We had to observe it.

Like the compiler I built for Lifesource, human beings can take instructions in words and translate them into actions executable on the "neural hardware" of their biological brains. I can ask you to count to ten, and you can then count to ten. I can ask you to count backward from ten to one while thinking, *David is cool*. We can even read the rules of Scrabble and somehow figure out how to play.

So yes, the human mind is emergent like a school of fish or a cyclone. But something much profounder has emerged. Instead of a storm, we are emergent computers that think, feel, and even dream. Computers unlike any silicon simulacra, for we are the real thing, capable of simulating *and* being. When you imagine an elephant, you *see* it. When you introspect and ask, *How am I today?* you *feel* the answer.

We take it all for granted—being, language, thought itself. How could we not? Telling your partner that you'll run to the supermarket after picking up the kids is so commonplace it doesn't rise to the level of comment. But stop for a minute to consider it. Molecules built of atoms, chemical reactions that cleave molecules, and DNA, encoding capabilities inherited across generations. Networks upon networks upon networks, all evolved over billions of years to get us to this point of planning and communicating a mundane chore. A mind—that most special of emergent properties—watches the show unfold. To tell, to make sense, to interpret, to create, to feel—this is the gift of being human. And an absolute miracle when you stop to admire it.

It should be no surprise that things could go wrong in something so complex and adaptive. Dysfunction, breakdown, collapse; they seem almost inevitable. But unlike simpler systems—unlike schools of fish or weather patterns—the human mind possesses the unique capability to study itself, to understand itself, and thereby, potentially, to reshape itself. When supported by the right conditions and connections, perhaps these same networks that make us who we are could also remake us when we're broken.

25

Just Say Everything

Dr. Laquercia invited me into his office. An older man, he was dressed in a smart brown suit, and despite his age had a full head of short-cut salt-and-pepper hair. His office was filled wall-to-wall with bookshelves, and sunlight filtered in from large windows looking over a courtyard garden. At the far end of the room, adjacent to a leather chair, was a blue couch—I assumed that was where patients lay down.

We shook hands and sat facing each other in two chairs. Dr. Laquercia asked me some preliminaries. Over the next half hour, I explained my panic attacks and outlined the contours of my last year in Boston.

Finally, he asked, "So, you want to give this a shot?"

I took a breath. "Okay."

"In sessions, some people choose to sit, but most people lie down." He gestured toward the couch. "Your choice."

I shrugged, went over to the couch, and lay down. Dr. Laquercia got up and took a seat behind me in his analyst's chair.

I stared at the books on his bookshelf for a minute. Finally, I said, "So, how does this work?"

"Just say everything," he responded.

"Well, how does that work, then? Should I free associate? A cat reminds me of a dog reminds me of a bone reminds me of—"

"No need to free associate. Just say everything."

"What if I'm embarrassed?" I asked.

"Even better. But there's no need to go spelunking through your worst memories. Just say everything as it comes up. When you're ready to say it."

Silence.

Finally, I said, "A lot of smart people think Freud was a fraud and his theories were bullshit."

"A lot of his theories *were* bullshit. Lucky for you, this process isn't. Let me worry about Freud. You worry about saying everything."

More silence.

"How can saying everything make people better?" I asked.

"Nobody really knows. Science hasn't yielded much insight," he said.

"That's not exactly encouraging."

"No."

"But you say this thing works?"

"I'm certain of it."

"How do you know?" I asked.

"Decades of personal experience and many, many anecdotes."

"I was hoping for a little more."

"Frustrating, right?"

Silence.

"So, what's the catch?" I asked.

"Psychoanalysis can take a long time," Dr. Laquercia replied.

"How long?"

"It depends on what you want to get out of it."

"I don't want to be afraid anymore," I said without hesitation.

"Perhaps half a year to a year and a half," he said.

"That long? I'm wigging out over here!"

"I can refer you to a psychiatrist if you'd like medication for short-term relief."

Just Say Everything

Silence.

"What happens if someone sticks around longer?" I asked.

"They overcome their resistances. Possibly, they reach their full potential."

"And how long does that take?"

"Many years. Decades, even."

"Dang. Did you go through this?"

"Yes."

"And did it help?"

"It made me who I am today."

Our session ended, and I agreed to see Dr. Laquercia the next week.

Over the next few sessions, I learned that psychoanalysis is a never-ending, one-sided conversation. You talk and talk, and when you're done with that, get ready for some more talk. This was different from both the therapy sessions I'd had as a thirteen-year-old living in Virginia and what I'd seen portrayed in popular culture where the therapist spoke a fair bit.

Over the next couple of months, each time I returned to Dr. Laquercia's office, I tried to draw him into a dialogue, but he resisted it. When I pushed him, he'd stay quiet, content to wait me out in the silence. When I brought it up explicitly, he explained that this was my time, repeating what became his mantra, "Just say everything." Eventually, I accepted the dynamic and began sharing all my experiences, emotions, and inner dialogue with him. Being from a group home and sharing so much with so many roommates as a kid, I think this came easier to me than it would to most folks, and I also found the process became easier over time.

Dr. Laquercia would speak on occasion, though, perhaps four or five minutes in a fifty-minute session.

In one of our early sessions, I said, "I wish I'd never moved to Boston."

"How come?" he asked.

"Because then I would never have had these panic attacks. None of this would have happened to me."

"Come on. You think moving to Boston caused all this?"

"Well, no. Obviously, I had a hard childhood."

"And do you really think you could have avoided confronting that childhood?"

I was silent for a minute but finally admitted, "No."

"Honestly, it's a gift you had this crisis," said Dr. Laquercia. "Most people stay in the same depressed rut for decades before they finally hit rock bottom and seek help."

"Doesn't seem like much of a gift to me. Panic attacks suck." I thought for a minute. "Have *you* ever had one?" I asked. "I mean, a real, all-out, the-world-is-fucking-ending panic attack?"

"You haven't lived until you've experienced dread," he responded.

And so a year passed as I worked with Dr. Laquercia. It was clear that my attempt to live alone in Boston had failed, so after a month of therapy, I quit my job at Lifesource and moved down to New York City to be closer to family and friends. Dr. Laquercia had offices in both Boston and Manhattan, so I was able to continue my sessions with him. I found and rented a studio apartment a few blocks away from Elliot and Moira, who also had an apartment in Manhattan, and we agreed that I'd come over once a week for dinner to stay in touch.

I found a job programming at a financial software company. The task was to translate old business code written for IBM mainframes in the '60s and '70s to modern code that would run on updated servers. This new job was *quite* a step down from what I'd accomplished professionally—both at CMU and in Boston, but I didn't care. I was looking for stability and a paycheck, in that order, and nothing more.

But the job was intensely dull, so instead of rewriting the code by hand, as my manager expected of me, I wrote a compiler to do it and then sat back and played *Quake II*, always keeping a side-eye out for my boss, should he stroll by.

I gave jogging a try, although I couldn't say why. That's the funny thing about psychotherapy. You start making changes to your life you can't quite explain. Perhaps I'd heard running was a healthy thing to do. But I observed that my mood stabilized whenever I exercised regularly. I brought up this observation in my sessions with Dr. Laquercia, and we both agreed it was a good idea to turn jogging into a habit. The frequency and strength of my panic attacks decreased significantly.

That first year in New York wasn't much in the way of a life, but my emotions stabilized, and I began flirting with the idea that my future was actually something I wanted to be a part of.

In Dr. Laquercia's office, I finally started getting to the heart of the matter.

"Dr. Laquercia, I have to admit something to you that's very embarrassing," I said.

Silence.

"I feel egotistical," I continued. "And I'm not sure I can bring myself to say it." I took a deep breath. "I think my childhood convinced me I had to be perfect. Perfect like a god."

More silence.

"You know, it's funny," I continued. "Religion got me all fucked up, but it helped me, too."

"How's that?" Dr. Laquercia asked.

"Take my favorite line from the Bible, 'Seek, and ye shall find. Knock, and it shall be opened unto you.' I've had that memorized ever since I was given my first Bible."

"It's a good verse."

"Maybe I'm in this office because of that Bible. That verse was my mentality when I called you, you know."

"What were you seeking?" he asked.

"A way to move forward. A way to live…to be at peace in my own head, I guess," I responded. "That stuff about being perfect, amazing, the greatest…I think that's why I got to a place where I was pushing myself so hard. If I was perfect enough, if I could just outshine everyone, then maybe someone would pay attention to me."

"Neglect has profound and long-lasting effects on children," Dr. Laquercia responded. "Your developing mind shaped itself around a world utterly beyond its control."

"No. You don't understand. I thought I might be able to do it…to *be* perfect. That's the shameful part. I think that's why I got so bugged out."

"I *do* understand," Dr. Laquercia retorted. "You lived it, so you're too close to see the broader context. This was your childhood survival strategy. There's no shame in that. Now that you're an adult, you can recognize it for what it was—a way to survive desperate circumstances—and learn to move on. In fact, you should be proud."

"*Proud?*"

"Of course! You survived! Think of all the different ways kids at those group homes behaved to get their needs met. Any guesses where they are these days?"

"Who the hell knows," I responded.

But that wasn't entirely true. I knew about Esther.

"So, how did you two get together? And what's he like?" Moira asked Esther about her fiancé, Jack. By this time, I'd been living in New York for about a year and a half, and Moira, Elliot, and I had flown down to Austin, Texas, to reconnect with my sister.

During my college years and afterward, each of us had had our ups and downs with my sister. Her behavior could be erratic. She'd lash out at you if you tried to help her, and she was prone to seeing slights where none were intended. Things hadn't been easy for Esther, but often she was her own worst enemy.

"We met at one of those Landmark Forum weekend retreats," Esther replied. "We have so many of the same interests. He's just lovely, super handsome, too. And his family is *loaded*." She giggled after she said it out loud.

"Does he treat you well?" Elliot asked.

Her smile disappeared, and Esther stared at Elliot for a second. "Better than anyone else ever has."

Moira laid her hand on Esther's. "Well, it's wonderful to see you so happy. We can't wait to meet him."

Later, Jack rolled up in his 1975 black Cadillac Eldorado convertible to take Esther and me to a party they'd planned. They'd invited all their family and friends for a celebration of their move to Austin. We'd drove to the venue with the top down and music booming. Esther and I were in the back, belting out the tunes and hanging halfway out of the car. My sister could always party like a rock star, and I found it easy to have fun with her when alcohol lowered her defenses.

Marrying a billionaire would have been Esther's crowning achievement. Just as I had survived through attempting to outshine everyone with brilliance, Esther had developed her own strategy—an almost instinctive ability to present herself as a damsel in distress. It had shaped her entire life. By the point she'd met Jack, I'd watched it play out repeatedly—dramatic scenes, tearful pleas for help, desperate requests for money, hastily purchased plane tickets to new cities. Now, after years of perfecting this technique, she'd focused it, laser sharp, into two words: *I do*.

Esther came within a hair's breadth of pulling it off, too. But drama had become her reality. When the inevitable crisis came, the relationship imploded. Esther found Jack's gun and threatened to kill herself if he broke off the engagement. He freaked and called the cops, and she took a weeklong vacation in a mental hospital.

Her life, at least what I knew of it, seemed to stall.

My life, on the other hand, was coming together. My panic attacks had completely disappeared within two years in therapy, though I was still on edge about the future and what my life held. Both Dr. Laquercia and Elliot regularly assured me things were going fine.

After spending those same two years meandering through bookstores, bars, and side streets, I decided to finish my education. I missed the intellectual challenge of writing that compiler in Boston, even if the pressure had been too much at the time. Now, stabler and with better support systems in place, I felt ready to contemplate a return to academia.

I thought back to the conversation I'd had with Mike Dino, my student adviser, when I'd decided to leave CMU. Never before had an administrator shown me such respect through their candid communication, and I wanted to reciprocate by letting him know of my commitment to completing my degree. When I reached out to Mike, we talked about how I might wrap up my few remaining classes. With his guidance and support (and a couple of classes from Columbia University and Brooklyn College), I successfully graduated from CMU with a degree in computer science a year later.

While finishing my degree, I quit that job modernizing mainframe code and joined another start-up company, this time as chief technology officer. This was a grossly overblown title, but it was the age of the early internet, and I had a ton of internet programming experience under my belt. For this new gig, I'd be responsible for the complete technical development of a website in the spirit of eBay, where we'd support an online marketplace for home improvement work. While less technically demanding than the work I'd done in Boston, it was a big step up in leadership responsibilities. I even convinced my buddy Sport to move to New York City to join the company.

I discovered online dating, which suited both New York City and me perfectly. Manhattan can be a surprisingly anonymous place. So I put my profile on a dating website, tweaked it a bit over a couple of weeks, and the next thing you know, I had dates lined up anytime I wanted one.

Three dates in, I met Joline. She was a lovely, creative young woman, an artsy nerd whose laptop had a giant collection of colorful stickers. She was all of twenty; I was twenty-three. In a rash decision a couple of months into dating, we moved in together.

Six months had passed since I'd first moved in with Joline. I walked into Dr. Laquercia's office, ready to punch walls.

"Joline brought a dog home," I told him once I settled in to open the session.

"Great!" he said.

"No, not great, Dr. Laquercia. Not great at all. She and I had explicitly discussed this. We both agreed *not* to get a dog."

I studied the books on his shelf as I fumed. There were the complete volumes of Freud, alongside a bound volume that read *PhD Dissertation for Theodore Laquercia*.

Fucking shit, I can't believe I'm going to talk about this. I continued looking at the bookshelf. Farther down were C. S. Lewis's *Chronicles of Narnia*. Over to the right was—

"Where's your mind, David?" Dr. Laquercia asked.

I began crying.

"What's up?" Dr. Laquercia asked again.

"You know what's the most shameful thing I've ever done?"

Dr. Laquercia didn't respond.

Through tears, I said, "Back when I was thirteen, I used to kick my aunt and uncle's dog Bean." Quietly, I said, "I'm terrified I'm going to do it again."

I talked at length about Bean and the terrible guilt I felt when I allowed myself to think about it. I spoke about the rage I'd contended with as a child, the beatings I'd received. I recalled the challenges of living with James and Beverly, the manifest unfairness of group-home life, all of it.

After I'd finished, Dr. Laquercia said, "Bean was quite the teacher. Your acknowledgment of your capacity to harm others is an enormous step forward." He paused. "That same capacity is in every one of us."

"Including you?" I asked.

"Of course!" Dr. Laquercia said. "You. Me. Mother Teresa, even. It's a part of being human."

Silence.

"So, how do I control myself?" I asked.

"You know how I always say 'Just say everything'?" Dr. Laquercia asked.

"Sure do."

"Well, it works when you're alone, too. As a matter of fact, you don't even have to speak out loud. Just keep saying everything in your head. With any luck, it's been happening for a while now."

I thought for a second. "Yes, actually…now that you bring it up."

"Then you are self-analyzing; this is sometimes called *mindfulness*. When you self-analyze, you give yourself a crucial moment. You give yourself a chance."

I thought about the implications of his words. "So…these last few years…I've been practicing?"

"For this very moment. When you're mindful, you can safely feel *all* your emotions and think *all* your thoughts. You don't have to kick the dog, David." He paused. "It's when you're unaware of what's in your heart and head, that's when you're in real danger."

I wiped tears from my eyes and laughed. "That's some wax-on wax-off shit right there!" I said.

We were getting somewhere.

I learned to manage my anger and slowly built a life of harmony with Joline's dog, Roxy. The hardest moments came when I'd return home from work to find evidence of misdeeds—shredded toilet paper strewn across the apartment, or garbage picked through and scattered across the kitchen floor. In those first seconds, that familiar rage would surface, as potent as it had been when I was thirteen.

But now I understood its source. It wasn't about Roxy at all but an echo from my years in group homes, where any misbehavior meant swift, harsh consequences. Perhaps I'd even taken on identification with the housefather, the rage Mr. Clodfelter may have felt at any sign of disrespect from one of the boys. In those moments, walking into my apartment only to find a mess, my anger was very real, but it wasn't Roxy's to bear.

Thanks to my Aunt Beverly's early instruction, I was comfortable with dogs and knew how to handle them. More importantly, thanks to Dr. Laquercia, I now knew how to handle myself. It wasn't easy at first. I'd take deep breaths as I gathered the scraps of paper or swept the floor, but I kept remembering Dr. Laquercia's words about being mindful of what was in my heart and head, allowing myself to feel the anger without acting on it.

Roxy and I developed a routine. We'd head out for long runs through Central Park, burning off both her pent-up energy and my lingering tension. Over time, something shifted. The anger, when it came, grew less intense, less demanding of release. I began to trust myself around Roxy, even in moments of frustration. We developed a deep bond—I trained her, even teaching her to roll over and play dead, and she became my faithful running partner. The fear of losing control simply faded away.

About six months after the conversation with Dr. Laquercia about Bean, I visited James and Beverly in Virginia. I'd made the trip south under the guise of taking a small break from work, but my real intention was to repair our relationship. We hadn't spoken much over the years; I'd receive the occasional holiday card or the infrequent, brief phone call that skirted around anything real.

Beverly had suggested I come for dinner, and as I sat at their kitchen table, watching her cook sage-seasoned chicken breasts in a cast-iron skillet, memories of Bean flooded back. She'd been gone for years now, but her presence still lingered in this kitchen. Their new Lab, Maple, dozed at James's feet while Beverly poured us each a glass of wine.

With trepidation, I led the conversation back to the time when I was in the eighth grade. All three of us had learned to avoid the topic.

"I have to admit something to you both," I said. Then I blurted it out before I lost my nerve. "I used to kick Bean."

Beverly put down the spatula and turned around to look at me.

"It didn't last long," I said as I began crying. "But I definitely abused her…and I sincerely apologize for that."

Both my aunt and uncle took a moment.

In the silence, I looked at Beverly and then at James. I spoke again. "I want to thank you both for taking me in."

Beverly was openly crying now as well, leaning against the kitchen counter.

James spoke up. "We're sorry for what happened between us. One of my deepest regrets was how I handled that conversation with you in the woods. At least Milton Hershey School was better than that children's home in Albuquerque."

"Well, if we're honest today," I said, "I'm not sure it was." I went on to explain how difficult my student home at MHS was and how crazy my housefather had been.

"Why didn't you tell us about this?" he asked, clearly pained.

"I didn't feel welcome." I looked up at Beverly. "Being ghosted by you was one of the most painful things I've ever endured."

That night, we had an honest conversation about one of the most challenging periods in any of the three of our lives. By the end, we were all a mess of tears, but we'd all forgiven one another and agreed to let bygones be bygones.

Joline and I might have worked out had it not been for 9/11. But a terrorist attack in your city has a way of forcing you to reexamine relationships. That day forced so many of us to reevaluate what truly mattered, leading some couples to split up in search of deeper connections while others rushed headlong into forging new families. When Joline moved out, taking Roxy with her, I coped by staying in and listening to sad country songs.

After a month or two of wallowing, I finally threw myself back into online dating, though a long string of unsuccessful dates nearly broke my resolve. Just as I was about to delete my profile, I met Robin, and we agreed to meet for a beer at an Irish bar in Soho.

The first thing I noticed about Robin was that she had a crooked smile. She had almond-shaped, hazel eyes, fair skin, and that dark brown hair often associated with Scottish or Irish heritage.

"Well, you're beautiful!" I said as she approached.

"Sure am! The mannequins they make for the clothing stores are *totally* based on me." She laughed as she extended her hand. "Hi, I'm Robin."

She ordered a Guinness, and we got to chatting. The next thing you know, she'd spilled her stout all over my lap.

"Darn it!" she said and dashed over to the bar for napkins. She apologized, trying to clean beer off my leg and thigh. I simply broke out into laughter.

The awkwardness broke any remaining ice. Robin was an artist and had moved to New York to get a master's degree from Pratt in interior design. We ended up chatting for a couple of hours. When it was time to go, I walked her to the subway and told her to call me when she got home. I gave her a kiss on the cheek.

I called her a few days later, and we went on another date. Then another and another. Soon, things were serious in a good way, her company enriching my life. I introduced her to Elliot and Moira, who were immediately taken with her, and she began accompanying me to our weekly dinner at their place.

The following summer, she and I took a road trip across the United States in Robin's old red Jeep Cherokee, "Big Red." We must have broken down in three different national parks. Together we camped and hiked through the Badlands, Yellowstone, the Grand Canyon, and every Podunk state park from New York to New Orleans. I introduced her to New Mexico. We got drunk on Bourbon Street, ate soul food in Savannah, and toured the Washington Mall together. We returned from the trip tanned, road weary, and with enough inside jokes to fill the two-person comedy club of the apartment we'd decided to share.

26

Attractors

In 2000, the dot-com bubble burst, and, as our potential for further funding disappeared, my start-up popped right along with a zillion other early ventures. At least I got to keep the black, plastic plaque printed with *David Sussillo, Chief Technology Officer.* Back when I'd worked with Barrett to help start up OHM my junior year at Carnegie Mellon, I'd felt overeducated and under-skilled. After four years grinding it out in software, the situation had very much reversed. Something was missing.

I longed for the thrill of discovery I'd first experienced inventing new algorithms on my TI-81 calculator in high school or the heady explorations of theoretical computer science I'd been exposed to in classes at CMU—those moments of pure wonder when the shape of a problem would crystallize, leading to the all-consuming search for solutions. Research had always been my refuge, from my childhood days of mastering video games—learning their patterns, testing strategies, pushing for that next level—to the complex mathematics of my college years. It was a place where my creativity could flourish without the baggage of my past. While I was addressing the traumas of that past through psychoanalysis, I still craved the intellectual hunt.

So one day, shortly after the dissolution of the start-up, I hopped on the subway to Columbia University to take a look around. It turned out that part of the university's compensation package for full-time employees included two free classes per semester. This was a no-brainer. I applied for a UNIX systems administration job on campus, received an offer, and immediately accepted. I'd be a cyber-plumber, keeping the computers running, and in return, I'd receive a modest but living wage, all while taking free classes toward a master's degree in electrical engineering.

Over the next two years, I crawled under the floorboards to replace wires and repeatedly rebooted the email server because one professor persisted in emailing the entire contents of his computer's hard drive to his personal email account. You haven't truly lived until you've performed open-heart surgery on an email server, manually repairing the inodes and superblocks of its file system, with sixty-three frustrated professors breathing down your neck about not being able to send or receive email.

But aside from occasional server meltdowns, life at Columbia suited me. I once heard a comedian joke that grad school was the snooze button on the alarm clock of life. For me, that wasn't remotely true. Just listen to some of the topics from my electrical engineering masters: wavelets, Fourier transforms, infinite impulse response filters, information theory. Doesn't it all sound so mysterious and magical? Like maybe you could build a spaceship or perpetual motion machine in your basement using nothing but a soldering iron, some baking soda, and the guts of an old Nintendo? Or perhaps you could learn to fry someone you really disliked with electricity coming out of your hands? Yep, grad school was definitely for me.

"It's been almost five years, David. Your panic attacks have been gone for a while now, yes?" asked Dr. Laquercia.

"That's right. I've forgotten how to find them, even if I wanted to, which I sure as hell don't."

"That was your goal when you first came to see me—to be rid of your anxiety. It's time to revisit this. Do you want to continue?"

"What's left if I keep going?" I asked.

"Well, life doesn't stop throwing challenges at you. But it's more than that. Psychoanalysis is the discovery of the self. How your past combines with the present to create your future. You can explore what you want to achieve. *Why* you want to achieve it. It goes as deep as the mind itself." He paused. "I also think you might benefit from joining my therapy group."

"Whoa, whoa, whoa. It's hard enough just sharing with you sometimes. Talking about heavy stuff with a group of strangers sounds awful."

"Sometimes hearing others' stories helps us understand our own more deeply. They benefit from your experiences and perspective, too. And they don't stay strangers for long."

I thought about it. "Well, I have grown to enjoy our weekly meetings. I don't have to stop those, do I?"

"Of course not," said Dr. Laquercia. "The group would be in addition to our individual sessions. If you want to."

"I'll think about it," I said.

"So, what's next?" Dr. Laquercia asked. Though he sat behind me, I could tell he was smiling.

By now, I knew something about this process; it was up to me to give it shape. "I know it sounds hokey, but given what I've been through, I'd like to do something that helps us understand mental illness or the human condition."

"I don't think that sounds hokey."

"I was considering a PhD. Maybe neuroscience. There's a subfield I heard about called *theoretical neuroscience*. It's kind of like trying to understand how the brain works by treating it as an incredibly complex computer, or maybe how a physicist might try to understand the properties of some strange, new material. Apparently, it can get pretty mathy."

Dr. Laquercia listened while I hatched plans over the next few months. The more I looked into neuroscience, the more fascinated I became. Most theorists in the field had focused their attention on an experimental subfield called *systems neuroscience*. The goal here was to address head-on how neurons are organized into the circuits that give rise to computation, and thereby to perceptions, emotions, thoughts, and mind. It'd been clear from my introductory neuro classes that the field understood quite a few details but was nowhere close to understanding the big picture. And from a career perspective, between mental illness, neurological disorders, and general interest in the mysteries of the mind, it seemed to me that there was no shortage of opportunities for impact.

So in the fall, I applied to neuroscience PhD programs all over the country. And by early spring, I'd received rejection letters from all over the country. The only program I'd yet to hear from was Columbia University.

A PhD is an enormous commitment—five to six years—so when students receive an offer from a program, they're also typically invited to come visit for a weekend. I was up at Columbia every day, so I'd caught wind that their weekend for prospective students had come and gone. My heart sank. But one of those prospects must have chosen another program at the last minute, because fully a month after all the admissions business should have been settled, I received a personalized email from the department head.

Attractors

Dear David Sussillo,

This is John Koester from the Neuroscience Department here at Columbia. I believe we've met once or twice. I apologize for the delay, but I'm writing because I'd like to offer you a position in the 2003 incoming class for our PhD program. In particular, we're considering opening a center for theoretical neuroscience. With your technical background, we believe you'd be a great fit. We'd love to have you! Please let me know at your earliest convenience.

Warm regards,
John

"Fuck yes!" I screamed at the top of my lungs. Robin came bounding into the room, and once I told her, we hugged and laughed and jumped up and down and all around. Then I gathered myself and replied that I would be honored to join.

The following fall, I began my training in neuroscience. The theoretical center that John had alluded to wouldn't open for at least another year, so I joined Professor Douglas Ravenholm's experimental lab. Doug wanted to "unlock the deepest secrets of the brain," as he regularly put it, meaning he wanted to tease apart the circuits and function of the neocortex, that outer layer of mammalian brains thought to subserve everything from vision to motor control to high-order cognitive processing like decision-making.

Identifying how the cortex functions is like searching for neuroscience's equivalent of the ideal gas law ($PV = nRT$). This is the simple equation many of us learn in high school chemistry, stating that a gas's temperature (T) rises proportional to its pressure (P) or its volume (V), assuming the other is held fixed. This elegant relationship is surprising because, when physicists looked under the hood, they discovered that it emerges from the cacophony of countless molecules bouncing around randomly. Just as that equation connects the microscopic motion of gas molecules to macroscopic properties like pressure and temperature, neuroscientists seek fundamental principles that would link the electrical activity of billions of neurons to higher-level brain functions like memory or decision-making. In short, neuroscience is searching for the bridge between scales that might connect neurons to cognition—its own "PV = nRT."

One promising idea of how brains might bridge these scales was developed by John Hopfield, who created simplified artificial neural network models to provide explanations for specific kinds of biological computation. *Hopfield networks*, now named after him, use *attractor* dynamics to model potential mechanisms of pattern completion and memory recall in the brain.

The activity in these networks can be visualized as a landscape with valleys and hills. The state of the network—the pattern of electrical activity across all neurons—moves across this landscape like a marble rolling downhill, naturally settling into valleys that represent stable patterns or memories. When you try to recall your neighbor's dog's name, for example, you might start with fuzzy details like floppy ears or a wet nose—with an underlying pattern of neural activity close to the full memory, but not quite. As your neural activity "rolls downhill" into an attractor valley (literally a pattern of activity that the network moves toward), more details emerge until you reach the complete memory: sweet, little Luna. Once there, the network activity settles, making it unlikely you'll forget the name again moments later. This ability to find order from fuzzy or incomplete information through collective dynamics is a hallmark of neural networks.

And so we return to Professor Douglas Ravenholm at Columbia and his quest to unlock the deepest secrets of the brain. While Hopfield networks demonstrate how attractors might work in simplified artificial networks, the challenge remained: Could we find evidence of these principles operating in real brains? When I began my PhD in Doug's lab back in 2003, this search was just beginning. The hypothesis was also experimentally compelling: If memories in biological neural networks operated through attractor dynamics, we should be able to observe neural activity settling into these states because they stick around—they're stable. But testing this required watching many neurons simultaneously, a technique that had only recently been invented.

Historically, neuroscientists recorded neurons one at a time—like trying to understand a movie by watching a single pixel. You might eventually glean something about the story, but only after long, exhausting work. Doug's team employed a groundbreaking technique called *calcium imaging*, which revolutionized neuroscience by allowing us to observe thousands of neurons simultaneously. The technique uses fluorescent molecules that glow when neurons fire electrically, creating a mesmerizing movie where active neurons light up, revealing their synchronized dance as they perform computations.

Doug hoped that analyzing these movies would reveal fundamental principles of brain function—that macroscale understanding akin to the ideal gas law. His hypothesis was that we would see evidence of attractor dynamics—neural activity being drawn toward stable states that would persist long enough to be observed in experiments and, in so doing, validate Hopfield's theory.

For my part, I was honored to join Doug's lab as an experimentalist in training. Theory can only get one so far; you have to take measurements if you are going to call it science. Under the mentorship of a postdoc, I'd perform the imaging experiments and meticulously analyze the resulting data to uncover meaningful patterns in the hopes of uncovering evidence of attractor states.

I'd been working in Doug's lab for nine months, and my first real shot at becoming a neuroscientist wasn't going well. Despite my enthusiasm for the science, when it came to the experimental work, I was all thumbs. The imaging experiments required a delicate touch I hadn't yet developed, and I could sense Doug's growing frustration with my clumsy attempts at the bench.

But the real tension centered on an analysis I'd shown him six months earlier, where I thought I'd found evidence of the attractors he was so passionate about. Doug had latched onto this preliminary result with an intensity that made me increasingly uncomfortable. Every biweekly check-in devolved into the same conversation about that analysis, with Doug pressing for updates and me growing more certain that my initial finding had been a mistake.

The postdocs in the lab had warned me about Doug's single-minded focus and had advised against telling him outright that I thought the analysis was a dead end. But watching his evident disappointment meeting after meeting as I failed to reproduce the result was wearing me down. My inability to get along with Doug wasn't helping, either. At first, I thought it was just me, until I started attending happy hour and discovered my labmates' endless grousing about Doug's management style.

I began to wonder if my struggles with Doug reflected a deeper incompatibility. He'd taken a risk inviting "the theory guy" into his lab full of experimentalists, and I felt the weight of that opportunity. But more than that, I understood the stakes; your first-year lab often defines your entire PhD trajectory, and switching labs can brand you as difficult. With no clear path to success in Doug's lab and no obvious way to transfer elsewhere, I began to feel trapped in an increasingly unstable situation.

The irony wasn't lost on me—here we were studying attractor dynamics, looking for stable states in neural activity, while my relationship with Doug seemed to be anything but stable. In fairness, deciding when to walk away from an uncertain result is tricky business. Perhaps he just wanted to ensure I'd explored every possible avenue before abandoning the result. But as the months wore on with no progress, I could feel the growing distance between us, my initial excitement about experimentally validating theoretical concepts giving way to a gnawing uncertainty about my future in science.

Unsure of how to handle the scenario, I decided to forgo the postdocs' advice. It was time to rip the Band-Aid off.

Doug had a little pocket notebook he kept. Whenever he'd meet with you, he'd pull it out, go offline for a minute as he reviewed the relevant details of your project, and then return to the present and commence the conversation. As the meeting progressed, he'd write little notes. I guess he didn't need them this time, because he pulled up a chair, sat down next to my desk, and asked, "How is the attractor project going?"

I took a deep breath and went for it. "I've got to level with you, Doug—I think I showed you an artifact that first meeting. A complete mistake."

Ravenholm's brows furrowed. "These tools are the apex of neural observation." He turned and gestured around the lab. "You're at the wheel of a research Ferrari, David." Then he looked back at me. "Don't you want to unlock the deepest secrets of the brain?"

I swallowed. "Yes, Doug. Of course."

"Well, get to it, then. Time's wasting." With that, Doug abruptly ended our one-on-one.

Relating the story at my next therapy session with Dr. Laquercia, I said, "Of course I want to unlock the deepest secrets of the motherfucking brain. But I'm starting to feel like I might not be able to do anything at all productive in that lab." I wasn't producing the result Doug wanted, and for my part, I couldn't understand how he could perseverate over a single analysis for so long.

Dr. Laquercia listened, and together we strategized about the best ways to avoid antagonizing my PhD adviser.

There was a larger problem. I wasn't getting all my academic needs met. When I'd joined Columbia, I'd hoped to gain training in theory as well as experimental neuroscience. But the center for theoretical neuroscience that John had promised had yet to materialize. So early in my second year, I brought up to Doug that I might apply for a Fulbright grant to study abroad my third year with a theoretical neuroscientist in Austria, Professor Friedrich Mueller. Doug and Friedrich knew each other professionally, and they were both eager to collaborate. So Doug agreed to my applying for a Fulbright. I figured he went along with it because of the added bonus: It'd clear the deadwood—namely, me—from his laboratory, at least for a year.

Things in the lab were rough that second year, but my relationship with Robin had blossomed. Elliot and Moira had gifted us a weekend at their home in the Berkshires, so Robin and I had driven the two hours north for a winter getaway. I'd made a reservation at our favorite restaurant, the Old Mill, and we were nestled in a cozy nook at the bar. Lost in thought, I kept folding and refolding my napkin into ever smaller triangles.

"Hey, space cadet," Robin said, placing her martini in front of my face. "Stop worrying about your PhD."

"Okay," I stammered, "just...hold on. I need to use the bathroom."

I crossed to the front of the restaurant and found the coatrack, digging into my coat pocket until I pulled out a small box. I jammed it into the front pocket of my pants, which resulted in a ridiculously large bulge. There was nothing for it, so I put my hands in front of my pants and recrossed the floor, returning to Robin at the bar. I took a shaky sip of my manhattan.

"What is *up*?" asked Robin. "You are completely out of sorts."

"It's, well, I was thinking...about how much I love you."

Robin smiled. "Okay. I can work with that."

My nerves were taut; it was now or never. I cleared my throat and took a deep breath. "I wanted to show you how much I...well...hold on..." I crammed my hand into my pants pocket, unable to remove the box. "Hang on a minute." I stood up and went on my tippy-toes to fumble some more. The box wouldn't budge.

Robin broke out into nervous laughter as she glanced at the other people at the bar and then back at me. With a jerk that nearly sent the box flying, I finally pulled it out. "Here!" I said. "I got you something."

Robin picked up the wrapped box, her face a mixture of surprise and curiosity. She shook it near her ear and then started opening it.

Once the wrapping paper fell away, she realized it was a ring box. Her eyes widened, and she stopped.

"Open it," I said.

She opened the box, and inside was a platinum ring with a green demantoid garnet, the bright kind they used in the old-timey Tiffany jewelry. Robin had been very clear about her love of colored gemstones, and I'd taken the cue.

"I found out a month ago," I said. "I got the Fulbright. I'll be leaving for Austria this summer, and I want you to come with me. Will you marry me?"

Robin's hands trembled as she handled the ring. She looked up at me as tears filled her eyes. "I...Of course! Yes! I'll come!"

"And the marriage part?"

Robin slid the engagement ring onto her finger. "Marriage? Of course I'll marry you!"

The adrenaline had both of us shaking like leaves, but we managed a kiss. The bartender had caught wind of the proposal and had wisely laid off. Once he saw happy tears and an embrace, he brought over a bottle of champagne. Robin and I toasted our future together.

The following summer, just before we were to leave for Europe, Robin and I were married at Elliot and Moira's country home in the lush green of late summer. We invited a hundred close friends and family, including Dr. Laquercia, his wife, and the group therapy circle I'd decided to join near the beginning of my PhD. Sport and Don were both there as my groomsmen. All my aunts and uncles attended. Esther didn't come.

The bagpipes were cued—Robin had really wanted those—and my aunts and uncles walked me down the aisle in place of my parents. They all held one long ribbon to symbolize their shared participation in helping me survive my childhood. Radiant in her white dress, Robin walked down the aisle, hand in hand with her parents.

As I stood there, watching her come down the aisle, all the reasons I loved Robin overwhelmed me. Her homemade lasagna, our deep conversations—even the silly ritual of feeding our cat his green beans—each reason combining to create a desire to spend my life with her. Her artistic genius had transformed our apartment. She'd even cleverly disguised a missing brick in the fireplace with a printout of a perfect brick, turning a flaw into a quirky detail. There was never a judgment about my past, despite her roots in blue-blooded Wellesley, Massachusetts.

Uncle Elliot opened the ceremony, our buddy performed "Lush Life" on his tenor saxophone, and then Robin and I took the stage. There, in the backyard of Elliot and Moira's property on a perfect sunny, summer day, we consecrated our vows in front of family and friends and pronounced ourselves husband and wife.

I caught up with Doug for my final check-in a day or two before Robin and I were set to leave for Austria.

"I'm really excited for you," he said. "You'll love Europe."

"Thanks again," I said. "I really appreciate you agreeing to this arrangement. I think I'm going to learn a ton from Friedrich."

"But—" Doug lifted his index finger. "I want you to think broadly about your time there, because when you return to the US, you will not have a spot in my lab."

"What?" I said, color draining from my face.

"Like I said, think broadly while you're there." Doug stood up and tucked his little notebook and pen into his shirt pocket. "You're a bright guy; you'll figure it out." And with that, he retreated into his office.

I was shocked. I knew Doug had been disappointed in my performance over the last two years, but I didn't know he was *that* disappointed.

I found a couple of cardboard boxes and brought them over to my desk. As I was tossing all my crap into a box—my textbooks, a whole bunch of notebooks, my picture of Robin—other members of the lab began looking over. Finally, the postdoc I'd been working with, Wei Lun, walked up to me.

"Look," Wei Lun said, shaking his head, "nobody here thinks you're deadwood. You've been really helpful to my project, especially with the software and data analysis. Even some of your experimental data is going to end up in our papers."

"What did I do?" I shook my head. "I thought a PhD was supposed to be as much an apprenticeship as book learning. Training takes time!"

"Of course that's right. I don't know what you did to set him off." Wei Lun held up his hand and looked around. "One sec." He walked over to see if Doug was in his office. Then he walked back. "Must be teaching. For what it's worth, I think this is only partly about you. You know he just got the PIAN award, right?"

I nodded. "Yeah, I heard." Doug had recently been invited to join the prestigious Perseus Institute for Advanced Neuroscience.

"PIAN provides big bucks," Wei Lun intoned. "But that money comes with enormous pressure, too. In five years, Doug has to go up for renewal. PIAN judges a lab's quality not by the stack of papers it's produced but by only the lab's top *five* papers."

"Huh. So Doug thinks I'm not going to be a driver of one of those five papers?"

"Well, otherwise, none of this makes sense."

"Man, that's some realpolitik bullshit right there," I said as I loaded the last of my odds and ends into my box.

"I know. It *is* bullshit. You'll be an author on at least two papers already. Anyway, everyone knows you're more theoretically oriented, so maybe it's not the worst thing."

During my next session with Dr. Laquercia, I unloaded. Ravenholm giving me the boot was a huge setback. What if it got me ejected from the PhD program altogether?

After listening for most of the session, Dr. Laquercia finally responded, "David, blame all you want, but what's done is done. It's over. The one and only person you can change in this world is *you*."

Once I stopped seething, I was forced to agree. The truth was that over the last seven years with Dr. Laquercia, I'd grown ever more into the habit of looking in the mirror. Living in group homes had taught me to be hypervigilant about authority figures—to watch their moods, anticipate their reactions, and adapt my behavior accordingly. With Doug, I found myself slipping into those old patterns, becoming more guarded and less authentic in my interactions. It wasn't that examining these patterns would have changed Doug or his decision, but understanding them *would* help me navigate future relationships more effectively.

During my time in Austria, I continued my sessions with Dr. Laquercia over the phone. We examined the situation from every angle, how I might have contributed to the dynamic, ways that I may have unconsciously associated Doug with a housefather figure, what behaviors that might have provoked in me. After a year's worth of analysis, I was certain of two things: I wasn't going to let Doug wreck my plans to become a neuroscientist. And I wasn't going to allow unhelpful, vestigial behaviors from my childhood hold me back, either.

27

Useful Networks

After a blissful year in Austria, I returned to the US and the smoldering ruins of my PhD. Frankly, I was stumbling into my fourth year. By this point, a candidate should be cozied up in a lab and well on the way to picking a question that'll be the crown jewel of their dissertation. You should be kicking ass and taking scientific names. I was doing neither.

Desperate for guidance, I sent an email to John, the neuroscience department head, asking what he thought I should do. He replied that Columbia's Center for Theoretical Neuroscience had finally come together and that he would try to find me a position with a professor there.

He reached out to Professor Larry Abbott, a physicist-turned-neuroscientist who had risen to prominence in the field during the previous decade. I later found out that Larry wasn't overly thrilled about taking on a fourth-year reject from another lab, but John wouldn't take no for an answer. Larry agreed to a three-month trial period.

And so, in arguably the greatest stroke of luck I've ever had, I blundered ass-backward into being advised by the one and only, the great Larry motherfuckin' Abbott. Yet one more back door—barely ajar and closing fast—that luck or fate or vanishingly small odds allowed me to slip through.

Useful Networks

Over the next few months, it became clear that when it came to science, Larry and I were practically reading each other's minds. We were both intuitive, conceptual thinkers with similar ideas about computation and the brain. When my three-month trial ended, Larry welcomed me as one of his full-time students.

Before falling head over heels for biology and neuroscience, Larry had an entirely separate career in theoretical physics. In 1983, he published a paper in which he and his colleague suggested that the axion, a hypothetical subatomic particle that might be important for understanding how matter is organized, could be a major component of dark matter in the universe. The paper went unnoticed by the scientific community for a whopping *three decades* before finally gaining recognition due to several ongoing searches for dark matter. It's now Larry's most highly cited paper.

Despite his mathematical prowess, when it came to neuroscience, Larry always tested his neural network ideas in a real-time simulation he'd programmed on his computer. When he introduced this simulator to me, I got it immediately: Instead of playing *Ms. Pac-Man*, Larry "played" research. There were programmable buttons, sliders, moving graphs, and colorful charts with dots and lines and everything. If a simulation went belly-up, you just rewound time with a flick of the slider, tweaked a parameter or two, and bam! You could see the difference in the results right then and there. We were playing video games, but instead of chasing high scores, we were chasing scientific breakthroughs.

About a year into my mentorship, I asked him about this approach. "Math simply isn't enough," he said, turning away from a whiteboard covered in nonlinear differential equations. "*That*," he said, pointing his dry-erase marker at his beefy computer workstation, "is the only thing that separates us from hundreds of years of thinking about science." Larry was in his mid-fifties, balding, and going gray. But when he got amped up about science, his energy made him seem decades younger.

"Another thing," he continued. "Always pay attention to problems people say can't be solved. This stuff just becomes dogma. Humans are lazy thinkers. Unless there's mathematical proof, call bullshit on these blanket statements. Hell, even if there is proof, look for a loophole."

His words proved prescient. Over the next two years, through a process of interactive research, simulation, and math, I discovered a solution to a well-known problem that would become the meat and potatoes of my PhD dissertation. In fact, we managed to pull something off that everyone thought was impossible. Together, Larry and I figured out how to train chaotic recurrent neural networks to actually do something useful. What does that mean?

Ever since the 1940s, when McCulloch and Pitts proposed the first mathematical model of a neuron, scientists dreamed of building networks that mimicked the brain's incredible computing power. Their groundbreaking work showed that even simplified artificial neurons, when connected in the right way, could perform complex computations. This insight sparked an entirely new field dedicated to understanding artificial neural networks.

Over the years, researchers made significant progress with various models—from Hubel and Wiesel's discoveries about how the visual cortex processes information through increasingly complex feedforward cascades, to Hopfield's attractor networks that helped explain memory and pattern completion. These contributions built a foundation for understanding neural computation, but a core challenge remained unsolved.

Understanding the human brain requires us to move beyond feedforward models of neural activity. Unlike a factory assembly line where products move neatly from station to station, our brains operate more like a bustling conversation, with information constantly looping back between neurons, evolving, and influencing ongoing processing. Neural networks, the mathematical models used to study brain function,

Useful Networks

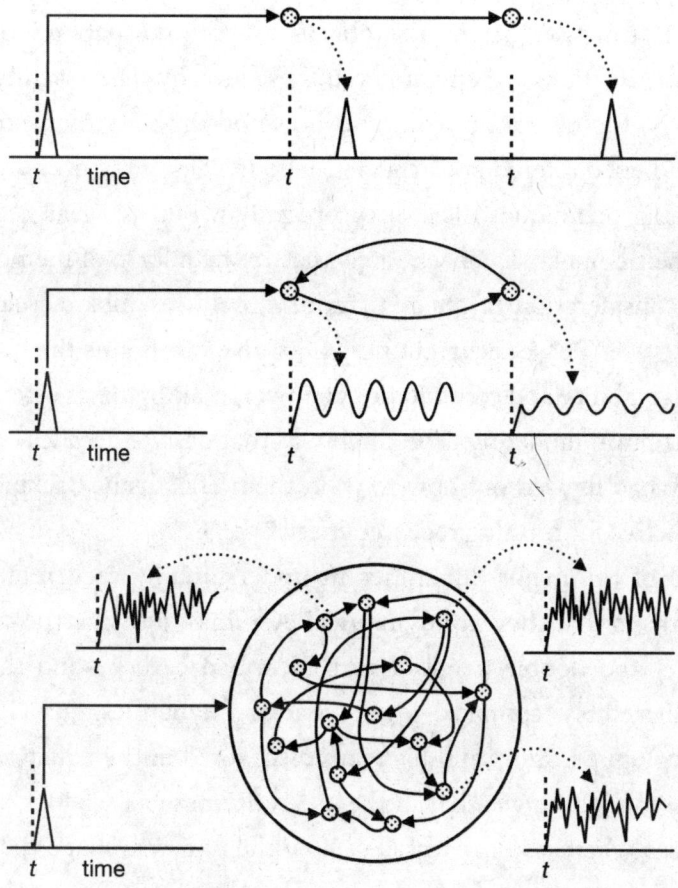

Caption: A feedforward network processes inputs in a straight, sequential path (top row). Here, a brief pulse of activity enters at time t and is passed forward through two additional neurons, with each responding in turn before going quiet. In contrast, a recurrent neural network (RNN) contains feedback loops (middle row, note the backward arrow), allowing past activity to influence future responses. The same input pulse now produces sustained oscillatory activity, as one neuron feeds back onto the other in a simple loop. Finally, when the network contains many interconnected neurons (bottom row), even a brief input can give rise to rich, complex dynamics—sometimes chaotic—revealing how recurrence transforms neural networks into dynamical systems. These systems are ideal for modeling memory, time-dependent processes, such as the weather, and even the brain itself.

come in two main varieties that mirror this distinction. Feedforward networks function like the assembly line, with information moving in just one direction. We encountered these already when we discussed ALVINN, the neural network that powered the self-driving military truck I'd encountered at Carnegie Mellon. These networks are trainable using techniques like backpropagation. But *recurrent* networks, with their complex feedback loops that create a form of memory and allow consideration of context, more closely resemble actual brain architecture. These recurrent networks give our brains their remarkable adaptability and computational power, making them essential for realistic brain modeling. The catch was that despite decades of effort, nobody had figured out how to train them effectively. Backprop was not effective for training recurrent networks.

One of the major difficulties in understanding recurrent neural networks is that they are dynamical systems—just like the weather patterns and double pendulums I described earlier—and they can have incredibly complex—even chaotic—dynamics, just like the meteorologist Lorenz and his team discovered in the equations they used to model the weather in the 1960s. Remember, chaotic systems are those where you can't predict how the past will shape the future due to sensitive dependence on initial conditions. To repeat the same behavior exactly in a chaotic system, you have to set its initial state with infinite precision, which is impossible in practice.

And this is what Larry and I figured out: how to *train* chaotic recurrent neural networks to do useful computations. Now, by the time I began my work with Larry in 2006, most AI researchers had abandoned neural networks altogether, and those who still worked with them had completely written off recurrent networks. Most neuroscientists believed that recurrent nets *were* the right choice for modeling brains via computer simulation, but nobody believed you could train them.

This is where Larry and I made our breakthrough, which we called *FORCE* learning. Instead of trying to tame chaos directly, we found a way to work with it. Imagine a wild horse—that's like a chaotic network. It's got tremendous potential, but it's running around unpredictably, not doing anything useful. Traditional training methods were like trying to saddle that mustang while it's bucking and rearing. With FORCE learning, we took a different approach. We exposed the network to a strong, consistent pattern—like having a wild horse follow a lead mare walking a steady path. As the network synchronized with this pattern, we gently guided it toward the behaviors we wanted it to learn, gradually shifting its internal landscape without fighting against its inherent chaos.

What made this approach revolutionary was that it didn't try to eliminate the chaotic nature of these networks. Rather, we harnessed it, because we knew the chaos provided the computational richness and flexibility that made these networks so powerful. By working with this chaos rather than against it, we found that recurrent networks could learn to generate precise patterns and solve complex problems that had previously seemed impossible. The wild horse could now perform skilled jumps or dressage—still wild at heart, but with the discipline to channel that energy into something purposeful.

The implications for neuroscience were significant. FORCE learning gave researchers the ability to build artificial networks that performed the same tasks as used in neuroscience experiments, such as determining which of two tones is higher in pitch or remembering sequences of lights. Researchers could then attempt to analyze how these artificial systems solved these problems, which could then be translated into hypotheses about real brain function.

It would turn out that this approach would provide unprecedented neuroscientific insights, allowing scientists to generate testable hypotheses about the neural mechanisms underlying cognition and behavior.[3]

During my time working with Larry, I couldn't help but see the irony. Here we were, trying to tame these wild, chaotic recurrent neural networks. My very own childhood had been marked by that same chaos and uncertainty. The sensitivity to initial conditions that made these networks so difficult to train mirrored the way small, seemingly inconsequential events had altered the trajectory of my own life.

Mentorship under Larry and Dr. Laquercia, as well as the support of Robin and my aunts and uncles, were the guiding forces that helped me navigate this complex landscape. Just as the strong, consistent stimulus in FORCE learning helped to guide a chaotic network toward a more organized and productive state, their unwavering support and belief in me provided the stability and direction I needed to channel my own potential. Their guidance helped me to find that delicate balance between chaos and order, to dance at the edge of possibility—without tipping over into the abyss as I nearly had in Boston.

My tumultuous past had given me a unique perspective on the world. The very chaos that had once seemed like an insurmountable obstacle could be a source of strength, resilience, and especially creativity. And just as these recurrent networks achieved their greatest feats when operating at the edge of chaos, I came to understand that it was in navigating the delicate balance between my own internal order and disorder that I, too, could unlock my full potential.

I defended my PhD in computational neuroscience from Columbia after three intense years collaborating with Larry. Most of my family attended, and Robin's parents came down from Boston to support me as well.

My dissertation received the honor *with distinction*—a designation indicating that, beyond demonstrating the ability to produce novel research, I'd made a major contribution to the field. When we submitted the work to the prestigious journal *Neuron*, Larry declared it one of the top five neuroscience papers he'd ever been involved with. His assessment proved prescient; fifteen years later, among the three hundred papers he's authored, our work on FORCE learning remains his third most-cited research publication in neuroscience.

After my defense, we all went out to a family-style Italian restaurant to celebrate my PhD. Near the end of dinner, my Aunt Maria showed me a picture of the two of us standing side by side on the shore of Masten Lake: I an ungainly teenager and she my mom for a few precious months every summer. It struck me, possibly for the first time, how much I'd depended upon having that kind of a respite during my Milton Hershey years. That periodic reassurance that I could connect was reassurance of my own humanity.

Leaning against Maria there in the restaurant, I ugly-cried—and I mean a full-on, minutes-long meltdown—in front of Larry and other colleagues, longtime friends like Sport, and my family. Maria, teary herself, rubbed my shoulder, full of warmth, as I realized just how much she, Brad, and my cousins had done for me and how much I loved them.

28

What Remains

Six months after my PhD defense, I received a call from my Aunt Moira. My father was very ill. Nearly half a century of drug addiction had finally caught up with him. The doctors had diagnosed cirrhosis of the liver, and it seemed likely he would die within a few weeks. My aunt suggested I make the trek to New Mexico and take what would be my last chance to make peace with my father—or, at the very least, confront him.

The news transported me back to my therapy session years earlier, when Dr. Laquercia had first suggested I join his group therapy circle. I'd been hesitant, nervous about exposing myself to people I didn't know. But I'd joined anyway and discovered he'd been right—to understand our own story, sometimes we need to hear it reflected in others.

One particular session, a woman in our group had arrived in tears, devastated by her father's sudden death in a car accident. The group had given the woman the space to tell her story, and in her telling, I'd grown ever-more despondent and withdrawn, until Dr. Laquercia had turned to me and asked, "What's on your mind, David?"

With effort, I shared with the group the story of my mother's death and her funeral. I explained that I hadn't grieved at all, how my father had come up behind me and put his hand on my shoulder, and how I'd then cried just a little.

I buried my head in my hands, overcome by unexpected emotions. Tears streamed through my fingers. "Fuck that fucking fuck!" I said, voice raised.

"Be careful, David. There's a lot to tease apart here," said Dr. Laquercia.

"I understand just fine what's going on!" I shouted as sobs racked my body. "When my father put his hand on my shoulder, I felt safe. It allowed me to cry. Which meant I loved him."

Dr. Laquercia stayed quiet, and so did the rest of the group.

"He didn't deserve it. Children don't have a goddamned choice."

"No, they don't," said Dr. Laquercia.

The heartache in that room was close to unbearable, but together, the nine of us held it for an hour. In doing so, I was able to grieve my mother's death in a safety not dissimilar to what my father had momentarily provided.

Thanks to that group session, I'd begun the process of acknowledging my parents' profound failures and laying the responsibility for my childhood where it belonged. It didn't belong with the Albuquerque Christian Children's Home or Milton Hershey School, and certainly not with James and Beverly. As hard as it had been for me to bear, the blame belonged squarely at the feet of my parents.

That realization from a couple of years ago now weighed heavily on me as I considered Moira's call. But as I wrestled with the decision to visit my father, it wasn't his face that I saw in front of me but rather that of my mother. With her, there could never be resolution, no tearfully or angrily answered questions. I'd never know who she was or who she might have been. So I hopped on a plane to Albuquerque; I'd confront my father and learn whatever I could.

But as I made my way to his halfway house, my mind was churning—*What am I doing here? And how the hell am I going to keep my anger under wraps?*

I'd not seen my father for almost twenty-five years. When he opened the door to his modest apartment, he appeared thin but not frail, darkly tanned, and his still-brown hair had receded several inches. His eyes were lively. Honestly, he looked great for his sixty-one years, and to look at him, I'd have never guessed that he was a lifelong heroin addict with only weeks to live.

"Hello, son," he said.

He had no teeth.

So there are signs. "Hello," I said. There was no way I was going to "Dad" this motherfucker.

He ushered me in, raising his arms to hug me.

"No, sir," I said, pushing past him into his apartment.

The room was plain—barren, in fact. The white walls had no art or decoration. There was a blue sofa, which I assume converted into a bed. A cream-colored sheet hung in front of the window, but it wasn't flush, so sunlight made it through at the corners. There was a single-person table at standing height and a stool next to it.

My father motioned to the sofa. "You don't mind if I sit, do you?" he asked.

I shook my head and took the stool.

Once settled, my father said, "Wow, look at you! I hear you're a professor at Columbia University!"

There wasn't enough time in the world to explain that I wasn't a professor, just a recently graduated PhD student—and what the difference was. In that single sentence lay a lifetime of missing context. My father had never completed high school.

"I'm really proud of you, son. I always knew you were smart," he said.

"Thanks."

My father started talking about the Bible study group of recovering addicts that he led.

"I don't want to talk about Jesus," I said.

"Oh, okay. What do you want to talk about?"

"Tell me about the night when I was five years old, when you tried to light our Lori Place apartment on fire and nearly killed all of us."

My father studied me for a minute. I stared back at him; I wasn't there to make nice.

"Wow. Okay. Cut right to the chase, man." He took a deep breath. "You remember that family rehab place, Dare?"

I nodded.

"Even after Dare, your mother and me, we were constantly high."

"I thought you were supposed to be clean."

"That's what we told your grandparents. Well, the night that fight went down, we'd stolen a bag of drugs from a pharmacy."

"A *bag* of drugs?" I asked.

"Someone's prescription. Mother's-little-helper-type stuff. It was a grab-and-run."

"My mother was involved in this?"

"Of course. And she was every bit just as disappointed that we didn't find any painkillers. We hadn't scored in a while." My father thought for a second. "I don't know why I started the fight...maybe just in a destructive mood. So I popped those downers."

"Were you trying to kill yourself?"

"No. I'd tried that about a month before that fight. Ended up in the hospital. James came out, took care of me, tried to get me into rehab."

"So why'd you do it, then?"

My father looked away at the wall, and a few seconds passed.

"Well?"

He didn't respond.

"Esther and I were in that apartment!" I yelled.

"I honestly don't remember." He turned back to me. "I was pretty messed up."

"Jesus! So just say you're high, and you don't have to explain yourself?"

"I'm sorry, David."

"Apologize to Esther," I said, calming down somewhat. "It's her life you fucked up the most."

"I apologize, David. Truly." Judging from his downcast expression, it looked like he meant it.

How could I forgive this guy? His decisions had made my childhood hell, had messed up my sister something awful, and had contributed to my mother's demise.

A minute passed without conversation. I took a deep breath and then spoke. "Did you and my mother even love each other?" My parents had been married for nine years. During most of my childhood, I'd been aware of the duration of their marriage and had taken pride in it.

"At the beginning."

"Why'd she stick around, then?"

"She was a freewheeling hippie who wanted a man who knew how to score drugs or find shelter and food in the wilderness." He spread his hands. "I was that guy."

"And you?"

"Well, first, it was fun; your mother was beautiful. Then Esther came along, and your mom got heavy. Then you."

"So, no love between you? Really?"

"Like I said, at first. Afterward, we were partners more than anything. Stealing, thieving, whatever it took."

My father talked for the better part of an hour about life in those days, and I came away with a significantly darker view of my early years than I'd had before. For all that, it was cathartic to hear him put his voice into the story of my childhood, to have his full attention for at least an hour.

As he spoke, I found my anger dissipating somewhat. Though I could never forgive him, I found myself coming to a semblance of peace with him. Or perhaps with the idea of his impending death. My father was a goddamned drug addict, but a nice guy, maybe even a thoughtful guy. That's as much as I was going to get, and it wasn't nothing.

When it was time for me to go, he got up from the couch and showed me to the door. He stood there in the doorway for a couple of seconds. "Goodbye, son," he said.

I turned around to look at him one last time. "Goodbye."

He just stood looking at me, arms at his side. He'd clearly given up on the hug.

I knew this guy was about to die. I couldn't leave him hanging like that. *Goddamn this fucking fuck, but it's the right thing to do. For him.* I stepped back into his apartment and hugged my father. *And for me.*

As I turned and headed for the stairs, I heard him close the door. I headed down to the street level, shaking my head, wondering for the thousandth time how the hell I'd ended up in that place at that moment. Of all the possible arrangements of matter in all the possible universes, here I was, saying goodbye to my estranged father, who'd spent the entirety of his adult life chasing and then consuming a molecule to the exclusion and detriment of everything and everyone else.

I'd seen my father maybe two dozen times since he and my mother divorced, and I'd never much cared for him. But there at the end of his life, I respected him for leveling with me.

The doctors hadn't been wrong; he passed away a month later.

* * *

After my visit to Albuquerque, I returned to New York City and immediately got back to work. Perhaps it was because my father had had such a minimal impact on my life, or because I was so accustomed to drama, but his death didn't affect me much. Growing up, I'd learned to manage the daily context switch between the Albuquerque Christian Children's Home and public school, and this felt like a similar transition.

What proved to be far more challenging was Esther's behavior, which began to spiral completely out of control. Since Esther was living in Albuquerque, she'd agreed to collect our father's ashes after his cremation. Driven—I guess—by spite, she refused to relinquish them to Moira, who'd wanted the ashes, even though Esther herself had no interest in keeping them. For a month, she used my father's remains as a tool to torment our aunt, taunting her with comments like "Maybe I'll send them to you, maybe I won't," or "What will you give me in exchange?"

A month after that drama died down, I received an unexpected call from a Social Security administrator who worked in a branch office just outside Albuquerque. She apologized for calling, saying it was extremely irregular, but that she believed that Esther was trying to steal my portion of the meager Social Security inheritance left to us from our father's sporadic work over the years. When I called Esther and confronted her, she admitted to the scheme. Unapologetic, she asserted through some inexplicable logic that she wasn't stealing but rather taking what was rightfully hers.

An attempt at outright theft of many thousands of dollars was uncharted territory, and it frightened me. It dawned on me that my sister might be capable of hurting me or someone I loved. So I severed all communication with her. Though I continued to hope she might find a way into psychotherapy or some other kind of help, all evidence pointed toward a life falling into chaos.

29

Ten Thousand Seats

As my PhD drew to a close in 2009, Larry's and my research with FORCE learning hit a snag. The recurrent networks that he and I trained were revolutionary but were also true black boxes; we had no idea whatsoever about how they might function, which is critical if you want to use them to understand how brains work. It was a problem of reverse engineering.

Imagine you wanted to understand how *Ms. Pac-Man* worked, but you knew nothing about electronics or programming. Where would you start? You might begin by opening up the arcade cabinet to poke around its innards. With some effort, you might identify the game's "brain"—the microprocessor. You might deduce that this processor is programmed rather than hardwired for specific functions. But the real challenge remains: What makes Ms. Pac-Man chase power pellets or flee from ghosts?

Modern reverse engineers—and yes, that's a real job title—tackle such problems by analyzing program code, tracking electrical signals between components, and documenting behavior under different conditions. Eventually, they build a complete picture of how the system operates. But here's the thing: An arcade game, while complex, is still a human-made machine designed with logic and purpose. What if you wanted to reverse engineer something far more sophisticated—something that emerged through billions of years of evolution?

This is exactly the challenge neuroscientists face when trying to understand the human brain. For decades, this challenge seemed insurmountable. How do you reverse engineer a system when you can barely measure its components, let alone understand how they work together? And the sheer complexity is staggering: billions of neurons, a thousand trillion connections.

Instead of only studying real brains, what if neuroscientists could create simplified versions that we could fully examine? That's where artificial neural networks come in. Through FORCE learning, the neuroscience community gained its first reliable way to train recurrent neural networks—simplified stand-ins for living brains—to execute tasks similar to those performed by their biological counterparts.

But these networks, trained through examples rather than explicit programming or design, also have inscrutable innards. A network trained to classify images of dogs and cats might excel at the task, but you wouldn't have a clue how it works. If we can't even understand how this artificial brain functions, how could we compare it to the real thing?

This apparent obstacle is an incredible opportunity in disguise. If we can crack the code and figure out how artificial neural networks perform their impressive feats, we might stumble upon entirely new concepts and algorithms that could revolutionize various scientific fields. In short, training by example and then reverse engineering neural networks is a method for generating new hypotheses, algorithms, or designs.

It's a bit like searching for novel drugs in the rainforest. Evolution has forced plants to develop unique chemical defenses to survive in a hostile environment. These compounds, honed over millions of years, often have therapeutic properties that pharmaceutical research couldn't have designed from first principles. Similarly, neural networks trained by example develop solutions that human intuition might never conceive.

Let's bring this back to neuroscience. Want to know how a chickadee's remarkable brain remembers the locations of the thousands of seeds it gathers and stores? Train by example a recurrent neural network to tackle the same or analogous problem, then reverse engineer it. Assuming you can understand any of it (and that's a big if), the network's solution becomes a hypothesis about how a chickadee's brain solves this memorization task. Armed with such a hypothesis, an experimental neuroscientist can test it in real bird brains by taking careful measurements.

Driven by my fascination with complex systems, I enrolled in an advanced graduate course on nonlinear dynamics. Although mathematically demanding, we delved deep into chaos and attractors, and I learned a powerful technique: identifying attractors—stable states that systems naturally move toward—and the simplified dynamics around them to grasp a system's overall behavior.

I approached several mathematically inclined postdocs at Columbia, asking about the potential of these textbook approaches for reverse engineering–trained recurrent networks. The consensus was overwhelmingly negative; recurrent networks were far too complex for such methods to work.

When I reached the desk of another postdoc in the theory center, Omri Barak, he said something different. "Why *wouldn't* it work?" He took off his rectangular glasses, preparing himself for some critical thinking. He walked over to the whiteboard and said, "Let's take the simplest task we can think of...a simple yes/no decision." Then Omri started sketching a three-dimensional landscape, adding a couple of valleys to represent the attractors. After a few minutes, he looked back at me. "You might be onto something here. But a recurrent network is too high-dimensional to solve in closed form. You'd have to automate the process of finding the attractors on a computer. How are you going to do that?"

"I'm not," I said, pointing at Omri and giving him my best grin. "*You're* gonna do it. Wanna collaborate?"

Finding these attractors and analyzing the dynamics around them became our method of reverse engineering recurrent networks. Think of a grandfather clock with all its complex gearing. It seems daunting to simply open one up and figure out how it works. However, there are key positions—like when the clock's pendulum reaches the peak of its swing or settles at the bottom—where the motion becomes predictable. At these points, the clock's behavior simplifies, so by studying these special positions, we can grasp the overall dynamics without getting lost in the complexities of the gear mechanism.

In the end, it was a culture crossover play, taking classic material from mathematics and applying it to fertile ground in theoretical neuroscience. Omri and I cooked up a bunch of examples of recurrent networks performing a variety of simple tasks like memory storage or generating rhythmic patterns. The results were a revelation. Even for these simple tasks, we'd initially had no idea how the networks worked. After we'd applied our technique, we could see exactly how the network stored information in different attractors and how the dynamics moved between them.

For the first time in my career, I felt like I had the tools to make sense of something profoundly complex.

★ ★ ★

Over the three and a half years of my mentorship under Larry Abbott, he and I had become good friends. He knew the story of my childhood as well as the details of my exit from Ravenholm's lab. As we discussed what might come next for me scientifically, we both understood my success would depend on finding an environment that was, at a minimum, nontoxic, and—reaching for the stars—perhaps even supportive and collaborative.

Our conversations kept returning to Stanford University and the laboratory of Professor Krishna Shenoy. Krishna had a growing reputation as a world-class scientist, and his laboratory was producing unbelievable neuroscience, one incredible paper after another. The guy seemed to have his own dedicated phone line to the editors at *Nature*, the premier science journal. More importantly, within the community, Krishna had a growing reputation as a world-class scientific *mentor*.

Krishna's group was at the forefront of applying techniques from dynamical systems to understanding brain function—the perfect place to test out my modeling ideas on actual, living, squishy brains. I'd developed models that worked: FORCE learning to train recurrent neural networks and the reverse engineering techniques to understand them, but I had yet to deliver on any hard neuro results. Moving to Krishna's lab for a postdoc would provide an opportunity to test the framework, with huge implications if successful. It would mean that neuroscientists really could use artificial neural networks as hypothesis generators in a way that might help guide their research. Larry made the introductions, and Krishna gave the green light. So Robin and I moved out to the San Francisco Bay Area.

While I would ultimately produce a series of impactful papers with Krishna's lab, it was an early chance encounter that would transform both my career and possibly even our understanding of how brains make decisions. Thanks to the open seating area in which we all worked, I happened to rub elbows with Bill Newsome, a titan in systems neuroscience who had spent decades unraveling how the brain processes visual information and makes decisions based upon it.

Neuroscience struggles with a fundamental paradox: the homunculus problem. Imagine a tiny person sitting inside your brain, watching screens of incoming sensory information and pressing buttons to make decisions. But this creates an infinite regress: Who's inside the homunculus's head making decisions? And who's inside that one's head? This thought experiment illustrates the true difficulty of brain science: At some level, the rubber must hit the road—just as fish work together to school, neurons and synapses themselves must directly implement even our most high-level cognitive processes, such as decision-making.

After a PhD where'd I'd innovated how to train artificial neural networks and developed tools to peer inside them, I believed I might have something to offer. When Bill invited me to present my ideas to his group, I knew this could be the moment where theory met reality—where neural networks might finally help us understand real brains.

The room's response to my talk revealed the stakes. Some were bewildered by the mathematics. Others were openly skeptical—after all, it was 2010, and the idea that artificial neural networks could illuminate brain function was considered pure fantasy. But a few saw the potential, including a postdoc named Valerio Mante who'd spent years collecting neural recordings that defied conventional explanation.

After my talk, Valerio approached me, his appearance—buzz-cut hair and synthetic wool fleece jacket—matching his direct Swiss manner. "I have these neural recordings from animals making contextual decisions," he said. "Very difficult experiments, years of data collection. But I'll be honest—I have no idea what to make of any of it. Could your recurrent networks help?"

The *contextual decision-making* that Valerio referenced can be understood within our own daily activities. Imagine you're at a crosswalk at a busy intersection in New York City while cars zoom up and down the avenue. If you want to cross the street, you pay attention to the motion of the cars so you don't get mowed down. Yet if instead you want to hail a cab, you pay attention to that iconic NYC yellow cab color. This is contextual decision-making in action. Depending on the task—whether you want to cross the road or hail a cab—your brain engages in different visual processing—attending to either the motion or the color qualities of the visual scene.

Since much of human decision-making can be cast into this kind of contextual framework, if you care about how humans make decisions, fully understanding even a simple instance is of vital importance. And the implications are far-reaching. If we have a fundamental understanding of decision-making, then we might be able to understand why, when, and how humans make poor choices that detrimentally affect their own well-being and that of others. Lord knows I had a personal stake in that particular mystery.

Bill and Valerio had devised a video game version of the crosswalk scenario. Then they'd painstakingly trained animals to play the game in an experimental rig where they could monitor the brain as it made decisions. Using electrodes that listen in on individual neurons, Valerio had collected reams of neural activity from the prefrontal cortex, the brain area implicated in complex thinking. They'd also recorded the exact behavior and decisions of the animals. So they'd figured they'd be in a position to grasp how the prefrontal cortex made decisions.

But they hadn't been able to do it; the data was too complex. The neuronal activity seemed almost random, defying comprehension. To contrast, in early visual processing, things are more straightforward: Hubel and Wiesel worked out that if you shine a bar of light in the visual field, cortical neurons activate reliably and vigorously in patterns that reflect the bar's orientation and brightness.

The responses that Bill and Valerio were confronting within the prefrontal cortex were all kinds of crazy. Bill had spoken about it to academic audiences many times, introducing the problem's difficulty by talking about the "prefrontal zoo." If you squinted, you could see some relationship between a neuron's response and the stimulus, but by and large, neural activity in the prefrontal cortex was unintelligible. This was most definitely *not* how an engineer would build a decision-making system.

If an animal makes a wrong choice in the wild, it could die. How could such a confusing neural system possibly implement something so important? In essence, Bill and Valerio were grappling with the homunculus problem. Without a central command center, or a "little man" inside the brain to direct traffic, how do the neurons in the prefrontal cortex sift through this cacophony of neural signals to produce informed decisions?

This was *exactly* the kind of problem I'd been preparing to tackle: a real brain solving a complex task in a way that challenged our intuitions about neural computation. Valerio and I began meeting daily to see if my reverse engineering approach could deliver a hypothesis that might explain the prefrontal zoo. And so began the collaboration that would define both of our careers as neuroscientists.

The routine that Valerio and I developed is that I would train the recurrent neural networks to mimic the behavior of the animals playing the video game, incorporating whatever innovations we'd brainstormed since the last iteration. I'd make sure it functioned correctly and then pass the network to Valerio, who would compare its behavior and artificial neural activity to the animals' decisions and neural activity. We both agreed there was no point reverse engineering the network—a difficult, open-ended, and time-consuming process—until it matched the neural data from the animal's prefrontal cortex.

This cycle of innovation and analysis went on for at least a year, and I was beginning to lose hope for the project, until one morning, Valerio burst into the Clark Center. He was out of breath and had a huge smile on his face.

"David, they're the same! The neural dynamics are the same!"

"Slow down. What are the same?" I asked.

Valerio threw down his backpack. "The brain! The recurrent neural network! The traces of their dynamics are the same."

"Are you sure? What changed?"

"I had to find the right way to look at things," responded Valerio.

Our conversation quickly became a whirlwind as Valerio continued, "I started thinking about different ways to analyze the data. Had to get the visualization subspace correct."

"How'd you do it?"

"I inverted the task regression! Once I found the regressors for the behavioral variables in the brain data, I used the regressor weights to point back *into* the data."

I thought about it for a few seconds. Such an approach could provide real insight, but only if you weren't pointing at junk.

"And the variance explained?" I asked. "Is it large enough?"

Valerio nodded. "I had the same concern. It totally checks out."

I grinned and pulled a second chair over. "Take me through your code."

Breaking down the jargon of this exchange was the fact that Valerio and I had been toiling away, painstakingly crafting the inputs and outputs to the recurrent network and tinkering with its architecture in the hopes of making a clean comparison to the brain data. But something was always off. Valerio had made a creative leap over the weekend, and after he'd applied whatever glitch-in-the-matrix insight he'd come up with, the neural data now looked an awful lot like the traces from the recurrent network.

So I reverse engineered the network in the hopes that we could use it like a decoder ring to understand the prefrontal cortex's decision-making abilities. What we discovered was nothing less than the precise mathematical detail of how the network solved the task. At a high level, the network used what neuroscientists call *neural population dynamics*—the coordinated activity patterns of many neurons working together. This allowed the context—crossing the street versus hailing a cab—to subtly change how each neuron responded to color versus motion inputs.

The neurons in the artificial network also perfectly matched the "zoo-like" behavior Bill and Valerio had observed in the prefrontal cortex. Individual neurons in both our artificial network and the brain appeared to encode task information almost randomly—not because they were confused but because this mixture was a natural consequence of the way the network solved the problem.

From that point forward, Valerio, Bill, Krishna, and I knew we were onto something big, and we worked together constantly for the next two years. While we couldn't prove the brain used the recurrent neural network's internal solution, the brain data matched the artificial net's activity so closely that we felt confident we had uncovered a completely novel hypothesis for how the prefrontal cortex *might* solve contextual decision-making.

* * *

During this time, I found my way back to Columbia University to give an early talk on the work. If anyone could understand what we'd accomplished, it would be the folks at the Columbia Center for Theoretical Neuroscience. After the talk, Larry and I retreated to his office, and I took him through the project in all its gory detail. We worked through some of the more challenging aspects of the math for a couple of hours.

Once we'd finished on the whiteboard, and he finally grasped all the details, he said something I'll remember to the day I die: "This'll go down as one of the greatest papers ever written in neuroscience." He shook his head in amazement. "To imagine that the four people on the planet who could have pulled this off happened to be working in the same building at the same university at the same time."

"I'm honored, Larry," I said. "That means a lot coming from you."

"It's one thing to say that dynamical systems can explain motor control. It's another thing altogether to show that cognitive processes like decision-making can be explained using the same language and with the same tools." Larry scratched his head. "You know, I've been invited to give the Grass Lecture at the Society for Neuroscience conference this year. What would you think if I presented your work there?"

"Larry, you could present my work to an empty room, and I'd be honored," I said. "Which one is the Grass Lecture?"

"The big one."

Later that year, Valerio and I pushed open the double doors to the auditorium at the Society for Neuroscience. We were met with an enormous space filled with scientists taking their seats. Some were chatting quietly; others were crafting emails on laptops. Walking into the lecture hall from the back, I could barely see the speaker's lectern. The space was about the size of a football field.

Neither Valerio nor I had ever received anything close to this level of attention. You'd better believe we were making our way up front. "How many seats do you think are in here?" I asked.

"Ten thousand?"

I shook my head in disbelief.

Valerio and I entered the third aisle from the front and made our way to the center.

A few minutes later, the auditorium darkened, and the society president walked to the lectern. She waited to allow the din to die down, then introduced and invited Larry to the stage.

There was resounding applause as my PhD adviser approached the podium. "Today I want to tell you about some exciting new work from my colleagues at Stanford. It's a new movement in computational and theoretical neuroscience called *computation through neural population dynamics*. By using artificial neural networks as ball-and-stick models of brain circuits and combining them with high-dimensional neural data now available through calcium imaging or multiprobe electrodes, we are at the dawn of a new age in neuroscience. An age where we may finally understand how neurons give rise to the neural dynamics that explain behavior." And with that, Larry launched into his talk about our work.

I settled into my seat, legs stretched out, basking in scientific glory. I looked over at Valerio and gave him a wink.

After the talk, conference bigwigs and neuroscience luminaries milled about near the stage. Valerio and I had the honor of meeting the one and only Torsten Wiesel, the Nobel laureate whose groundbreaking work with David Hubel had revolutionized our understanding of the visual cortex. The wild-haired octogenarian found his way to us and shook our hands as he congratulated us on the work.

The following year, after a mountain of effort and an eternity of waiting, our paper, "Context-Dependent Computation by Recurrent Dynamics in Prefrontal Cortex," was published in *Nature*, the world's top scientific journal. The "Mante Sussillo" paper, as it's now called, has come to be one of the most heavily cited works in modern systems neuroscience.

Our work, related research from other laboratories, and Bill's skillful advocacy led to an important development: The Simons Foundation, a private philanthropic institution, established the Simons Collaboration on the Global Brain, which would go on to fund this new kind of neuroscience for over a decade. For my part, I would go on to collaborate with other neuroscientists, demonstrating the reverse engineering's broader applicability across different neural systems. Today, using artificial neural networks to generate hypotheses about brain function has become the dominant approach in neuroscience—a global standard that, in some small way, began with the work we did.[4]

From where I started, it still feels impossible.

30

Get the Free Life

"I had the craziest dream last night," I said in my phone session with Dr Laquercia. My paper with Valerio had just been published.

"I love dreams," Dr. Laquercia responded.

"I'm back in my grandparents' house in Albuquerque. I don't think anybody's home. There's an evil presence, a feeling of ill intent, you know, like only David Lynch can do.

"I'm walking through the kitchen, and just then, time fractures. A clock floats off the counter, and I hear a loud buzzing in my ears. I look out the window; a twenty-foot-tall eagle—maybe an angel?—is perched on the top of the tree I used to climb as a boy. The United States or the church as a guardian or something?

"I walk into the den, where my grandparents and my mother used to visit together. And there's this evil spirit standing there. But it's also you, Dr. Laquercia. *You're* the evil spirit! Your face is scarred, and your eyes are black pits.

"I start levitating and scream, *'I CAST YOU OUT OF HERE!'* as I melt you—well, the demon you—with electricity coming out of my fingertips.

"Dr. Laquercia, it was amazing; I shot up out of bed like a bolt of lightning had struck me! Robin woke up all confused, convinced there was an earthquake."

Dr. Laquercia chuckled. "Dreams are almost never a single truth, but I'd guess things are going pretty well for you."

That dream marked a turning point. It was the moment when the present and future seemed to hold more weight than the shadows of my past. My life is no longer defined by what happened to me but by who I've become, by what I create.

Now, looking back, I think of the conversation I had with that young server at the Princeton Neuroscience Retreat. Her eyes wide, her question heavy in the air: "How did you do it?" I'd stumbled through a few platitudes, stymied by the inadequacy of words and the impossibility of her request.

My life appears to be a kaleidoscope of fragments that somehow coalesced to create something larger and more complex than I can possibly understand. Of course, there was grit and luck, as I'd said to the server. But it was more than that. Each fragment includes a moment of kindness, a flicker of humanity in the darkest corners. A best buddy to share adventures with, an air-guitar-playing elementary teacher who took notice of me, a housemother who had me tested for the gifted and talented program, a group-home big brother with whom I could plan escapes and dreams, a first love in college.

And there was family. Aunts and uncles who involved themselves, who didn't sit idly by, who invited me up for vacation in the summer, and who were there for me when life became unbearable.

And of course, there were those who acted from afar, the Federico Faggins, the Seymour Paperts and Cynthia Solomons of the world, working to improve and to better, indirectly or directly improving opportunities for everyone, including one young boy in an Albuquerque group home.

But "making it" wasn't just about external forces. Nor is my life solely focused on career, as it may have seemed from the perspective of the Growing Up in Science series lecture I gave at Princeton's retreat. It also comes from the two boys who coexist within me, twins of a sort. One surfaces from time to time in the form of knee-jerk emotional reactions and whispered cynicism, but he no longer holds the reins. I see that kid coming from a mile away now, and wisdom has shown me this boy's merit; he keeps me honest and watches over my well-being in his own nervous way. To hold this boy close is to remember and acknowledge my roots.

But there's the other boy, the one who still geeks out over *Super Mario Bros.*, who blasts old-school hip-hop, and who busts out the Running Man or Cabbage Patch in front of the mirror. This guy leaps at the chance for a road trip with Robin, heading down the Pacific Coast Highway to Big Sur in his convertible. It's his laughter coming out of me when I'm noodling over new ideas and algorithms.

All these parts, once disjointed, unused, or unacknowledged, have become integrated, like the murmuration of a million starlings, to produce the emergent phenomenon I call *me*. In short, I became whole. And if I had only a single sentence, that's what I should have offered to that earnest and courageous server who made herself vulnerable: I found a way to become whole.

I will admit, however, that the process of becoming whole was far from simple. One of the most significant factors was my decades-long journey with psychoanalysis under the guidance of Dr. Laquercia. The scientist in me finds this somewhat disturbing because nobody truly grasps how psychoanalysis works; the scientific evidence for its efficacy is thin. This stands in contrast to drugs like Prozac, which, thanks to the success of reductionist science, we have a basic understanding of, at least at the molecular and cellular level. Prozac blocks the quick reabsorption of serotonin—a chemical used in communication between neurons—into the surrounding cells. We think this enhances communication in the neural networks that process emotions. Beyond that, things become murky. Still, it's a start.

Yet reductionist science stumbles here, too. While we can trace Prozac's effects at the molecular level, its precise circuit-level magic remains elusive. Our main tools to determine drug efficacy are self-report and longitudinal studies of outcomes after treatment. We retreat to statistics because we really have no idea how molecules such as Prozac impact neural population dynamics that likely subserve the computations underlying behavior.

On the other hand, to make sense of talk therapies like psychoanalysis, one begins with something high-level and intuitive, such as Dr. Laquercia and I speaking with each other, inducing emotional simulation in each other's minds—so-called transference and countertransference—and then working downward. But beginning at this intuitive level does not make it simpler to understand. *Far* from it. We must navigate the tangled jungle of emotions and thoughts, down through the cognitive gears, then deeper still to the brain's speech and emotion circuits, and ultimately cellular and even molecular underpinnings. After all that, one builds everything back up to the state of emotions and thoughts to understand what changed. This is an impossibly complex undertaking, one that will require generations of scientists to fully unravel.

Comprehending how either Prozac or talk therapy changes a brain holistically are both monumental puzzles, but understanding talk therapy is simply a different order of business. There's no molecule to hold on to, rather there is an adaptive, recurrent system composed of a billion billion pieces changing itself in a highly complex, top-down fashion.

Still, I would argue that the act of talking *is* therapeutic. That with Dr. Laquercia, I *was* changing myself through emotional and situational simulation. By remembering my childhood experiences in a safe environment and processing their echoes, can there be any doubt I was reintegrating the entirety of myself and my experiences on a mechanistic level? Was I not subtly rewiring my brain's very circuitry, even if we cannot yet explain what happens or how it works?

Such top-down "simulation therapy" isn't unique to the West. Eastern traditions, such as the Metta meditation, where you bathe yourself and the world in loving-kindness, literally imagining self-love and love of others, offer a different dialect of the same language. What neural re-architecting might such practices achieve over years of mindful immersion?

And what might computational neuroscience tell us about mental illness? Theories about how neuronal activity gives rise to or signals mental illness are nearly absent from the psychotherapies implemented today. The *Diagnostic and Statistical Manual of Mental Disorders* (*DSM*), the quintessential book used by therapists and psychiatrists to diagnose mental disorders, brims with symptom checklists. Take, for example, borderline personality disorder.

It's described as "a pervasive pattern of instability in interpersonal relationships, self-image, affects (the felt quality of an emotional state), and marked impulsivity." Note the *DSM* doesn't say, "Borderline personality is characterized by a decrease of serotonin in the amygdala, leading to a decreased ability to accumulate sensory evidence regarding emotional signals." While I haven't read the 947-page tome front to back, I've come across very few neurobiological markers or even low-level genetic or chemical markers in the text. I'd wager there are zero references to neural computation or to brain circuits that might subserve it.

One day, we'll have math and computer models to explain disorders such as borderline personality. With a better understanding of the brain and improved diagnostic technology, it's my sincere hope that future descriptions in the *DSM* will invoke a computational language, things like, "The principal eigenvalue of the line attractor in the Tac1 network in the medial habenula isn't balanced at unity, leading to an under-integration of rewarding stimuli and thereby to pathological levels of reward-seeking behavior." It's okay, you aren't meant to understand that, but trust me, it's appropriately mathematical and describes a middle layer of understanding, bridging the gap between molecule and mood.

Such a mixture of math and emotions is the bread and butter of an emerging field called *computational psychiatry*. This community hypothesizes that many mental illnesses arise from pathologies in the *neural network*—for example, in wrongly guided information flow or erroneous computation, even if the underlying causes are genetic or molecular. The name of this nascent field is based on the idea that we should first understand neural computation before we can most effectively treat mental illness.

In the summer of 2020, I was hiking with Robin near Mammoth Lakes. I didn't think I had cell service there, but a call from my Aunt Moira came in.

She was incredibly upset. Two uniformed police officers had shown up in their backyard the night before at 2:00 a.m. Elliot had opened the back door bleary-eyed and confused. Upon hearing the questions the cops had directed at him, he'd became suddenly wide-awake and self-conscious about the casual placement of his hands in his pajama pockets. Someone had called my aunt and uncle's local police department claiming that Elliot was high on drugs, that he had a bunch of illegal guns, and was threatening Moira.

Moira finished, "After we talked to the police, they indicated that these claims were made by a woman from Idaho."

"Idaho?"

"We think it's your sister. Have you heard anything from Esther recently?"

"Sorry, last I heard about her was from you," I responded, feeling a knot form in my gut. Despite all my sister's aggression and unpredictability through the years, Moira had found a way to stay in semiregular contact with her. Whenever I visited with my aunt and uncle, we'd spend some time discussing her.

"Well, I talked to Paul, and he called this 'being swatted,'" Moira continued. My cousin Paul was Moira and Elliot's son, now in his early thirties. "Elliot and I are really confused by this." She paused. "Is this something we should be worried about? Esther's had a hard life; I don't—"

"Hell yes, you should be worried! People have been killed from being swatted."

There was a pause. "That's what Paul said."

Two weeks later, while the family was still calling around to different police departments in New York, New Mexico, and California to determine how best to protect themselves, I received a call from a police officer from Idaho.

"Hi, I'm with the sheriff's department in Idaho Falls. My name is Officer Cross. I'm looking for a Mr. David Sussillo."

"Yes. I'm David Sussillo. How can I help you?"

"Hello, Mr. Sussillo. Can I confirm that you're the brother of Esther Sussillo?"

"Esther is my sister."

"Can I confirm that your parents are both deceased and that you're Esther Sussillo's next of kin?"

I knew this was bad. "Yes, Officer, my parents are deceased. If you mean closest blood relative, then yes."

The officer took a deep breath. "Mr. Sussillo, I'm sorry to inform you that your sister died last night."

Officer Cross explained that Esther had been staying in a motel in Idaho Falls for the last few weeks. She'd intentionally overdosed on a cocktail of drugs and alcohol, in a reproduction of my father's behavior that night at the Lori Place apartments forty years earlier. Realizing she'd made a terrible mistake, Esther called 911 and was rushed to the emergency room. Upon entering the hospital, she expressed regret for her decision before slipping into a coma. Esther passed away in the middle of the night. She was alone.

I hung up and began to cry. Each time I contacted another family member to share the news, I cried still more. By the end of my sister's life, I'd truly loathed her. She'd behaved horrifically before the swatting incident: to me, to my wife, to just about anyone who'd ever treated her with kindness or generosity. But at that moment, I was blindsided by grief and sorrow.

The intensity of my feelings betrayed the hard truth of what I owed Esther. She'd done her best as a young girl to be a surrogate mother to me. We'd shared experiences that most folks couldn't possibly relate to. We might have been a source of strength for each other. Instead, she'd become unbearably difficult, entitled, demanding—dangerous, even. I'd chosen to avoid her, which had only served to enrage her further.

Esther's death was all the more tragic because I learned in the aftermath that she'd found love in the last years of her life and had married. Though they were estranged at the time of her death, her husband spoke forcefully and lovingly about Esther. He said that she'd had a kind heart, despite all her problems, which, by the end of her life, had included her own addictions. She'd made it her purpose to help other people in need, he told me during our brief conversation.

While I didn't disbelieve him, it was hard to imagine. After our father's death, Esther's life had really started spiraling. Throughout the following decade, she'd been arrested a dozen times, mainly for DUIs, evading and obstructing arrest, and even battery charges. In her final years, Esther took to leaving rage-filled voice messages for Robin and me—Robin's professional work was rubbish, my parents never loved me, I was cheating on Robin, whatever she could think of that would be most hurtful. Esther's last message, about six months before her death, was a thinly veiled threat: "You think you are better than me? You have no idea. You have no idea what's going to happen now."

In that respect, she was right. She swatted Moira and Elliot as her final fuck-you two weeks before taking her own life. She'd orchestrated an assault on the family members who, more than anyone else, had loved her and had taken the deepest and most enduring interest in her well-being.

For years now, before her death and since, I've returned many times to what Esther's life meant, and what my life means, and the counterpoint we provided each other. The same question arises when I think of my second-grade buddy, Shiloh. How can two kids, who started off in roughly the same place, end up so differently? More than any other person I've ever met, more than my mother, and even more than my father, who was addicted to heroin by fifteen, it often seems to me as though Esther never stood a chance.

Esther wasn't academically minded, but she was nobody's fool, and she had her own formidable gifts, including an incredible intuition about other people. When she was healthy and stable, her charismatic powers knew almost no limits. She'd damn near married a billionaire she'd randomly met at a retreat. And she would have made a hell of a psychotherapist had she been able to overcome her own personal traumas. (Most therapists are "wounded warriors," as Dr. Laquercia once explained to me.)

It may have been that Esther endured a trauma early in life from which she never recovered, even above and beyond what I know about, though our shared experiences would have been more than enough to contribute to the kind of mental illness she suffered from. Perhaps she concluded that her childhood was too painful to examine in any detail.

Possibly Esther's survival strategy, manipulating people—especially men based on her beauty—was a crutch that ultimately held her back.

But my scientific training and respect for the complexity of matter and mind are at odds with these kinds of explanations. The ideas about emergence explored here lead me to think that simple stories with just-so narratives are things I tell myself in the face of a world that has no easy answers or perhaps no answers at all.

Ultimately, I don't know why my sister turned out as she did, or how I made it out alive and relatively whole. And I don't know that I'll ever fully understand the broad strokes of Esther's life or my own. Our lives appear to be a slow accumulation of apparently inconsequential decisions and occasional advances, of lucky breaks and bad turns, each new moment determined by a multitude of unseen factors that provide choices and opportunities that were unavailable just moments before.

Now when I close my eyes and think of my sister, I try to think back to the time Moira and Elliot took us out of the Albuquerque Christian Children's Home for that glorious trip around New Mexico and Arizona. How happy Esther had been when she and my aunt had floated together effortlessly in the hotel pool in Gallup, New Mexico, all those years ago, when we were seen for perhaps the first time, by loving adults, as ourselves.

In the aftermath of Esther's passing, I began to feel a soft but persistent pull back to New Mexico. I decided to make the journey, hoping to reconnect with old friends and explore the roots of my past.

Ahead of my trip, I'd checked Facebook for contacts still living in New Mexico and had reconnected with an old buddy from the Albuquerque Christian Children's Home, Bobby, the kid who'd used his baby blues to get what he needed. Bobby told me Omar was still in New Mexico. He was doing well. Bobby suggested the three of us meet when I was in the area. And so it came to pass that I drove to Albuquerque to meet my old ACCH roommates for the first time since we were children.

Bobby had grown up to be as attractive a man as he'd been a child. He looked like Elvis or Buzz Lightyear. Omar was middle-aged now, pushing fifty, but fit. He had short, black hair and wore a pair of shades on his head. His mustache was graying, as were the sides of his temples. I was much taller than he was, but I could see from his arms that he could still twist me into a pretzel if the mood were to strike him.

We sat outside for a late brunch, with a perfect view of the sheer rocky outcroppings of the Sandia Mountains. I shared a bit of my story, getting a PhD, and all the rest. I went light on the details, but they were like family; the details didn't matter. They wanted to celebrate me and my success. *Our* shared success.

"You used to read those old encyclopedias we had at the home," Omar said. "I just wanted to go outside."

When it was his turn to catch me up, Omar shrugged. "Man, things were starting to go my way when you left. This family from Farmington agreed to pay my way through college and everything. All I had to do was stay out of trouble." Omar grinned. "But I was seventeen and a knucklehead."

Omar had left the group home a rebel, set loose and half-crazy with his newfound freedom. During a few years of surrounding himself with bad influences from his old neighborhood, he'd made terrible choices. In his early twenties, he found himself driving fast cars and planning a drive-by shooting. He'd been arrested, and it appeared he might go to prison.

But it also turned out that Omar had found his way to the Coca-Cola Company, faithful to those conversations we'd held so long ago. So, when it came time to go to court, Omar told his manager at Coca-Cola that he might not return.

"Why not?" the manager asked.

"I may be going to prison," Omar replied.

"Well, if you end up in jail, give me a call, and I'll bail you out. I'm there for you."

The case ended up going Omar's way, so he avoided incarceration. Then Omar did the hard part; he took stock of who he'd become. After the trial, Omar returned to work. He found he didn't want to disappoint this manager who'd offered to help him in his darkest hour. Over time, the manager became a mentor at work and then a mentor in life.

Omar invented reasons to avoid trouble; he stopped hanging around his old friends. Over the next decade, he found Christ, made a family, and graduated with a degree in accounting from the University of New Mexico. He'd spent the following years as a trucker and then as a manager of truckers. By the time I met up with him—and in a miraculous coincidence with my own career in artificial intelligence—Omar was working for a self-driving trucking outfit, proving adept at communicating the intricacies of driving trucks to the engineers.

Bobby chimed in, "I've been driving trucks for a long time now, too. It's good work and pays good. Plus, I like being out on the road, seeing New Mexico and the countryside, you know?" He smiled warmly.

After the server laid our food out, Omar said, "Let's say grace." Both Omar and Bobby lowered their heads. I couldn't remember the last time I'd prayed, but I didn't want to disrespect my old friends, so I lowered my head.

Omar looked up at me as he cut into his burrito smothered in New Mexico Hatch green chile, "I'm a preacher now, David! I preach at a Spanish-speaking congregation here in Albuquerque. I even got Bobby here to see the error of his ways." The two of them exchanged a nod. "I baptized him myself."

My eyebrows went up. "Omar, of all the kids at the home, you'd be the last I'd have pegged to get all religious," I said.

"It's changed my life completely. And it could change yours. I'm still available for a baptism." He laughed but gave me a questioning look.

"Naw. I was baptized back at the ACCH," I said.

With this, the conversation turned to the group home, the house-parents, all the stunts we'd pulled, and all the looney-tunes kids we'd grown up with. Omar and Jake were now in semiregular contact, occasionally traveling together on Christian missions to build low-cost homes in developing countries. We laughed out loud retelling crazy moments, like when Peter and Janet fell through the ceiling after they'd climbed into the rafters for some hanky-panky, or when a random drunk woman walked into Cottage 3 in the middle of the night and crawled into bed with one of the boys to pass out. We talked about the time Juanita and Jessica had snuck over to our room in the dead of night and me hiding in the closet before my first kiss in the sixth grade.

"Whatever happened to Jess?" I asked.

"I don't know the details," Bobby said, "but I'm pretty sure she's in prison now, doing hard time."

"What for?" I exclaimed.

"Murder, I think."

We talked on, shaking our heads at the apparently random outcomes of many of our former group-home siblings. "What about other kids? Jackson? Diamond? Juanita?" I asked.

"I don't know about them, but Lucia is living in Tennessee. She's a technician in the aerospace industry," said Bobby. "But honestly, I haven't been able to find most of them. They aren't interested in staying in touch. Don't want contact, don't want to remember. Me? I remember it like it was yesterday. *Yesterday*, bro."

I understood every bit of that. Even though it'd taken me thirty years to reach out, the memories from my childhood were as vivid as if they *had* happened yesterday.

"I was really sorry to hear about your sister," Omar said.

I inclined my head in acknowledgment. "She never really left the home."

Both Bobby and Omar nodded solemnly. They knew what I meant. We talked for hours.

When it was time to go, Bobby insisted we shouldn't be strangers. We all hugged one more time and agreed to stay in touch. I got back in my car and headed up to Santa Fe. As I left the outskirts of Albuquerque, a sense of peace and gratitude enveloped me. I was proud of Omar and Bobby. I was proud of myself—proud of *us*. We three group-home brothers had made it despite overwhelming odds.

Cruising up I-25 to Santa Fe, my thoughts drifted to Shiloh. I hadn't seen or heard from him since our single chance encounter in the Santa Fe Plaza during my college days, when he'd looked to be adrift and homeless. When reconnecting with Omar and Bobby online, before our meetup, I'd also searched online for Shiloh. What I'd discovered was a relentless cycle of incarceration. Shiloh's rap sheet stretched back two decades: arrests for public disturbances, trespassing, burglary, methamphetamine possession, the list went on. All painted a stark picture of a mentally unwell existence.

I found almost twenty mugshots. It was the most haunting collection of photos of a single person that I'd ever seen, and it chronicled Shiloh's transformation from a young thirtysomething to a weathered soul nearing fifty. From drugged-out and tweaking to filthy and homeless, from lost and forlorn, to rebellious and even whimsical. In some photos, he had short hair and was clean-shaven; in others, he had long hair and a Jesus beard. There was even a hint of amusement that flickered in a few of the photos. Yet the one constant was the orange prison jumpsuit.

Beneath the hardship, though, I still glimpsed my old friend, my funny eight-year-old buddy. And this provoked in me an unbearable sadness for him and for a world that could allow such a thing to happen. But for chance, it could have been him looking at mugshots of me outfitted in orange.

Once back in Santa Fe, I decided to take a walk in the old neighborhood we'd lived in. I walked past the tiny apartment where I'd lived in second grade. The small complex looked unchanged, but its modest dwellings had been converted into small businesses offering acupuncture, hair extensions, fancy nails, and the like. I walked a bit down Berry Street to where Shiloh's trailer park had been. The trailer park was gone, paved over for an apartment complex and Toyota dealership. Thanks to the asphalt parking lot, there was no chance of finding buried eight-year-olds' promises.

That year, we'd been in second grade. Shiloh and I had raised hell. Dumpster-diving. Thieving. Total pyros. Begging for quarters. For all that, we'd been innocent—children surviving in a world unconcerned with the needs of children.

He'd been my first best friend, a first love when it came right down to it. Though our paths had diverged, a fragment of him remained with me and had paved the way for future relationships, from Omar to Serra to Robin. We'd taught each other how to trust and how to have fun, just months before the shield of my childhood innocence would shatter.

We were always trying to go play *Ms. Pac-Man* in the arcade on St. Michael's Drive, first tearing apart his trailer or searching the streets for pennies to parlay into a quarter. Then we'd bound over to the arcade. We'd insert our quarter into the console, ready to take on the world. How we cheered and shouted at each other in encouragement, determined to rack up enough points to earn an extra life and keep the fight alive.

Get the free, Shiloh! Get the free life! I wish with all my heart that there were a way for him to get that extra life.

For no reason I can point to, I have.

AFTERWORD

In the science sections of this book, I've focused mostly on discoveries of the past: how neuroscience has laid the foundation for the AI technology that we use today. Yet neuroscience research has always moved slowly for both practical and ethical reasons. In comparison, AI's growth—fueled by vast, preexisting databases—has virtually exploded, leaving neuroscience in the dust. Where will this accelerated growth lead us?

Many of the current headlines reflect an atmosphere of deep anxiety: "Artificial Intelligence Could Lead to Extinction, Experts Warn," "ChatGPT Can Help Doctors—and Hurt Patients," and "The Rise of the Deepfake and the Threat to Democracy." These breathless proclamations paint AI at the very least as a job killer and, at their most extreme, an ominous existential threat. I don't think these concerns are entirely unfounded—AI *will* disrupt industries and create unprecedented challenges around misinformation, privacy, and content ownership. It *will* render some skills obsolete while creating demand for others, presenting both legitimate concerns and extraordinary opportunities.

This is a pattern we've seen throughout technological history. When automobiles replaced horse-drawn carriages in the early twentieth century, many professions—from blacksmiths to carriage makers—faced upheaval, while cities required major redesigns. But automobiles also created entirely new industries.

Focusing solely on potential harms often overshadows AI's real contributions. In my own field, the use of artificial neural networks now allows paralyzed patients to control computer cursors or enable the decoding of speech from neural activity. In medicine, AI systems are demonstrating promising capabilities in diagnostics, beginning to assist with treatment personalization, and accelerating drug discovery. In addressing global challenges from climate change to food security, AI significantly enhances human researchers' ability to process and interpret complex data. The true reality of AI isn't captured in either utopian or dystopian extremes but rather exists in the messy middle, where technological progress brings both opportunities and challenges requiring thoughtful navigation.

Surprisingly, despite AI's remarkable achievements, today's artificial neural networks actually remain highly simplistic compared to the human brain. They rely on operations like matrix multiplication, a function called *attention* that allows the network to selectively focus on relevant information, and a few nonlinear transformations to invoke the magic of emergence. Coupled with massive web-scraped datasets, this simple recipe powers advanced language models and image generators. Frankly, I'm amazed at how much can be achieved with data, scale, and repetition of these operations.

These advances have also brought about an ironic twist. These same systems—born from our attempts to understand the brain—are now forcing us to reconsider what we thought we knew about *thinking*. If one simplistically defines thinking in an operational manner—as the manipulation of language for the logical processing of concepts—as we do all the time in our own heads, then, in my opinion, the answer to whether or not chatbots think is an unequivocal yes.

Yet traditionally, not just language but consciousness was defined by thought: "I think, therefore I am," as Descartes famously declared. This brings us to a core tension: AI surprises us not because it thinks like we do but because it thinks *at all*. These chatbots don't have bodies, they aren't alive, and they certainly aren't conscious. They make stupid mistakes humans would never, ever make, like confidently citing a nonexistent scientific study claiming churros make excellent surgical instruments. And at their core, their training is no more sophisticated than learning to predict the next word in human-generated sentences. For example, a chatbot is trained by learning that when it sees *I'm going to the*, it's likely that the answer is either *store*, *fridge*, or *bathroom*, so it should output one of these words with equal probability. If instead, the phrase was *Can you hand me the milk? I'm going to the*, then it becomes much more likely that the answer is *fridge*. And so, through the ever-increasing context of language, chatbots work their magic.

Despite the occasional absurd mistake and a simple method of learning, chatbots also demonstrably engage in complex reasoning, generate sophisticated responses, and even simulate a surprising degree of understanding. If you play around with a chatbot long enough, I think you'll agree that they often seem to "get it," that regardless of the simple methods by which they are trained and behind mere language processing, they nevertheless appear to be very adequately manipulating ideas and concepts.

This tension between how things appear from the outside and the level of depth on the inside reminds me of my and Robin's lovable black cat, Hercules. His ability to leap effortlessly to the top of the refrigerator or to track the quick movements of a laser pointer might suggest equally sophisticated mental capacities. But let's be honest, cats are getting over on charm. Hercules is no exception; he's not exactly Mensa material. No amount of training would ever teach him language or logical reasoning. Often, I jokingly compare him to one of those plastic, black Magic 8 Balls, basically a random number generator in fur: And the answer is: *Food!* But for all his endearing simplicity, there's no question in my mind that when Hercules saunters over for a snuggle, he's truly with us; he's present. A gift of evolution embedded somehow in his brain in ways we simply don't yet understand.

It's in this sense that chatbots—and artificial neural networks more generally—are decidedly *not* like us. Hercules is present with perhaps minimal thought, while today's large language models are thoughtful without being present. We, with our messy, magnificent biological networks cobbled together over eons of evolution, have only limited abstract processing capabilities, and we must focus hard to use them. Hercules fails here as a matter of course. But Hercules exists in the world, as do we: We live, eat, and breathe, maintaining homeostasis. We love one another; we reproduce, we play sports and dance. Today's AI bots, on the other hand, don't interact with the world at all; they aren't embodied. They aren't even alive. *All* they do is think, again in the reductive, operational sense of manipulating concepts via language. So from a philosophical standpoint, I'm content to sit with the idea that we are witnessing the first examples of thinking without being.

If there's anything that has accurately summarized the course of AI, it's not from neuroscience but a short thought piece written in 2019 by renowned AI pioneer Rich Sutton. He argues that pretty much every time AI researchers have attempted to improve an algorithm using real human insight gleaned from studying a problem, the results have been disappointing. Instead, another algorithm comes along that uses a brute-force approach, learning from vast amounts of data. This algorithm then outperforms the one generated from the human's insight or experience. Sutton named this piece "The Bitter Lesson."

We've seen this repeatedly. In the '90s, chess-playing algorithms that relied on human-crafted strategies were outperformed by those that simply analyzed millions of chess positions. In 2016, DeepMind's AlphaGo, which learned to play Go by studying hundreds of thousands of human games and playing against itself, defeated the world champion for the first time. Even in image recognition, AlexNet's 2012 victory in the ImageNet competition demonstrated the power of deep learning over traditional, human-designed feature detectors. Of course this lesson is bitter, because we naturally value our own understanding and expertise.

Because this pattern has repeated so often, Sutton reasons that we may as well admit defeat in the face of brute-force, data-thirsty algorithms. All we need for progress is lots of data, cheap computers, and fast algorithms with tons of capacity. Indeed, today's neural networks can process vast amounts of data when paired with GPUs, one of the reasons recent AI has been so successful. The Internet is filled with decades of accumulated human data and culture in the form of text, images, songs, stories, videos, and news articles. And if you need more capacity in the neural network model, simply add more layers to the deep network, like adding more processing units to a computer.

Which brings us to the crucial question: Where is today's AI renaissance heading? I can't give you a direct answer, because I can't predict the future, but I can give you a pretty good indirect answer. We're going to discover the limits of the bitter lesson. How far can we take our simplistic artificial neural networks, our massive datasets scraped from the web, and our cheap computers? How many cool ideas and applications can we build from this paradigm? So far, we've got incredibly useful chatbots, image-generation algorithms, instantaneous language translation, and voice-to-text applications. I think it'll go *much* further: all manner of business-to-business applications, a complete revolution in diagnostic medicine, and flawless image, music, and video generation. Self-driving cars are absolutely within reach. I imagine that every piece of technology from our cars to our coffee makers will interact with us through spoken or written language. From automated scientific hypothesis generation, to drug discovery, to manufacturing optimization, I think the world is in for some big changes over the coming decades.

There's a long history of deep pessimism whenever new technology emerges. Consider the concerns about the telegraph speeding up the world, the blame cast upon elevators for crime waves, and the fear of early cinema captured in hand-wringing headlines like VILE MOVING PICTURES CORRUPTING THE MORALS OF COUNTLESS CHILDREN. The impulse to blame technology for societal decay or outright calamity has always been strong. One gem from 1982 reads, DO WE REALLY NEED HOME COMPUTERS?

Even in serious academic circles, there's an honest debate happening. On one hand, you have pessimists, championed by Geoffrey Hinton and others, who advocate approaching the technology with extreme caution, suggesting even a moratorium on using current technology to catch our breath before we proceed further. On the other, you have optimists like Yann LeCun, another AI luminary, tirelessly reminding us of science's historic role in improving human lives. Both Hinton and LeCun have made tremendous contributions to AI, and both of their perspectives deserve serious consideration.

But what about the *big question*? Are we headed for a truly *conscious* artificial general intelligence anytime soon? Here, I offer a reasonably confident no. Currently, we have no path to Hercules. Re-creating a cat's brain—an artificial cat that's present when you snuggle—is so far

Afterword

out of reach as to sound preposterous. We have nothing that is living or conscious, and it's not at all obvious that scale alone can provide this. Because, again, *that's* what today's AI renaissance really is, an exploration of the limits of scale. Even self-driving cars, requiring vast time and treasure for data collection, exemplify this data-driven, bitter lesson approach. In summary, I am doubtful whether scale alone can ever bridge the gap between "thinking" and "being." Achieving true consciousness and physical presence may require fundamentally different approaches and, returning full circle to neuroscience, a far deeper understanding of biological brains than we have currently achieved.

Personally, while I strive for nuance and acknowledge a future with infinite outcomes—including terrible ones—I just can't envision a world with robot overlords, or any other existential threats to humanity caused by AI. And though I share concerns about more prosaic problems of AI technologies, such as the potential for disinformation in politics, issues of copyright for creative works, or widespread job displacement—my optimism about AI runs deeper than these worries. Honestly, I see a new toolbox overflowing with potential for creativity and discovery. And I suspect that most of my colleagues in the field view things in a similar light.

I often reflect on my youth, playing video games or screwing around on a personal computer. In part, I am who I am because of those experiences. Video games didn't just entertain me—they taught me about systems, logic, and possibility. Computers didn't just help me escape—they gave me a career path I never could have imagined. I think about that eleven-year-old boy, pecking away on an old IBM personal computer, frustrated by a Pascal programming book that was too advanced for him to understand alone. Today, that kid could have an AI tutor walking him through every concept, answering every question, available 24/7.

Afterword

I think about a child today who is currently engaging with an AI chatbot, attempting to get it to say *shit* or *fart*, as I would have done, or attempting to trick it into generating a dirty limerick. But look beyond the giggles. What skills will this kid acquire? From something as straightforward as developing the motor skill of typing, to writing their first "David is cool" program, to contemplating language. Perhaps they're engaged in something as profound as the inventors of LOGO envisioned—learning how to think by reflecting on thought itself. *Is that chatbot alive? How would I know? I wonder if I can trick it. What does it even mean to be alive?*

My own journey from group homes to a career in neuroscience is a living example that one of technology's greatest powers is in expanding human potential. The same neural networks I've spent my career trying to understand are now offering new pathways for connection, creativity, and discovery. For all the uncertainty ahead, I believe that AI—like many tools before—will, in the end, be shaped by the best of our human intentions.

ACKNOWLEDGMENTS

This book would not exist without Elizabeth DeNoma, who read my earliest draft, encouraged me to publish, and championed the project from the beginning. My literary agent, Jenna Land Free, took a remarkable risk on a first-time author. She always made time to advise or listen, and encouraged me to weave my science into the personal narrative in ways that elevated the story. In many ways, my editor at Hachette, Karyn Marcus, taught me how to write—her influence is on every page. I'm thankful to Jane Isay for conversations that helped me "popcorn" my way to beginning the book with my strength: video games. I'm also grateful for the thoughtful edits and comments from Judith Bloch and Sarah Fuchs during the early stages of this project. Many thanks to Wei Ji Ma and everyone involved in the Growing Up in Science lecture series, which helped me open up publicly about my childhood and inspired the framing of this memoir's opening. My early readers sustained me through countless drafts with their support and encouragement: Jody, Jeff, Elliot, Moira, Maria, James, Larry, Robin, Cheryl, Tania, Michelle, Helen, Bill, Nicole, Stephanie, and Jesse. Special thanks to Larry Abbott for helping to ensure the scientific accuracy of this work, and to Dr. Laquercia and Dr. Rauch for helping me process the emotional weight of these memories as I put them on paper. To Robin,

Acknowledgments

who created the illustrations and showed endless patience with a husband disappearing into his laptop for months on end—thank you for everything. Finally, thank you to Ian Dorset, Fred Francis, Nan Thornton, and the entire team at Hachette for bringing this book into the world.

NOTES

1. Anyone familiar with elementary school math can grasp the basic concept of matrix-matrix multiplication: It's all about multiplying and adding numbers within and across rectangular grids of numbers used to represent objects and transformations of those objects from one form to another. One application where matrix multiplication shines is in the realm of graphics processing.

   Imagine juggling countless physical objects in a vast 3D space. Each object can be represented by a list of its 3D coordinates—x, y, z—neatly stacked together into a matrix. Now, picture performing crucial transformations like rotating, moving, or resizing these objects—fundamental operations in creating realistic graphics. Amazingly, these transformations can be elegantly represented by another matrix. To apply a transformation (e.g., a rotation), we multiply the object's coordinate matrix (e.g., a teapot's x, y, z position data) by a rotation matrix, resulting in another matrix that represents the rotated teapot. This powerful mathematical operation allows us to seamlessly apply almost any desired manipulation to our 3D objects.

   Finally, when it's time to bring these transformed objects to the screen, we call upon yet another type of matrix, aptly named a *projection*. It translates the intricate 3D scene onto the flat 2D canvas of your monitor's screen, ensuring that perspective and depth appear realistic, creating the illusion of a 3D world on a flat screen.

   In a nutshell, matrix-matrix multiplication acts as the mathematical engine driving the breathtaking visuals we experience in graphic-rich gaming environments.

Notes

Its ability to efficiently handle 3D geometry and transformations makes it an indispensable tool for creating the stunning worlds we explore in games and movies.

Because matrix-matrix multiplications can be executed in parallel, a GPU can process multiple transformations simultaneously, rather than applying them sequentially to each 3D object. It's this parallelization that leads to the GPU's incredible speedup.

2. Just like manipulating countless 3D objects in graphics, matrix-matrix multiplication found another use case in the world of neural networks. Imagine each data point—whether a weather record or a cat picture—converted into numerical form and structured as a matrix. Now, picture feeding these data points through the layers of a neural network. Passing the data from one layer to the next involves a matrix multiplication.

GPUs' parallel processing enabled researchers to train and deploy deep neural networks on massive datasets, driving advances in fields from image recognition to medical diagnostics.

3. While narrating my journey, it's crucial to acknowledge the broad and dynamic landscape of neural network research during this period. My work on recurrent networks was built upon the foundational insights of researchers like Friedrich Mueller and, in particular, Herbert Jaeger, as well as the collaborative efforts of Kanaka Rajan and Haim Sompolinsky with Larry, in their mathematical exploration of driven, chaotic systems.

More broadly, neural network research has thrived for decades, with branches both inside and outside neuroscience developing their unique approaches and methodologies. For instance, unbeknownst to Larry, myself, and most of the neuroscience and AI communities at the time, in the mid-'90s, Sepp Hochreiter and Jürgen Schmidhuber were pioneering and applying a novel type of recurrent neural network called a Long Short-Term Memory (LSTM, popularized in the AI community by Alex Graves in the mid-2010s), which could use the backpropagation algorithm for training. Their groundbreaking work would only gain widespread recognition five years after my PhD. Meanwhile, near the end of my PhD and beyond, the neuroscience community was increasingly gravitating toward FORCE learning as the method of choice for training recurrent networks.

4. While my work with Valerio, Bill, and Krishna changed many skeptical minds about the value of trained artificial neural networks in modern brain research, it's important to acknowledge the history of using neural networks to understand brain function. Here are just a few notable examples that impacted both me and the field.

In the 1980s, David Rumelhart, James McClelland, and Geoffrey Hinton developed the influential Parallel Distributed Processing framework, while David Ackley, Geoffrey Hinton, and Terrence Sejnowski invented the Boltzmann machine. These early connectionist models laid the groundwork for much of the research that followed, including our work.

A seminal paper from this era is David Zipser and Richard Andersen's 1988 study, which showed that a feedforward artificial neural network trained using backpropagation to transform retinal coordinates together with eye position signals into head-centered coordinates generates gain fields in hidden layer units, mirroring a type of coordinate transformation found in neurons of the posterior parietal cortex.

These studies, among others, showcased the potential of artificial neural networks for modeling and understanding specific brain functions, paving the way for our research on contextual decision-making in the prefrontal cortex.

In the 2010s, Daniel Yamins, James DiCarlo, and others trained feedforward networks for object classification and showed that their intermediate representations resemble those in the primate ventral visual stream. Building on the conceptual foundation laid by Bruno Olshausen and David Field's mid-'90s work on unsupervised sparse coding, this supervised, task-optimized approach demonstrated how recognition training can also give rise to cortical-like hierarchies of visual processing.

ABOUT THE AUTHOR

David Sussillo spent five years in the Albuquerque Christian Children's Home and four years at the Milton Hershey School as a child. After graduating high school, he ultimately received a PhD from Columbia University in computational neuroscience. Now David is an adjunct professor at Stanford University and has been a scientist at the Google Brain group (recently featured in the book *Genius Makers*) and Meta Reality Labs. In his professional pursuits, David researches brain-machine interfaces to develop the next generation of computers. David was the recipient of a Fulbright research grant and is an internationally recognized neuroscientist with over forty publications. He works to understand the ghost in the machine—how cells in our brain collectively give rise to the computations that determine behavior. David has been happily married these last twenty years to his wife, Robin.